Crisis, Agency, and Law in US Civil-Military Relations

"How can the vitality of America's civil-military relations be objectively analyzed? In the disciplines that study these relations, there has never been a consensus. With his legal background, Dan Maurer complements moral and political arguments as he weaves the fiduciary duties of candor, loyalty, confidentiality, and scope of responsibility into a jurisprudential form of agency theory as a basis for such norms. His cases and analysis are impressive, and the field of modern civil-military relations is now analytically the richer for it."

—Don M. Snider, *Colonel (retired), PhD, Professor Emeritus, West Point, and retired Professor of Profession and Ethic, US Army War College.*

Daniel Maurer

Crisis, Agency, and Law in US Civil-Military Relations

palgrave
macmillan

Daniel Maurer
Office of the Staff Judge Advocate
Fort Sill, Oklahoma, USA

ISBN 978-3-319-53525-8 ISBN 978-3-319-53526-5 (eBook)
DOI 10.1007/978-3-319-53526-5

Library of Congress Control Number: 2017937395

Cover image: WENN Ltd/Alamy Stock Photo
Cover design: Tom Howey

Printed on acid-free paper

This Palgrave Macmillan imprint is published by Springer Nature
The registered company is Springer International Publishing AG
The registered company address is: Gewerbestrasse 11, 6330 Cham, Switzerland

To "Household Six" and my squad of three brilliant little Jedi…
…may you, someday, be assigned to read this for class

Contents

1	**Introduction**	1
	Notes	15
2	**The Opening Statement**	17
	The Strategic Civil-Military Relationship Problem	20
	The Scholarship Gap: The Inability to Diagnose Poor Civil-Military Relationships	24
	Applying the Law of Agency	27
	Notes	27
3	**The Case-In-Chief: What the Law Does (Not) Say**	37
	The Constitution Structures Civil-Military Relations	37
	Legislation Organizes Civil-Military Relations	41
	Case Law Remains Silent on Civil-Military Relations	48
	Administrative Regulations Focus on Undue Personal Gain, not Civil-Military Relations	53
	Military Doctrine Looks Down and In, not Up and Out	55
	Notes	60
4	**The Expert Witnesses: A Cross-Examination**	75
	Huntington, Professionalism, and Two Forms of Control	75
	Janowitz, Civil-Military Fusion, and the Military as a Pressure Group	78

Cohen and Unequal Partnerships 79
Feaver, Agency, and Rational Actors 82
Notes 89

5 **The Expert Witnesses: The Fingerprints of Agency** 95
Notes 98

6 **The Rebuttal Witnesses: From Agency to Norms to Diagnosis** 101
Jurisprudential Agency 102
Notes 105

7 **Exhibit A: Scope of Responsibility and Authority** 109
President-General-Soldier-in-Chief: The Case of Jefferson Davis 110
McClellan's Megalomania and Ridgeway's Recalcitrance 117
The Case of the True Believer: Maxwell Taylor 119
Notes 125

8 **Boundaries, or a "Poverty of Useful and Unambiguous Authority"?** 131
Notes 136

9 **Exhibit B: When Fidelity and Frankness Conflict** 137
Revolt of the Admirals 142
Lincoln's Spy 145
Notes 150

10 **Exhibit C: Amending the Goldwater-Nichols Act** 155
Example Draft Text of an Amendment 156
[Amended] § 151. Joints Chiefs of Staff: Composition; Functions; Fiduciary Duties 157
Goldwater-Nichols Agency Applied 160
Notes 175

11 Exhibit D: The Future Fallacy: A Civ-Mil Dialogue 177
Notes 203

12 Closing Argument 211

Index 217

CHAPTER 1

Introduction

A little past noon, the *Bataan* slipped beneath parting clouds revealing a bright late-April sun over the Windy City. The few passengers onboard, peering from the windows at the sparkling lake shore below, may have been able to make out the odd but cheerful welcome sign aimed just at them—"Hi, Mac!"—composed in large white letters along Lake Michigan's beach by enthusiastic residents of Michigan City, Indiana, just outside Chicago. Touching down at Midway Airport minutes later, the still-uniformed hero emerged from the plane's cabin. At seventy-one years old, he was ripe with a self-righteous and self-assured vigor of a much younger man. "Mac" descended the stairwell to the ear-splitting cannonade of a seventeen-gun artillery salute and the embrace of an honor guard of one hundred and twenty men. They would escort this "great soldier-statesman" to a waiting coral red convertible where he took his seat next to his adoring wife and son. Thus enthroned, his plain tan uniform seemed, if only briefly, tinged with a royal purple.[1]

As the General's car pulled away magnificently from the airfield, it was trailed by a convoy of Chicago's police commissioner, mayor, the governor of Illinois, a squad of admirals and generals, members of Congress, and a bishop. The center of this public attention peered ahead through his sunglasses. He was likely warmed more by what one contemporary correspondent called this "great swelling chorus of acclamation" than by Chicago's famously breezy early spring. As twenty miles of road lay before him, three million faces jittered anxiously along the parade route for a

D. Maurer, *Crisis, Agency, and Law in US Civil-Military Relations*,
DOI 10.1007/978-3-319-53526-5_1

glimpse of the famous man in khaki, some standing ten deep in front of storefronts hastily boarded up by their owners worried about the hurricane-like crush of the crowds that afternoon. Keeping the spectators, fawners, veterans, and the curious at bay, and at a respectable distance from the forty-car motorcade, stood Chicago's finest.

This police force security detail had been augmented by more than a thousand firefighters, mobilized with no additional pay but satisfied with the belief that their service this day would ring with awe in the ears of their grandchildren one far-off day. Flowers and ticker-tape fell like rainbow-colored snow from the stone and brick towers downtown. The Chicago thoroughfares vibrated along its parallel sidewalks with a public aching for visions of glorious valor they expected, but would elude them in the coming years: the birth of non-noble terms like "police action," "armistice," and "cold war." These terms would fail to evoke the sense of honor, victory, and American military prowess the citizens largely demanded as their destiny.[2] It was a destiny personally embodied by the General sitting erect and waving to the spectators as his motorcade weaved through the city streets. And so he himself believed. This applause was his vindication, a very democratic endorsement of his ideal warrior ethos: When war comes, politics must fade away like old soldiers; the nation's economic, political, and military future is entrusted to a "military receivership" implied by the oath he swore to defend the Constitution, not an oath to the half-hearted policies of a diplomatically immature, timid, and—above all—*temporary* political administration. *These* fellow Americans on the other hand, he knew, understood well what was necessary to win and that he had never, despite the allegation, compromised his duty by so-called "insubordination."[3]

Hours later, inside the concrete coliseum of Soldier Field, the aged but animated warrior-diplomat was offered fireworks, school bands, laudatory speeches, and nineteen interruptions of applause as his final remarks climaxed. He managed to sound triumphant, regretful, and gracious all at once, an effect calculated to screen his true offensive maneuver—to "assail" the President's foreign policy and war strategy in the Korean conflict.

*****

Douglas MacArthur, five-star General, former Army Chief of Staff, former Commander of the Allied Forces in the Pacific Theater of World War II, former military governor of Japan, and Medal of Honor awardee, was more popular among his fellow Americans than any other public figure of his day. Thus feted by public coronation, he had—just two weeks prior to this glorious Chicago celebration—been fired, ingloriously relieved of command in Korea by President Truman, the popularly elected (though massively unpopular) Commander-in-Chief. Mac, after long consideration of, and long exposure to, the international affairs of the Far East, had concluded (and advocated) that more troops, fewer political restraints, and a much wider theater of battle into mainland China was the *only* way to assure the nation's, the United Nations,' and *his* total victory.

It was, in the end, simply a *military* conclusion, and everyone knew that the military must take its commands from the commander-in-chief, the president. But this military conclusion, and the General's attempts to execute it, was one "entirely at cross-purposes" with President Truman's intent to remain nested in a network of allies under United Nations authority and to contain the bounds of that conflict so that atomic escalation and World War III could be avoided (even so far as to draft a proposal for a cease-fire).

> The United Nations fighting forces are tough and able and well equipped… [the Communists] may take further action which will spread the conflict. They have that choice, and with it the awful responsibility for what may follow…[w]e do not want to see the conflict in Korea extended. We are trying to prevent a world war, not to start one…Why don't we bomb Manchuria and China itself? Why don't we assist the Chinese Nationalist troops to land on the mainland of China? If we were to do these things we would running a very grave risk of starting a general war. If that were to happen, we would have brought about the exact situation we are trying to prevent.[4]

It was a suffocating intent well known to MacArthur, and to American allies, when he presumptively published an inflammatory "military assessment" of the Chinese army and its effect in the war thus far. He had implied that the Chinese must (and should for their own good) retire from the field lest they suffer overwhelming military defeat. It was a threat, one of MacArthur's biographers later noted, that none of his political masters were willing to underwrite.[5]

More speeches, more laurels, more books, and a Congressional hearing still loomed ahead after MacArthur's visit to Chicago. But even now, at the general's public apotheosis, it was clear that his combative approach to strategic policy-making—at least when it did not align with his own military vision and subtle political appreciation—would provide a stage for a most apt study of the American "civil-military crisis." It was neither the first time nor the last time that Americans witnessed this strange form of ambiguous drama among the nation's senior uniformed leaders and its democratically elected suit-wearing leaders.

*****

In 1861, not long after the Union's startling loss to the rebel army at Bull Run (Manassas) in northern Virginia, President Lincoln installed a popular, anti-slavery, Major General John C. Freémont as commander of the Western Department, headquartered in St. Louis, Missouri. Akin to a modern day unified combatant command, like the U.S. Central Command, Freémont's assumption of considerable geopolitical responsibility (the Department covered Illinois, and all land between the Mississippi River and the Rocky Mountains) inevitably bumped into his designs for military campaigns, and thereby began his MacArthur-like clash with Lincoln. The political tripwire in 1861 was slavery. Specifically, the extent to which the Federal government was ready to emancipate slaves in the Confederate States was not nearly as wide as Freémont's desire for a sensational and aggressive splash early in the War. Lincoln was walking a finer line, delicately attempting to not alienate the then-neutral border (and slave-holding) state of Kentucky.[6] There was obvious risk to sensitive political considerations at the heart of sustaining strategic freedom along several major rivers in the frontier. Moreover, Congress had recently passed a law that authorized only the *confiscation*, not emancipation, of slave "property" of Confederates.

By that point early in the War, Lincoln had not yet been repeatedly disappointed by his generals and their tactical losses or inertia. Right before he dispatched Freémont to his command, Lincoln told him he had no specific instructions for how to establish and sustain the new Military Department, and remarked, "I have given you *carte blanche*; you must use your own judgment and do the best you can."[7] This—as we will see—was an extraordinary grant of authority, a limitless scope of responsibility that would prove, ultimately, to be *too* enabling, which led to the general's direct confrontation with his commander-in-chief. Despite Congress's limitation, and Lincoln's grand policy concerns, Freémont nevertheless declared martial law in his assigned territory, ordered the summary execution of captured guerillas, and issued his own emancipation proclamation that freed all slaves owned by Confederate activists in Missouri who were then overwhelming his federal forces with insurgent tactics.

A private letter from Lincoln to Freémont politely offered reasons why the general's unilateral edicts were strategically unwise. The president's letter was ignored with a "proconsular arrogance."[8] Lincoln's public order to rescind the emancipation and execution policy soon followed, with the general's removal from command not long after.[9]

*****

MacArthur and Truman, reenacting the Freémont Lincoln crisis from ninety years earlier, engaged in more civilized power-shifting political drama than those, in other less fortunate or less apathetic regions of the world, that manifest as a bloody and chaotic *coup d'état.* Truman and his Cabinet were "deeply shocked,"[10] but more by MacArthur's obvious and arrogant undermining of an awkwardly beginning diplomatic strategy to prevent more bloodshed in Korea than by the General's inability to control his strategic proclamations. And nobody seriously thought MacArthur might lead a uniformed revolt to usurp political power. But this was not the first time he made himself—as Truman observed in his diary entry of April 5, 1951—a "center of controversy."[11] MacArthur's interviews with foreign newspapers, in which he referred to the "artificial conditions" and "ludicrous" effect of political interference with military necessity, only added gasoline to the smoldering fire.[12] MacArthur's letter to Congressman Joe Martin finally sparked the blow out. Martin, a Republican and the House of Representatives' minority leader, had publically insinuated that President Truman was responsible for the "murder" of American soldiers sent to fight in a war that the Administration evidently was not in to win. MacArthur, upon reading the Congressman's remarks a month later in Japan, wrote back to Martin approvingly, admitting his own shock at why "some"—obviously the heads of state in the allied nations, his commander-in-chief included—still failed to believe that the fate of communism's advance across Asia, and then Europe, would be decided on the Korean peninsula. In such a case, he commented, "there is no substitute for victory."[13] Martin read MacArthur's letter into the Congressional Record, and it proved to be the "last straw" in an already too heavy pile of "rank insubordination."[14]

After Truman relieved MacArthur from command in the Far East, and the General's strangely ceremonious return to the United States, a new battlefront opened. The battle for public opinion was fought to outflank and envelop the enemy of the Constitution that each man believed of the other. President Truman worried that his sacking of the popular General of the Army, though needed to reassert proper civilian authority over the military, would make his request for defense appropriations stall in Congress, while the White House mail room surged with tens of thousands of letters supporting MacArthur.[15] Bumper stickers and major national newspaper editorials called for Truman's impeachment.[16] A Maryland woman attempted to send a telegram to the President, calling him a moron; after debate with the operator, she settled on the less offensive "witling."[17] The freshman senator from California, Richard Nixon, believed Truman's relief of MacArthur played directly to the spirit and desire of the Communists—it left the American fighting man's hands tied in knots.

The President's response was to split his effort and move in two directions at once. He went to the radio waves to defend the exercise of his constitutional power as Commander-in-Chief to the American people: "the cause of world peace is more important than any individual," he explained as if he had to apologize to a disciplined child with a "it was for a greater good" defense.[18] But the President nevertheless ordered a half-day schedule for government employees, so that they could greet MacArthur upon his heroic return to Washington, D.C. In the capital, the General delivered an eloquent and forceful speech before an assembled joint session of Congress, met 500,000 well-wishers on Pennsylvania Avenue, and was gifted a key to the city.[19] He was a modern day *strategoi* Themistocles, arguing the cause for a stronger military defense against the Red Empire, much as the Greek hero argued for Athenian resolve in the face of the invading Persian Empire.[20] And this was before his parades in the largest cities of the country. Truman, to dull the shine gleaming off the General after his speech and during those very parades, leaked the transcript of his meeting with MacArthur on Wake Island, during which the General made many pronouncements and military forecasts of Chinese capability that turned out to be wrong.[21]

*****

So who turned out to be victorious in this civ-mil battle of words? That answer is unlikely to ever be answered definitively. It would be pregnant with partisan views, and subject to the vagaries of historical interpretation and, probably, a dose of personality psychoanalysis. But it is not the most important question. We should really ask who was *right*. As historian H. W. Brands notes, the jubilation thrown at MacArthur at this time could be thought of as either celebration (of the General) or protest (against Truman, or his unpopular policies in Korea).[22] By what measure could we even determine what "right" is?

Clausewitz wrote that a stout defense was really a "shield made up of well-directed blows," that its purpose was preservation rather than conquest, and its force should swing heavily at the "decisive point" without reservation.[23] For MacArthur, the evidence of *his* self-preservation against the "grotesque" charge of insubordination and dereliction of duty,[24] levied by his political superiors, had already been introduced and admitted in the court of public opinion. And it was abundantly clear that therein lay the "decisive point" in this noncombatant drama. The hours of parades in New York City, Chicago, and San Francisco, the public schools in Oklahoma, New York, Illinois and Texas named in his honor, and the bronze statue standing proudly on the Plain at the United States Military Academy at West Point, with right hand clenched in a fist on his hip and left arm draped by a jacket and very likely a portrait of the man as he stepped off his plane that April day in Chicago, all testify to the enduring strength of that acclamation and esteem. It was clear he had no fear of a breached bastion wall by political critics, nor the lasting enmity of his President, none of whom could marshal up an offensive greater than MacArthur's ego and public reputation. Herbert Hoover wrote of the General, the "greatest combination of statesman and military leader that America has produced since George Washington," that MacArthur's deeds—however tainted—would "live forever after" him.[25]

MacArthur's relief, along with battlefield genius, has indeed lived forever after him. But, except for its extreme publicity and the pre-existing fame of the antagonist involved, the MacArthur-Truman "civil-military crisis" was not unique to American politics or war-making. Many military leaders preceded Mac, like Union Generals Freémont in the Western theater in 1861 and George McClellan in 1862 in the Eastern, in their vainglorious self-images and inability to work well with an amateur war strategist elected to the highest office of the land. Many also followed MacArthur, like General Matthew Ridgeway in the 1950s and General Colin Powel in the 1990s, both of whom—more than once—seemed to cash in their highly esteemed public reputations to openly criticized the administration's policy: debates over the how and when to deploy American troops abroad and more mundane but culturally (and therefore politically) sensitive issues like equal opportunity within the military's personnel policies. These latter day civil-military dramas, far from signaling an imminent coup, have nevertheless been labeled "crises" in the media and by pundits.

But there remains a critical problem. In and of themselves, they do not tell us whether the *quality* of civil-military relations during the episodes was improved by the political decision to fire the general (or not to) or was degraded by the general's apparent lack of (or too much) deference to civilian strategists. *Neither* in the law—the Constitution, federal statutes, cases and controversies, or even regulations and military doctrine—nor through conventional political science, history, or sociological studies of the subject, is capable of supporting the assumption that these episodes were pathological or a smear on one or both parties. In all cases, sufficient evidence can be laid on the table to show that the political decision, however unpopular, was constitutional and therefore "legal" and "probably right." But, equally defensible is the claim that the same evidence says nothing meaningful about whether the political decision *should* have been made; that, under the circumstances, the battle for more money or more troops or more institutional authority or battlefield discretion was the military's prerogative and should never have been invaded by a politician. Likewise, the senior admirals and generals that seemingly breach the boundaries of official propriety could either be fully justified by their sworn allegiance to the Constitution (rather than a particular government official or office) or condemned for exhibiting a political preference or political activity, as was MacArthur.

Like the division between strategy and tactics, the line drawn between breach of duty and devotion to duty is, strangely, not a bright one. The line of professional propriety seems to shift and spasm unpredictably within and between administrations. The spasm often seems entirely dependent on the peculiar personalities of the military and political elites involved, or—at best—simply a function of an observer's political preference. As a result, several important questions seem unanswerable: *Whose* loyalty was questionable? Loyalty to *what*, to *whom*, exactly? What other duty, if any, was breached? By what standard or norm do we consider it a breach?

In other words, diagnosing the health of the civil-military relationship, in context, appears to be without the proper generic measuring tool. It is not obvious, even after more than half a century, whether MacArthur's dismissal under the circumstances was symptomatic of a diseased civil-military relationship at the highest strategic level or was, instead, the appropriate remedy. If the latter, was it not evidence of a *well-functioning* immune system? Eleanor Roosevelt, in her syndicated column of April 9, 1951, represented this concerned view, skeptical of a field commander's political prerogative:

> I cannot feel, however, that a commanding general in the field, particularly when he commands for a group of nations, should take it upon himself to announce the policy that in his opinion should be followed in the area of the world where he commands troops. I cannot speak for any other citizen of the United States, and I know there are Representatives in the House and in the Senate who are in complete sympathy with the things that have been said lately by General MacArthur—but, for myself, I am unhappy about them.[26]

*****

This book is not biographical. It does not attempt a historical narration on individual military leaders and their sometimes collegial, oftentimes strained, and usually byzantine relations with the various political elites of the United States. Nor does this book promote a theoretical model of their behaviors in the hope that it will predict or explain, in quantifiable terms, their respective actions and reactions as they jostle for influence, credibility, and authority. This book does, however, aspire to a less-lofty but equally important goal: uncovering a method by which we—the public—and the parties mired in controversy themselves can diagnose the health of these critical relationships. I use the word "uncover" deliberately. The tool has been here all along, a function of the form these relationships take. My argument begins with three premises—premises that I hope are uncontroversial to the field of national security and defense, but significant enough to support the unconventional conclusions I draw later.

First, American politicians and appointed officials working for them, responsible for national security, are of a caste altogether different than senior military commanders and the Services' leadership in the Pentagon, despite the fact that they are on the same team roster, share the same ultimate objectives, and many former elite service-members cross over to civilian positions of elected or appointed authority. They are like long-separated twins, possessing memories of different professional and personal experiences, and relying on different forms (formal and informal) of training before being elevated to the strategic position they occupy—varying combinations of merit, popularity, good fortune, and reputation. They operate their day-to-day tactical affairs and longer-term strategic designs under different constraints and with apparently (but not necessarily real) different motives.

Politicians suffer the constraints of popular opinion, electoral ambitions, international approval, and peer expectations. On the other hand, for military leaders, constraints manifest as ambiguous or disliked policies handed "down from above" apparently without due consideration of their effect on the institutional prestige, legacies, or cultures of the Services or service-members (the key factor enflaming discrete episodes of civil-military strife, according to Professor and Navy veteran Dale Herspring). Constraints reveal themselves as a lack of adequate funding to support desired projects and programs, and they form as perception (real or imagined) that the civilians simply do not understand the military ethos or operations. Finally, they face constraints imposed by war itself—the terrible emotional and psychological cost of risking and losing lives of people they know or at least share their belief system and organizational culture and who are entrusted to their care. This cost inflates over time with the fog, fear, and friction (according to Clausewitz and modern strategy scholar Colin Gray) and unending uncertainty of enemy intentions and capabilities.[27]

These stark differences are only partially offset by the rules, regulations, and customs that have grown over decades, and have quite definitively forced these elites into different and unequal roles. Nevertheless, both camps include human beings and human beings, regardless of advanced training, schooling, temperament, a lifetime of rational and irrational decisions, the office held or the mission assigned, are all equally encumbered or ennobled by their passions, by their biases, and by their goals. MacArthur and Freémont were not all that categorically distinct from Truman or Lincoln. It would be silly, and largely ahistorical, to suggest that any rigid chasm of knowledge, perspective, interest, or influence divides civilian political leaders from the senior-most military officers of a state. Politicians are just as capable of appreciating the so-called "changing character of war,"[28] even if they have never served in one, as battle-tested generals are of appreciating that Congress does not act with one unified voice or on a schedule conducive to military plans, even if they have never held elective office. Courage, selflessness, and comradeship exist in political ranks no less than in the soldierly. Compromise, ideology, and ambition exhibit themselves daily in the E-ring corridor of the Pentagon and in command posts and headquarters around the world. These two castes then are not pure poles, but something symbiotic, though at times appearing to each other and to the casual outside observer as nothing other than personified antonyms, speaking and looking past each other and fumbling improbably into a semblance of successful cooperation. Even so eminent a military historian as John Keegan once wrote, contrasting the two and clearly coming down in favor of the heroic warrior, that "power corrupts . . . [but] [t]he life of the camp corrupts less than that of the court: battle tests the real worth of a man as politics never can."[29] Keegan never held an elective office nor wore a uniform in combat and illustrates that even detached scholarly study tends to assume some structural, intrinsic difference *must* exist and divide the civil from the military—whether it be a separation based on function or a separation based on form.

If Keegan and other separatists are wrong, though, why are there so many examples in our history of what appear to be debilitating civi-military tensions, especially in a culture where a military putsch is laughably improbable? What explains the successful wartime relationships in which a clearly domineering civilian elite overmatches his or her generals, determining not only strategy but tactics? What explains the successful wartime relationship in which a clearly deferential civilian leader treats his military strategist as a close partner? Why is there a no way to objectively determine whether such tensions are even pulling the parties asunder? For simplicity, let us call this first premise, and the questions it generates, the *Difference by Degree Principle.*

Building on the "unequal dialogue" perspective advanced by Eliot Cohen, my second premise is that these strategic roles include one that appears to the other as the "amateur" (at least in the field of national security) yet wields the undislocatable and supreme authority, and one that accepts the responsibilities and social respectability as the "professional" but who must be subjected to the legitimate authority over national security vested in others. Here, "amateur" does not pejoratively mean inadequate, junior, incapable, or comparatively less relevant. "Professional" does not necessarily mean better-informed, better trained, or usually right with the amateur colleague wrong on substance. Rather, this is the *Principle of Amateur Authority Over Professional Specialization.*

As a consequence, these elites find themselves acting as "choice architects"—a colorful and useful label coined by legal scholar Cass Sunstein and behavioral economist Richard Thaler. These elites must find ways and means, within the scope of their unequal but symbiotic roles, to "organize the context in which [others] make decisions;"[30] their chief goal in organizing the context is to influence, shape, and channel those decisions in a manner preferred by the choice architect.

*****

Many accomplished thinkers have descended on the broad interdisciplinary subject of American civil-military relations. This book owes a great deal to their analyses, most notably those of Samuel Huntington, Peter Feaver, Don Snider, and Cohen, all of whom will be discussed in more detail later. My third premise has evolved from Feaver's (and some others') view of the civil-military relationship as a principal–agent dyad. But rather than rely on a microeconomic, rational actor model of these actions and reactions, punches and counters, incentives and punishments (which Feaver admits to be slightly unrealistic), I focus on the point that such symbiotic relations exist ubiquitously in everyday life, and they more-or-less allow the world to go 'round. My professional background as a lawyer is both a testimony to that fact and, it turns out, a useful proof of concept. Just as clients rely on their lawyers for a suite of skills to achieve some goal, from creating a trust to merging a company to defending against a criminal prosecution, classic civil-military relations theory beginning with Huntington and continuing now with Snider emphasizes that the strategic civilian–principal relies on the strategic military leader-agent for three generic functions. These functions remain beyond the competence of, or at least the time available to, that principal: *Advice, Action, and Ability*. It is the agent's *advice* based on a detached perspective tailored to the known aims of the client and based on that agent's technical knowledge, experience, and judgment. It is the agent's *action* executed, managed, or planned to free the time of the principal to more freely act (or not act), supervise, and evaluate options and opportunities without being bogged down in detail work. That work, in turn, demands specialized *ability*, possessed by the agent. Let us call this the *Advice-Action-Ability Principle*.

The aim of this book is to describe, in an original but comprehensive way, the dynamic between the senior civilian American policy-makers. It is a diverse ecology: mostly in the White House, but also on Capitol Hill and rotating through the Pentagon, and their senior military officer advisors—the individual Service chiefs of staff, the collective corporate body of the Joint Chiefs of Staff, the geographic proconsuls we call Combatant Commanders and the uniformed leaders directing the employment, fighting, fitting, and training of the American Armed Forces. This relationship is, by virtue of both evidence from the field and an easily understandable analogy, a simple principal–agent relationship but defined as such in *legal* terms—no different in *form* than the dynamic between other principals and their agents, familiar faces from contemporary life like doctors and their patients, voters and politicians, a trustee and the beneficiary, and the lawyer and the client.

The examples on which to base a book like this are legion. While some—like the MacArthur-Truman episode—are obvious, others are less so. We can watch the strategic principal–agent dynamic play out in 2010 between General Stanley McChrystal and President Obama over apparent disrespect to the latter and his national security team—the first and only time the overall combat commander has been relieved by a president since MacArthur in 1951; between General Eric Shinseki and Secretary of Defense Donald Rumsfeld over who would predict the "right" size force for Iraq in 2003 and the ultimate characterization of that war; between President Eisenhower and his former colleague, Army Chief of Staff Matthew Ridgeway over the future role of the Army at the beginning of the Cold War; between President Kennedy and his Joint Chiefs—with an interloper in the form of Maxwell Taylor—in the time after the Bay of Pigs fiasco and during Cuban Missile Crisis; and between Senator John McCain and the Chairman of the Joint Chiefs of Staff, General Martin Dempsey, over how much the latter would reveal to the former about ongoing debates within the Obama team over possible military strategy in Syria's civil war.

Uncovering, and sometimes rediscovering, these historical and contemporary episodes and filtering them through the lens of agency relationships and against a backdrop of extensive scholarly studies was a daunting ambition. It was a challenge I chose in order to complete a Masters of Laws thesis requirement at the Army's Judge Advocate General's Legal Center and School in 2014. With the help and encouragement of many of my peer officers, the faculty, and several others, the next challenge was to amplify the material into this book—a subject much larger in scope and far more removed from the traditional topical areas analyzed with legal rigor at the JAG School. First, a large debt is owed to Colonel (Retired) David E. Johnson, Ph.D., the first director of the Army's Strategic Studies Group (SSG), who graciously hired me for a Fellowship on the SSG. For an exceptionally eye-opening year, I was surrounded by an intellectually diverse, interdisciplinary cohort of the finest and most creative thinkers, officers and two sergeants major with whom I have ever worked or known. Membership on that team allowed me to witness the tremors, quakes, and aftershocks of many contemporary civil-military debates and which kindled the questions that drove my initial research. Many others offered advice, suggestions, edits, and encouragement as I tinkered with innumerable drafts, surgically tailored them to academic requirements, and then began to translate them into this book: Lieutenant General H.R. McMaster, Colonel (Retired) Don Snider, Major Temi Anderson, Major Sarah Rykowski, Major Brendan Mayer, Major J.T. Soron, Major Elizabeth Turner, and of course my outstanding editorial team at Palgrave, Dr. Anca Pusca and Anne Schult. I owe special thanks to Dave Dillege, editor-in-chief of *Small Wars Journal*, who graciously permitted me to republish an earlier essay of mine as a slightly modified but complete chapter here (Chapter 10),[31] and to the United States Military Academy's *Modern War Institute*, which published a modified version of what has become Chapter 8.[32] My father, Lieutenant Colonel (Retired) David S. Maurer, and mother, Tina, never failed to spot a gap in logic or awkward phrase and patiently listened to my explanations like the model teachers they have always been to me. Finally, my wife and best friend, Jill, was my favorite (but most feared) editor, line coach, therapist, and cheerleader.

*****

My hope is that this book will be read by serious students of government, military history, and national security, as well as serving officers, civilian leaders, and the general civilian public—a population that currently has very little personal empathetic connection with either the governing class or the military, and whom I believe to be without the right tools to spot and diagnose the problems and conflicts we too often self-inflict.

Ultimately, democracy is based on accountability—both personal and as a body politic. As retired Lieutenant General-turned-philosopher James Dubik recently wrote, citizens "expect their leaders to account for their decisions or actions … explanation and justification—whether during a political campaign

[or] at a memorial service with the family of a veteran killed in combat, or among those with whom one just fought—go with the territory of leadership."[33] But we cannot establish accountability without judgment, but we should not judge without understanding first. We cannot understand, though, without context. We cannot establish context without discriminating among an ever-expanding universe of potentially relevant facts. We cannot discriminate among various facts without knowing what the "norms" are that give these facts some relative value. This book is about discovering and labeling those norms, and therefore a step toward accountability.

NOTES

1. The details of this Chicago welcoming can be found in Clayton Kirkpatrick, "America's Midwest Reception is Ready," *Chicago Tribune*, at 1–2 (April 26, 1951).
2. H.W. BRANDS, THE GENERAL VS. THE PRESIDENT: MACARTHUR AND TRUMAN AT THE BRINK OF NUCLEAR WAR 321 (2016) ("The millions of Americans cheering and shouting for MacArthur wanted the general to lead them, like a modern Moses, out of the Wilderness of uncertainty that seemed to be Americans' lot in the contemporary struggle against communism... if anyone could restore the certainty—the moral certainty, the civic certainty, the political certainty... MacArthur could").
3. WILLIAM MANCHESTER, AMERICAN CAESAR 751–56 (1978).
4. H.W. BRANDS, THE GENERAL VS. THE PRESIDENT 319–20 (2016) (quoting Truman's remarks by radio the night he relieved MacArthur).
5. MANCHESTER, AMERICAN CAESAR at 758–59.
6. DONALD STOKER, THE GRAND DESIGN: STRATEGY AND THE U.S. CIVIL WAR 44–55 (2010).
7. T. HARRY WILLIAMS, LINCOLN AND HIS GENERALS 33 (1952).
8. JAMES MCPHERSON, BATTLE CRY OF FREEDOM 352–54 (1988). Lincoln was forced, a year later, to address yet another "proconsular" general—this time, David Hunter commanding Union forces along the coast of South Carolina and Georgia—who summarily freed slaves without consulting or even informing the President first. Lincoln revoked the military order, and said "No commanding general shall do such a thing, on my responsibility, without consulting me... I reserve this [decision] to myself." *Id.* at 499.
9. WILLIAMS, LINCOLN AND HIS GENERALS 35–38 (1952).
10. MANCHESTER, AMERICAN CAESAR at 760.
11. President Harry S. Truman, diary entry (April 5, 1951), National Archives, available at https://catalog.archives.gov/id/7542750?q=korea%20macarthur%20truman.

12. MANCHESTER, AMERICAN CAESAR at 763.
13. *Id.*, at 764.
14. President Harry S. Truman, diary entry (April 6, 1951), National Archives, available at https://catalog.archives.gov/id/7542751?q=korea%20macarthur%20truman.
15. BRANDS, THE GENERAL VS. THE PRESIDENT 312.
16. MANCHESTER, AMERICAN CAESAR at 776; BRANDS, THE GENERAL VS. THE PRESIDENT at 313.
17. *Id.*, at 777.
18. http://www.pbs.org/wgbh/amex/macarthur/filmmore/reference/primary/officialdocs03.html.
19. MANCHESTER, AMERICAN CAESAR at 792.
20. THUCYDIDES, HISTORY OF THE PELOPONNESIAN WAR, 44 (trans. Rex Warner) (1972).
21. BRANDS, THE GENERAL VS. THE PRESIDENT at 329.
22. *Id.*, at 320.
23. CARL VON CLAUSEWITZ, ON WAR 204, 357 (Michael Howard, Peter Paret eds., trans., Princeton University Press 1984) (1832).
24. DOUGLAS MACARTHUR, REMINISCENCES 446 (1964).
25. *Id.*, at 461 (quoting a letter MacArthur received from former President Hoover, upon the General's return to the U.S. in 1951).
26. http://www.gwu.edu/~erpapers/myday/displaydoc.cfm?_y=1951&_f=md001877.
27. CARL VON CLAUSEWITZ, ON WAR 119–21 (Michael Howard, Peter Paret eds., trans., Princeton University Press 1984) (1832); COLIN S. GRAY, MODERN STRATEGY 41 (1999).
28. Colin S. Gray, *War – Continuity in Change, and Change in Continuity*, PARAMETERS 6–7 (Summer 2010).
29. JOHN KEEGAN, THE MASK OF COMMAND 89 (1987).
30. RICHARD H. THALER & CASS R. SUNSTEIN, NUDGE 3 (2009).
31. Dan Maurer, *The Future Fallacy: A Conversation About the "Certainty Principle,"* SMALL WARS JOURNAL (March 12, 2015), http://smallwarsjournal.com/jrnl/art/the-future-fallacy-a-conversation-about-the-%E2%80%9Ccertainty-principle%E2%80%9D.
32. Dan Maurer, *A Civil War Vignette that Explains Modern Civ-Mil Relations*, United States Military Academy, Modern War Institute, War Council blog (August 14, 2016), http://mwi.usma.edu/fidelity-frankness-collide-portrait-grant/.
33. JAMES M. DUBIK, JUST WAR RECONSIDERED: STRATEGY, ETHICS, AND THEORY 25 (2016).

CHAPTER 2

The Opening Statement

Theirs not to reason why /theirs but to do and die.[1] Though Tennyson wrote of the futile charge of a British brigade during the Crimean War, this speaks just as well of the tension between civilian political leadership and the military it commands. This tension between those who "reason why" about the employment of armed force and those that "do and die" has a long history. It creates two complimentary concerns in American politics. First, when does the military elite become too political or partisan, as President Truman believed of General MacArthur? Second, are the political elites too involved in tactical matters best left to the uniformed experts, as MacArthur believed?[2] Surprisingly, there is no way to currently answer either of those questions. Part of the explanation for that is these questions turn on when the "tactical" becomes "strategic" and where (if at all) the separation of responsibility over those domains might reside. Another part is the reality that in most cases, at the strategic planning and decision-making level, the line that divides the political choices from the military execution of those choices is rarely a crisp or neat one.[3] Without clear answers, this tension creates an unabated source of friction in American civil-military politics: The inability to distinguish between events that signal *symptoms* of unhealthy civil-military relationships from those events that are actually *remedies* for such conflict. This, in turn, means there is no objective way to diagnose the health of a strategic civil-military relationship.

D. Maurer, *Crisis, Agency, and Law in US Civil-Military Relations*,
DOI 10.1007/978-3-319-53526-5_2

This frustration, at its root, is a *legal* problem even if infrequently studied or described in such terms. It is a legal problem because it is fundamentally a fight over rights, authorities, and powers shared between two very different kinds of parties. It is a legal problem because of its Constitutional origins. It is a legal problem because laws have attempted with some, but incomplete, success in the past to engineer the lanes in which these two parties drive.

The animating concern underneath these fights has always been, on the one hand, the feared *coup d'état*, or the utter disregard or willful blindness to pragmatic military advice that costs lives of service-members needlessly.[4] However, the effects of these fights have been anything but uniform. History is replete with examples of firm, even if obtrusive, civilian control under a theory that all of war is politics anyway. Similarly, abundant are prescriptions for leaving the military's hands untied under a theory that a professionally educated warrior caste must not be micromanaged to death by civilians.[5]

Because civilian control of the armed forces is largely taken for granted in the United States, historically free from *coup d'états*, there remains an undiagnosed and understudied element to the expected tension between strategic civilian and military policy-makers. These separate and unequal partners tend to interact continuously in ways that leave one or the other directly (or perceived to be) disadvantaged, mistrusted, ignored, or recklessly employed. Such tensions risk unstable and unpredictable policy-making. As one prominent scholar has noted, "[t]he stakes are so high [and] the gaps in mutual understanding so stark [that] these relationships merit close attention... [t]hese peculiarities and conditions are unique and extreme, and they produce relationships far more complicated and tense than either citizen or soldier may expect."[6] Scholars, pundits, and the actual participants in these relationships, looking only at these harmful aftershocks, however, may misrepresent the underlying concerns and result in misdiagnosing a supposed "civil-military crisis."

Misdiagnosis is as persistent a risk as these recurring aftershocks. It is recognized by the academic field of civil-military relations traditionally dominated by history, sociology, and political science.[7] These studies reveal an apparent gap. They lack objective criteria or known norms for assessing the relative health of these relationships in context. Despite its fundamental nature as a legal challenge, neither law nor doctrine (the military's internal "law") fills in this gap with practical advice or standards for the parties to these relationships. Therefore, the chapters that follow offer a jurisprudential approach to this tension by using a form of legal reasoning to apply a legal concept and propose a legal change in order to suggest that such criteria are both desirable and relatively achievable.

Of course, Tennyson was not the only notable author to have thought about the difference—by degree—between civilian authority and military action:

> *The great thing about an Army officer is that he does what you tell him to do.*[8]
>
> *The particulars of your plans I neither know, or seek to know. You are vigilant and self-reliant; and, pleased with this, I wish not to obtrude any constraints or restraints upon you.*[9]
>
> *No major proposal for war can be worked out in ignorance of political factors; and when people talk, as they often do, about harmful political influence in the management of war, they are not really saying what they mean. Their quarrel is with the policy itself, not with its influence. If the policy is right—that is, successful—every intentional effect it has on the conduct of war can only be to the good.*[10]

Finding a common theme among Theodore Roosevelt, Abraham Lincoln, and Carl von Clausewitz is usually challenging. Their attitudes, however, on the complicated, contentious relationships between politicians and military leaders, revealed in these quotes, reflect the most conventional attitudes of participants in American strategic civil-military relationships. The first, coming from Roosevelt, reflects the presumption of military subservience to civil authority. The fundamental source most often cited for this axiom is the U.S. Constitution, and those duties are reflected by the officer's oath of office.[11] The second quote, in a letter from President Lincoln to General Ulysses S. Grant, reflects a belief that fewer political "restraints" ought to be imposed on competent military leaders during the exigencies of war, a common belief that some scholars, like Cohen, have begun to counter with contrary historical evidence. The third, coming from Prussian military philosopher Clausewitz in the early Nineteenth Century, foreshadows the contemporary view that the respective fields and actors of politics, policy, and war necessarily merge.[12] These men poignantly illustrate that the stresses in strategic civil-military relationship dynamics result from two fundamental causes.

First, there is no consensus about whether all three views are simultaneously true or, if not, which of these views is, or should be, dominant in

American politics or reflected in the law. Second, and in part because there is no consensus, there is no objective basis upon which to determine if the elite parties to these relationships are engaged in behavior that is self-destructive: unhealthy for a democracy or for the fighting in which it engages. These two factors yield the Strategic Civil-Military Relationship Problem.

The Strategic Civil-Military Relationship Problem

> I am here in a terrible place—the enemy have from 3 to 4 times my force—the Presdt [sic] is an idiot, the old General in his dotage—they cannot or will not see the true state of affairs. Most of my troops are demoralized by the defeat at Bull Run, some [regiments] even mutinous—I have probably stopped that—but you see my position is not pleasant... I am weary of all this. I have no ambition in the present affairs—only wish to save my country—& find the incapables around me will not permit it![13]

Three weeks after the first major battle of the American Civil War, at Bull Run, Union Major General George McClellan wrote this letter to his wife, Mary Ellen.[14] Though Mary Ellen likely supported her melancholic husband, it is doubtful that either she or the general understood how his plaintive, private note illustrates an important aspect of American democracy that continues today—the temporary, but tempestuous, marriage of civilian policy-maker and military leader.[15]

Among the consequences of American foreign policy since the terrorist attacks on September 11, 2001, senior civilian and military strategic decision-makers[16] have suffered, or have appeared to suffer, from the repetitive straining of their professional relationships. Senior civilian appointees in the Department of Defense publically criticized General Eric Shinseki, then Army Chief of Staff, for answering a question during a Senate Armed Services Committee hearing that departed from the Bush administration's asserted number of troops required to stabilize Iraq after its military defeat.[17] A polarizing Secretary of Defense, Donald Rumsfeld, was seemingly intent on using the wars in Iraq and Afghanistan as proving ground for his views on modernizing ("transforming") the military enterprise despite battlefield conditions that instead came to justify a high-manpower counterinsurgency strategy.[18] President Bush replaced the "embattled" and heavily criticized Rumsfeld with Robert Gates, after his Republican Party lost its majority in congressional mid-term elections.[19] In 2007, after nearly three years of command in Iraq, and in his first appearance before Congress as the Army Chief of Staff, General George Casey stated unambiguously that his Service was "out of balance"—that it could not accomplish all it was being tasked or was expected to do.[20] This candid admission, at odds with the Commander-in-Chief's wartime expectation, was remarkable if only because General Casey personally prompted the testimony himself—he was not asked by Congress for his opinion.[21]

Real or apparent conflict and tension did not abate with Barack Obama's election in 2008. Two consecutive commanding generals in Afghanistan, David McKiernan[22] and Stanley McChrystal,[23] were asked to resign in the first two years of Obama's initial term in office. Admiral William Fallon, the Combatant Commander overseeing two campaigns in the Middle East, also resigned over his tendency to publically discuss his strategic preferences despite knowing them to be at odds with the Administration's view.[24] Chuck Hagel resigned from his post as Secretary of Defense amid suspicion that his views on intervention in Syria were also unaligned with the rest of the Obama Administration, despite armed conflict in Ukraine, belligerent tension with Russia, Islamic State's rapid advance and occupation in parts of Syria and Iraq, a pandemic threatening in Western Africa, and other lesser-known threats to American security.[25] As of this writing, President-Elect Donald Trump has caused many, like Tom Ricks, to wonder when, how, and to what extent the military leadership will push back on what is assumed by some to be autocratic (and perhaps worse, unpredictable) decision-making.[26] It is a fair recap to conclude that the last decade and a half of strategic civil-military relations has been marred by misplaced trust, miscommunication, candor when and where it was inappropriate, and the absence of candor when it was needed the most.

As historian and retired Army officer Matthew Moten recently wrote of modern American political-military relationships, "[t]ension is natural ... [c] onflict is ubiquitous."[27] The early years of the Clinton Administration, for instance, provide an example of what the media and scholars described as substantial and deviant civil-military conflict—a "full blown clash."[28] As a result, *unhealthy* conflict and tension should be of concern and distinguished from conflict *per se*, or tension between the strategic military and political elites. Scholars have pointed to subtle dangers to the effective management of national security policy and war-fighting, such as generals who fail to advise about the "incongruence" between policy ends and military means.[29] They also see generals' foot-dragging and public dissent, unbridled criticism aimed at politicians and policy-making paralysis.[30] It is possible that these episodes of civil-military strife are really symptoms of a chronic illness: A "lymphoma" as one scholar has described it.[31] They could also be warning signs of an acute wounding—the proverbial stab in the back—to one of the parties, spurred by long neglect and mutual distrust.[32] Alternatively, they may be simply the unavoidable give-and-take of committed and knowledgeable professionals, one constitutionally subordinate to the other, pursuing divergent policy goals in a democracy.[33] Indeed, some successful wartime civilian leaders often micromanaged their subordinate commanders, second-guessed military strategy, and ignored military advice with amateur-like zeal.[34] For instance, Secretary of Defense Robert McNamara, emboldened by his successful plan to de-escalate the Cuban Missile Crisis and his dimmed regard for the senior military advice he received, personally managed the details of the early years of the Vietnam War, instilling nearly dominant political control over operations and strategy. One hundred years earlier, President Lincoln, not satisfied with being lectured by sluggishly moving General George McClellan on the political objectives of the Civil War, went so far—literally—as to visit his army in the field, personally interrogating several of McClellan's subordinate commanders on a range of subjects, from tactics and logistics to the health of the Union troops and the disposition of the Confederate forces. More recently, President Bush's controversial decision in early 2007 to approve the so-called "surge strategy" in Iraq put an additional 30,000 U.S. troops in that theater of war and emphasized population security over training the Iraq security forces, was over the objection and disagreement from key military leaders, including General George Casey (Commander of Multinational Force-Iraq) and Casey's superior, General John Abizaid (Commander of Central Command at the time).[35]

Despite a wealth of historical data in which to witness strategic civil-military relationships form, dissolve, and fracture, handicapping proper policy-making and combat operations, some observers steadfastly maintain that all is still well. One such author wrote:

> America's military operates comfortably within constitutional notions of separated powers, participating appropriately in defense and national security policymaking with due deference to the principle of civilian control. Indeed, an active and vigorous role by the military in the policy process is and always has been essential to the common defense.[36]

This defense of the status quo is quite reasonable if the assumption that anything short of a *coup d' état* is healthy civil-military relations in operation.[37] Moreover, the Services themselves seem intent on reminding their members and the public that they have always unquestionably remained, and will always remain, subservient to civilian government regardless of party identity, policy disagreement, or personal animosity. If the Services are addressing the subject of a professional "ethic" themselves, and no serious voice has expressed a concern that a military junta is inevitable, there appears to be no urgent need for a new way to envision the strategic civil-military relationship or spend time detecting symptoms of unhealthy relations. Indeed, some argue that the alleged controversies are too ominously portrayed by scholars and journalists anyway. Richard Betts, for example, argues that debates over whether to intervene in a foreign crisis with force empirically depict a military just as cautious and reluctant as civilian policy-making elites. Richard Hooker argues that the public and academic portrayals of civil-military crises reflect "poor history and even poorer political science" because these tensions are actually "deeply rooted in the American system of separated powers, regulated by strong traditions of subordination."[38]

Not all scholars are so nonplussed. Michael Pearlman observes that while pluralism and debate often prevent authoritarianism, they also generate ambiguity and inconsistency.[39] Publishing a prescription for military intervention in *Foreign Affairs,* as General Colin Powell did in 1992,[40] might suggest a general is no longer just implementing policy, but conceiving and driving it in a way that limits options available to a public opinion-sensitive Administration. In contrast, "living deeply in the tactical weeds"[41] might signal that a President, or a key civilian subordinate, has detrimentally emasculated the military because he or she no longer trusts the military expertise or advice being offered.[42]

Or, the *opposite* conclusions may be equally drawn. That two mutually exclusive conclusions can be drawn from the same data is easier to digest when considering the many plausible explanations for tension between strategic civil-military elites. Colin Gray suggests that the magnitude of the ever-present friction is a function of four factors, including a "culture clash," ignorance of how the other works, their distinct responsibilities, and finally the intrinsic difficulty of "relating military action and intended political consequences."[43] Peter Rodman, a veteran advisor in five presidential administrations, identified a cornerstone philosophical disagreement:

> In the back of our minds, perhaps, there is a technocratic model of government in which these professionals should be left to go about their business

> uncorrupted by politics or even by policy influence from elected or appointed officials who may have their own philosophy or objectives in the matter. But in truth, this is the wrong model. The political process that is the ultimate determinant of national policy is not a corruption; it is a source of legitimacy.[44]

There is no unambiguous answer. Looking at the gap in civil-military relationship studies and practice, the inability to objectively determine whether these and other similar episodes are good, bad, or inconsequential is becoming obvious. That inability, of course, has political consequences as well as military ones, and provides grist for presidential campaigns.[45]

The Scholarship Gap: The Inability to Diagnose Poor Civil-Military Relationships

The study of civil-military relations tends to split along several axes: demographic, personality, and operational.[46] When scholars, journalists, and pundits write of a harmful "crisis" or "gap" in modern American civil-military relations, they are typically referring to the perceived divide between military culture and the rest of society,[47] or a fissure between the President or politically appointed civilian leaders in the defense establishment and uniformed leaders of the Armed Services,[48] or the gulf between what Congress or the President is willing to allocate to support national security and that which is identified as a need by its practitioners.[49] Ultimately, these axes reflect three ways of viewing the same fundamental concern: the extent to which civilians remain in control of their military.[50]

There is another civil-military relations gap, at which Robert Gates hints in recounting his time as Secretary of Defense.[51] Unaddressed by the rich theoretical and empirical study and day-to-day practice, this gap is the inability to objectively diagnose a diseased, or at least unhealthy, relationship between these strategic policy-makers. Civil-military studies tend to conclude that there are indicators of "good" or "bad" relationships, but *admit* that no "simple standard" might do so definitively.[52] Such ambiguity has led to the American public's confusion when viewing these suspect relationships.[53] Richard Betts wrote that determining if the military's influence on policy is "too much" or "too little" does *not* vary with context, but rather "can only be a judgment that depends on one's political preferences."[54] Another scholar compared this challenge to that of the Supreme Court's definition of pornography: maybe we'll just know ["bad" civil-military relations] when we see it.[55] There is a palpable absence of what Rodman referred to as "neutral principles."[56]

From the perspective of either of the actors, or the American public,[57] this gap means that rifts form, tensions build, and relationships break with adverse consequences following. Budgets, for example, may be slashed, civilian officials may direct policy while ignoring military advice,[58] civil servants may become captured by special interests, senior officers may turn into political advocates or acolytes, wars that should be won are lost, and wars that should never have happened become inevitable.[59] As described later, these rifts are well documented in the relationship between American political and military strategy-makers. Not only are they prevalent in every administration and every period of armed conflict,[60] the framers of the U.S. Constitution anticipated and largely welcomed these kinds of episodes.[61] Though frequent, these contentious issues rarely rouse the American public to express grave concern because American political experience lacks the pressing probability of a *coup*.[62] Given the institutionalized tensions between the political and military elites, a long history of that tension becoming publically observable, and a relationship largely "take[n] for granted" by a "vast majority of Americans,"[63] the obvious question is whether any of this conflict between the top strategists is normatively good, bad, or inconsequential.[64]

The health of these normal and routine interactions is at question because there is no objective standard against which to contrast them, nor universally accepted expectations and norms.[65] Because there is a difference between dissent and disobedience that "unschooled policy makers or an uninformed population"[66] often fail to see, a frank and "productive exchange of views" is, by itself, an insufficient benchmark of healthy relations.[67] Reflecting on his time as the Army Chief of Staff, military representative to the President, and ultimately the Chairman during the beginning of the Vietnam War, Maxwell Taylor described what he believed was the

> importance of an intimate, easy relationship, born of friendship and mutual regard, between the president an the Chiefs [and which] is particularly important in the case of the Chairman [of the Joint Chiefs of Staff]... the Chairman should be a true believer in the foreign policy and military strategy of the administration which he serves.[68]

The *absence* of such a frank, candid, exchange of views is a similarly insufficient benchmark because, for some analysts, the "ultimate test" of this relationship's health is not the extent to which policy preferences of one party dominate over the others, but rather the degree to which the relationship overall enables or cripples military effectiveness in war.[69] This *in extremis* perspective, however, may not always be the most relevant: The relationship between civilian and military policy-makers exists regardless of whether troops are deployed in combat. Strain on those relationships may be caused and aggravated by events unrelated to wartime decision-making and advice.[70]

These episodes have little to do with direct war-time success, yet illustrate profound differences of opinion among the strategic policy-makers and senior military leaders. The only thing civil-military relations theory can say about these episodes is that they certainly depict overt and covert challenges to civilian control of the military. They might reflect the driving influence of personality conflicts,[71] external threats,[72] failure to live up to professional ethos and norms,[73] or the inability of the civilian and military elites to "converge" in agreement on certain essential policy issues.[74] Ultimately, however, current theory provides no way to gauge their relevance or impact in context against some objective standard.[75] Other than looking at the output, like publically disclosed expressions that may superficially look like conflict, strife, disagreement, balking, ignoring orders, or stonewalling, Michael Desch notes that civil-military relationship scholarship simply does not provide the means for this diagnosis.[76] Historian Andrew Bacevich, too, complains that the political scientists, sociologists, and historians who analyze this subject along certain narrow dimensions give the public:

> no salient context in which to evaluate the bickering, suspicion, and machinations that make their way to the surface, there to be reported by journalists who are themselves ill-equipped to interpret their significance... [and] [w]ithout such a context, the issue becomes mere news, of no more lasting import than a train wreck.[77]

Neither current law nor the individual Service regulations nor military doctrine, provide any objective criteria either.[78] However, the law of agency does have bearing on this subject and may provide the roadmap for establishing such norms and criteria—in effect, Rodman's "neutral principles."

Applying the Law of Agency

This book will employ basic concepts from the law of agency to draw an analogy. Just as a lawyer is as an "agent" for his client or "principal," in that he is authorized by another person to act for that person under certain conditions, senior civilian political leaders responsible for national security expect their military advisors and commanders in the field to perform with "utmost good faith, trust, confidence, and candor" and to "act with highest degree of honesty and loyalty."[79] The civilian policy-making principal demands and creates a de facto fiduciary relationship with the senior policy-executing military officer agents.[80] An agency relationship results because the military, individually and collectively, is subject to civilian control but the civilians must necessarily rely on the special expertise and capability possessed by their military subordinates in order to execute national policy.[81] This, we will see later, is *not* the agency of the simplified employer–employee relationship; rather, it is a complex set of shared and discrete responsibilities built on mutual understanding, mutual need, and mutual accountability.[82]

By thinking of the relationship in fiduciary terms, agency theory also provides a useful paradigm from which to establish transparent norms and expectations of the civil-military relationship.[83] Duties, such as candor, competence, good faith and loyalty, and scope of responsibility will be examined, analogized to the attorney–client model, and applied to the strategic civilian–military relationship. The premise can be summed up in four words, slightly amended a well-known service motto: *fiduciary* duty, honor, and country.

Notes

1. Alfred, Lord Tennyson, *The Charge of the Light Brigade* (1854), PoetryFoundation.org, http://www.poetryfoundation.org/poem/174586 (last visited March 19, 2015).
2. Gordon A. Craig, *The Political Leader as Strategist, in* Makers of Modern Strategy: from Machiavelli to the Nuclear Age 481, 482 (Peter Paret ed., 1986) [hereinafter Craig, *Political Leader as Strategist*].
3. James M. Dubik, Just War Reconsidered: Strategy, Ethics, and Theory 22 (2016) ("Such a strict role differentiation is too simplistic ... recognizing that the conduct of war includes more than fighting, [there are] mutually related responsibilities among those senior civil and military leaders who must wage war—that is, the responsibility to figure out war aims, identify and promulgate war strategies and policies, ensure that military and nonmilitary campaigns are

means toward the declared aims, and make both civil and military bureaucracies work well enough that they help achieve the aims set").

4. A *coup d'état* is a form of domestic military intervention involving a planned effort by military elites to seize national power from the incumbent political elites. It is generally less expansive in effect and participation than a national "revolution" and usually does not involve large elements of the mass military. *See* Rebecca L. Schiff, The Military and Domestic Politics: A Concordance Theory of Civil-Military Relations 21 (2009); *see also* Charles J. Dunlap, Jr., *The Origins of the American Military Coup of 2012*, Parameters, Winter 2011–12 (*reprint* from Winter 1992–93), at 107.
5. Eliot A. Cohen, Supreme Command: Soldiers, Statesmen, and Leadership in Wartime 2–3 (2002).
6. *Id.* at 2.
7. One outlier to this general academic trend is John Yoo, *Administration of War*, 58 Duke L. J. 2277 (2009). Professor Yoo applies rational actor-based agency theory, developed for civil-military relations theory by political scientist Peter Feaver (*see infra* Part II.C.4). Yoo suggests that general administrative law neglects the study of civil-military relations, but that administrative law scholars ought to study it as if it were any other constitutional and statutory interpretation problem involving the separate powers of the legislative and executive branches ("civilian control of the military is perhaps the most important principle of the American constitutional system of government"). *Id.* at 2281. Yoo asserts that looking to government "agencies" such as the Armed Services, through a principal–agent lens, may aid the effort to re-impose proper civilian control over a "shirking" military with an unfortunate "growing policy independence." *Id.* at 2292. Yoo's study, as distinguished from this thesis, does not apply fiduciary duties derived from the "law of agency," and does not address challenges to diagnosing the health of strategic civil-military relationships—it is silent on the question of whether specific "crises" are really symptoms of a pathological relationships.
8. Theodore Roosevelt, *quoted in* Morris Janowitz, The Professional Soldier: A Social and Political Portrait 379 (1960) [hereinafter, Janowitz, The Professional Soldier]. For a modern version of this sentiment, consider retired Lieutenant General Daniel Bolger's reflection on the current prevailing military views on the civil-military relationship: "[c]ivilian control of the military means the suits propose and the uniforms dispose… those on active duty almost always kept their opinions private [and] gave their views to the civilian officials in confidence behind closed doors." Daniel P. Bolger, Why We Lost: A General's Inside Account of the Iraq and Afghanistan Wars 423 (2014) [hereinafter, Bolger, Why We Lost].

9. Abraham Lincoln to Lieutenant General U.S. Grant, April 30, 1864, *quoted in* LINCOLN ON WAR 244 (Harold Holzer ed., 2011).
10. CARL VON CLAUSEWITZ, ON WAR 608 (Michael Howard, Peter Paret eds., trans., Princeton University Press 1984) (1832).
11. *See also* Barbara W. Tuchman, *Generalship*, PARAMETERS, Winter 2010–11, at 11, 20 (reprinting speech delivered at the U.S. Army War College, April 3, 1972):

    Traditionally, the American Army has been, and consciously has considered itself, the neutral instrument of state policy… [and] [w]hen it is ordered into action, the Army does not ask "Why?" or "What for?" In the past that has been a fundamental presumption.
12. *See, e.g.*, U.S. DEP'T OF NAVY, MARINE CORPS DOCTRINE PUBLICATION (MCDP) 1, WARFIGHTING 23–25 (20 June 1997), *available at* https://www.doctrine.usmc.mil/signpubs/mcdp1.pdf; *see also* GIDEON ROSE, HOW WARS END: WHY WE ALWAYS FIGHT THE LAST BATTLE 3 (2010), *and* COLIN S. GRAY, MODERN STRATEGY 30, 55 (1999), *and* LAWRENCE FREEDMAN, STRATEGY: A HISTORY 86 (2013).
13. THE CIVIL WAR PAPERS OF GEORGE B. MCCLELLAN 85–86 (Stephen W. Sears ed., 1992). The "old General" to whom he referred was General-in-Chief of the Army, Brevet Lieutenant General Winfield Scott. In an earlier letter home, he expressed his belief that Scott was "either a traitor or an incompetent." *Id.* at 81 (letter dated August 9, 1861).
14. *Id.*
15. Civil War historian Ethan S. Rafuse would consider this letter as "private grousing that should be treated as no more than that." Ethan S. Rafuse, *General McClellan and the Politicians Revisited*, PARAMETERS, Summer 2012, at 71, 83, n. 18. While this letter never made a public appearance, other conduct reveals that this "grousing" was symptomatic of a much more malignant and lifelong "disdain for politicians" (notwithstanding that McClellan ran for President in 1864). *Id.* at 74.
16. By "senior civilian and military strategic decision-makers," this thesis generally means two populations: (1) civilian elected and appointed officials in the federal government, who—by virtue of the specific office or by their scope of responsibilities—affect U.S. national security, and (2) active duty military personnel, usually of the rank of Lieutenant General or General (Army, Air Force, Marine Corps) or Vice Admiral or Admiral (Navy), in official duty positions in which their responsibilities include directly advising the civilians described previously and are the key leaders of the institutional Armed Services (e.g., the Chief of Staff of the Army) or commanders of organizations in the direct chain-of-command with the President and Secretary of Defense (e.g., Commanders of Unified Combatant Commands).

17. Eric Schmitt, *Threats and Responses: Military Spending; Pentagon Contradicts General On Iraq Occupation Force's Size*, N.Y. TIMES, Feb. 28, 2003, http://www.nytimes.com/2003/02/28/us/threats-responses-military-spending-pentagon-contradicts-general-iraq-occupation.html.
18. Donald H. Rumsfeld, *Transforming the Military*, FOREIGN AFFAIRS (May/June 2002), http://www.foreignaffairs.com/articles/58020/donald-h-rumsfeld/transforming-the-military. In an effort to impose strict civilian control over the "transformation" of the defense enterprise, some scholars assert that he deliberately muted the voices of his senior military leaders—whom he considered a "rival political faction"—in order to intentionally disrupt a bureacracy he viewed as a roadblock to new ideas, accountability, and military effectiveness. MATTHEW MOTEN, PRESIDENTS & THEIR GENERALS: AN AMERICAN HISTORY OF COMMAND IN WAR 345–47 (2014).
19. Michael A. Fletcher & Peter Baker, *Bush Ousts Embattled Rumsfeld; Democrats Near Control of Senate*, WASH. POST, Nov. 9, 2006, http://www.washingtonpost.com/wp-dyn/content/article/2006/11/08/AR2006110801180.html.
20. *Army Strategic Initiatives, Hearing Before the Committee on the Armed Services, United States House of Representatives*, 110th Cong. (Sept. 26, 2007) (statement of General George Casey), http://www.gpo.gov/fdsys/pkg/CHRG-110hhrg44632/html/CHRG-110hhrg44632.htm.
21. Bryan Bender, *Army is worn too thin, warns general*, THE BOSTON GLOBE, Sep. 27, 2007, http://www.boston.com/news/nation/washington/articles/2007/09/27/army_is_worn_too_thin_says_general/.
22. Ann Scott Tyson, *Gen. David McKiernan Ousted as Top U.S. Commander in Afghanistan*, WASH. POST, May 12, 2009, http://www.washingtonpost.com/wp-dyn/content/article/2009/05/11/AR2009051101864.html.
23. Helene Cooper & David Sanger, *Obama Says Afghan Policy Won't Change After Dismissal*, N.Y. Times June 23, 2010, http://www.nytimes.com/2010/06/24/us/politics/24mcchrystal.html?pagewanted=all&_r=0.
24. Admiral Fallon's resignation came on the heels of an article in the popular magazine *Esquire*, depicting him in heroic terms as blocking efforts and apparent desire in the George W. Bush Administration to instigate conflict with Iran. *See* Thomas P.M. Barnett, *The Man Between War and Peace*, ESQUIRE (April 2008), http://www.esquire.com/news-politics/a4284/fox-fallon/.
25. Helene Cooper, *Hagel Resigns Under Pressure as Global Crises Test Pentagon*, N.Y. TIMES, Nov. 24, 2014, http://www.nytimes.com/2014/11/25/us/hagel-said-to-be-stepping-down-as-defense-chief-under-pressure.html?_r=0.
26. Thomas E. Ricks, "Will the Generals Obey Trump?" *The Best Defense Blog*, ForeignPolicy.com (Nov. 16, 2016), http://foreignpolicy.com/2016/11/16/will-the-generals-obey-trump/.

27. Moten, Presidents & Their Generals, at 370.
28. *See* Richard H. Kohn, *Coming Soon: A Crisis in Civil-Military Relations*, World Affairs J. (Winter 2008), http://www.worldaffairsjournal.org/article/coming-soon-crisis-civil-military-relations; *see also Opinion: Who's in Charge of the Military?* N.Y. Times, Jan. 26, 1993, http://www.nytimes.com/1993/01/26/opinion/who-s-in-charge-of-the-military.html.
29. Paul Yingling, *A Failure in Generalship*, Armed Forces J., May 1, 2007, http://www.armedforcesjournal.com/a-failure-in-generalship/ (famously arguing that if a politician fails to provide the military with the means adequate to achieve his or her policy objective, the senior strategic military leader is under an obligation to advise the politician that the tool is simply not in the toolbox, or not sharp enough yet to be any real utility). Thomas Ricks refered to this as a "blistering attack" on the state of current civil-military relations. Thomas E. Ricks, *Army Officer Accuses Generals of 'Intellectual and Moral Failures,'* Wash. Post, Apr. 27, 2007, http://www.washingtonpost.com/wp-dyn/content/article/2007/04/26/AR2007042602230.html. Four yeares later, Yingling retired from Active Duty as a full Colonel. Paul Yingling, *Why an Army colonel is retiring early—to become a high school teacher*, Wash. Post, Dec. 2, 2011, http://www.washingtonpost.com/opinions/why-an-army-colonel-is-retiring-early–to-become-a-high-school-teacher/2011/12/02/gIQAB2wAMO_story.html.
30. Charles Stevenson, *The Still Nearly Impossible Job of Secretary of Defense*, War on the Rocks.com (November 25, 2014), http://warontherocks.com/2014/11/the-still-nearly-impossible-job-of-secretary-of-defense/.
31. Mackubin Thomas Owens, US Civil-Military Relations After 9/11: Renegotiating the Civil-Military Bargain 4 (2011).
32. *See, e.g.*, Frank G. Hoffman, *Dereliction of Duty Redux*, Foreign Policy Research Institute.com (Nov. 1997), http://www.fpri.org/articles/2007/11/dereliction-duty-redux; *and see* H.R. McMaster, Dereliction of Duty 5–7 (1997) (describing the Kennedy administration's tension with the Joint Chiefs of Staff, exacerbated by the failed Bay of Pigs operation in early 1961).
33. Thomas E. Ricks, The Generals: American Military Command From World War II to Today 450 (2013) ("sometimes contentious dialogue is a sign of healthy discourse").
34. Cohen, Supreme Command, at 4–8, 208–12.
35. Sam C. Sarkesian et al., Soldiers, Society, and National Security 117–18 (1995); Lincoln on War, *supra* note 11, at 139–42; Peter D. Feaver, *The Right to Be Right*, Int'l Security (Spring 2011), at 87, 89.
36. Colonel Richard D. Hooker, Jr., *Soldiers of the State: Reconsidering American Civil-Military Relations*, Parameters, Winter 2011–12 (*reprint* from Winter 2003–04), at 1.

37. Peter D. Feaver, Armed Servants: Agency, Oversight, and Civil-Military Relations 7 (2003) ("there is still a range of problematic activities in which the military can engage… 'solving' the problem of coups does not solve, in the sense of neutralize, the general problem of control on an ongoing basis").
38. Richard K. Betts, Soldiers, Statesmen, and Cold War Crises 4–5 and Appendix A, Tables A and C (1991); Richard D. Hooker, Jr., *Soldiers of the State: Reconsidering American Civil-Military Relations*, at 2, 6, 11.
39. Pearlman, Warmaking and American Democracy, at 13.
40. General Colin L. Powell, *U.S. Forces: Challenges Ahead*, Foreign Affairs (Winter 1992/93), http://www.cfr/org/world/us-forces-challenges-ahead/p7508.
41. Bob Woodward, Obama's Wars 37 (2010) (paraphrasing a discussion with retired Marine General James Jones had with Barack Obama in October 2008, before his election).
42. For a comparative example, consider Winston Churchill's authority and detailed direction of the British Armed Forces, especially in the first years of World War II. Craig, *Political Leader as Strategist, supra* note 2, at 499 ("he sent a directive for the conduct of the campaign in the Middle East that was virtually an operations order, including detailed tactical instructions, down to the forward and rear distribution of battalions, and giving minutely detailed orders for the employment of forces").
43. Gray, Modern Strategy, at 58–63.
44. Peter W. Rodman, Presidential Command 273 (2009).
45. Michael O'Hanlon, "Trump and the generals," The Brookings Institution, https://www.brookings.edu/blog/order-from-chaos/2016/09/14/trump-and-the-generals/ (Sept. 14, 2016).
46. *See, e.g.*, Eliot A. Cohen, *The Unequal Dialogue: The Theory and Reality of Civil-Military Relations and the Use of Force, in* Soldiers and Civilians: The Civil-Military Gap and American National Security 429, 430 (Peter D. Feaver, Richard H. Kohn eds., 2001), *and see* Peter J. Roman & David W. Tarr, *Military Professionalism and Policymaking: Is there a Civil-Military Gap at the Top? If So, Does it Matter?, in* The Civil-Military Gap, at 411.
47. Jason K. Dempsey, Our Army: Soldiers, Politics, and American Civil-Military Relations (2010) (surveying political participation, attitudes, and social opinions of Army service-members); Thomas E. Ricks, *The Widening Gap Between Military and Society*, The Atlantic Monthly, July 1, 1997, http://www.theatlantic.com/magazine/archive/1997/07/the-widening-gap-between-military-and-society/306158/; *see also* Andrew J. Bacevich, Breach of Trust: How American Failed Their Soldiers and Their Country (2013).

48. Charles C. Moskos, Jr., *From Institution to Occupation: Trends in Military Organization,* 4 ARMED FORCES & SOC'Y 41 (1977), *and see* Richard H. Kohn, *The Erosion of Civilian-Control of the Military in the United States Today,* NAVAL WAR C. REV., Summer 2002, at 9, 11–12 (using the metaphor of "two hostile relatives who feared and distrusted each other but realized they had to work together if both were to survive").
49. On the role of Congress as one part of the "civilian" arm of "civilian control," *see generally* CHARLES A. STEVENSON, WARRIORS AND POLITICIANS: US CIVIL-MILITARY RELATIONS UNDER STRESS (2006).
50. Suzanne C. Nielson, *Civil-Military Relations Theory and Military Effectiveness,* 10 PUB. ADMIN. & MGMT 61, 62 (2005).
51. ROBERT M. GATES, DUTY: MEMOIRS OF A SECREATRY AT WAR 83 (2014).
52. Deborah Avant, *Conflicting Indicators of 'Crisis' in American Civil-Military Relations,* 24 ARMED FORCES & SOC'Y, 375 (Spring 1998).
53. For instance, after President Truman famously relieved General Douglas MacArthur in Korea for escalating the war beyond the administration's limited political ambitions, public opinion majorities in the United States still supported the much-admired commanding general. A Gallup Poll in 1946 revealed that Douglas MacArthur was the "most admired" person in the world, among Americans, ahead of Dwight Eisenhower, President Truman, and Eleanor Roosevelt. AMERICAN INSTITUTE OF PUBLIC OPINION, THE GALLUP POLL: PUBLIC OPINION 1935–1971 584 (1972), *available at* http://www.ibiblio.org/pha/Gallup/Gallup.pdf. Yet, despite their favor, the public supported President Truman's policy of not attacking China and broadening the war—the express objective of the general they so admired. PEARLMAN, WARMAKING AND AMERICAN DEMOCRACY, at 16. Upon arriving in San Francisco, a week after being relieved for insubordination, MacArthur was greeted by "hundreds of thousands" of supporters, and a parade in his honor. *Cover page,* SAN FRANCISCO CHRON., Apr. 18, 1951, *available at* http://www.sfgate.com/bayarea/article/From-the-archives-MacArthur-welcomed-in-S-F-3164481.php#photo-2296939.
54. BETTS, COLD WAR CRISES, at xv; *see also* Jim Golby, Kyle Dropp, & Peter Feaver, *Listening to the Generals: How Military Advice Affects Public Support for the Use of Force,* Center for a New American Security (April 2013), *available at* http://www.cnas.org/files/documents/publications/CNAS%20Generals%20report%20updated.pdf (explaining their survey of how American public attitudes shift when military elites make their policy preferences publically known).
55. Richard H. Kohn, *Out of Control: The Crisis in Civil-Military Relations,* THE NAT'L INT. (Spring 1994), http://nationalinterest.org/article/out-of-control-the-crisis-in-civil-military-relations-343 (referencing Justice Potter

Stewart's concurring opinion in *Jacobellis v. Ohio*, 378 U.S. 184, 197 (1964) (Stewart, J., concurring)).

56. RODMAN, PRESIDENTIAL COMMAND at 4.
57. *See* Lieutenant General (Ret.) Karl W. Eikenberry & David M. Kennedy, *Americans and Their Military, Drifting Apart*, N.Y. Times, May 26, 2013, http://www.nytimes.com/2013/05/27/opinion/americans-and-their-military-drifting-apart.html?_r=1& *and see* SCHIFF, A CONCORDANCE THEORY, at 32–44.
58. *See, e.g.*, General Thomas D. White, *Strategy and the Defense Intellectuals*, THE SATURDAY EVENING POST, May 4, 1963, at 10 (complaining about the "pipe-smoking, tree-full-of-owls type of so-called professional 'defense intellectuals' [who are often] arrogant young professors, mathematicians and other theorists" brought to the Department of Defense by Secretary McNamara). For commentary on how foreign-policy pronouncements by senior military officers may, in the eyes of Congress at least, reduce their credibility as experts even on military-centric matters, *see* Suzanne C. Nielson, *Rules of the Game? The Weinberger Doctrine and the American Use of Force, in* THE FUTURE OF THE ARMY PROFESSION 627, 647 (Lloyd Matthews ed., 2005).
59. Roman & Tarr, *Does it Matter?*, at 411.
60. *See generally.*, COHEN, SUPREME COMMAND, *supra* note 4 (illustrating four wartime politicians: Lincoln, Clemenceau, Churchill, and Ben-Gurion).
61. *See, e.g.*, THE FEDERALIST NOS. 8, 24, 25, 69 (ALEXANDER HAMILTON); *and see* U.S. CONST. art I, § 8, and art II, § 2.
62. MICHAEL C. DESCH, CIVILIAN CONTROL OF THE MILITARY: THE CHANGING SECURITY ENVIRONMENT 3 (1999); SCHIFF, A CONCORDANCE THEORY, at 19; COHEN, SUPREME COMMAND, at 226.
63. A.J. Bacevich, *The Paradox of Professionalism: Eisenhower, Ridgway, and the Challenge to Civilian Control, 1953–1955*, 61 J. MIL. HIST. 303, 303 (1997).
64. OWENS, RENEGOTIATING THE BARGAIN, at 15.
65. Craig, *Political Leader as Strategist, in* MAKERS OF MODERN STRATEGY, at 482 ("it is difficult to frame a theoretical definition of appropriate roles that is not so general as to be meaningless").
66. Frank Hoffman, *A New American Military Ethic*, WAR ON THE ROCKS.COM (Aug. 6, 2014), http://warontherocks.com/2014/08/a-new-american-military-ethic/.
67. MOTEN, PRESIDENTS & THEIR GENERALS, at 367 (describing a dysfunctional pre-Iraq war civil-military dialogue between Secretary of Defense Rumsfeld and his civilian aides and the senior uniformed leaders of the Services and commanders).
68. GENERAL (RETIRED) MAXWELL TAYLOR, SWORDS AND PLOWSHARES 252 (1972).

69. LINDA ROBINSON ET AL., IMPROVING STRATEGIC COMPETENCE: LESSONS FROM 13 YEARS OF WAR (2014), http://www.rand.org/pubs/research_reports/RR816.html, *and see* BETTS, COLD WAR CRISES, at 1; *see also* Allan R. Millett, Williamson Murray & Kenneth H. Watman, *The Effectiveness of Military Organizations*, INT'L SECURITY (Summer 1986), at 37, 37 (observing that "political constraints" on how a military translates allocated resources into fighting power include "national and diplomatic objectives, popular attitudes towards the military, the conditions of engagements, and civilian morale"—in other words, civil-military relations).
70. For example, one month before the 1992 presidential election, the most publically respected and influential American flag officer in a generation penned an editorial in *The New York Times* advocating for a restrained deployment of military force into Eastern Europe, and lauding his president for "understand[ing] the proper use of military force" more than any recent administration. General Colin L. Powell, *Why Generals Get Nervous*, N. Y. TIMES, October 8, 1992, http://www.nytimes.com/1992/10/08/opinion/why-generals-get-nervous.html.
71. The Joint Chiefs of Staff that President Kennedy inherited from Eisenhower faced an administration with a "compartmentalized" personality and an informal "hallway style" of meetings that eschewed the transparency and formal hierarchy of previous national security processes. RICHARD REEVES, PRESIDENT KENNEDY: PROFILE OF POWER 19, 94 (1993). Far from Ike's structured National Security Council debates with his generals, Kennedy's initial handling of the Bay of Pigs operation lacked systemic dialogue between the senior civilian commander-in-chief and his principal military advisors. *Id.* at 102–103. For an overview of President Eisenhower's national security process and systems, *see* Raymond Millen, *Cultivating Strategic Thinking: The Eisenhower Model*, PARAMETERS (Summer 2012), at 56–70.
72. DESCH, CHANGING SECURITY ENVIRONMENT, at 13–14.
73. COHEN, SUPREME COMMAND, at 2; *see also* DON M. SNIDER, DISSENT AND STRATEGIC LEADERSHIP OF THE MILITARY PROFESSIONS (2008) (discussing the ethics of dissent by "strategic" leaders in uniform, based on a study of the 2006 public "revolt of the [retired] generals" in opposition to the Iraq war).
74. REBECCA L. SCHIFF, A CONCORDANCE THEORY, at 45–47.
75. The relevance of "context" of civil-military relations is discussed in an Army-sponsored RAND Arroyo Center assessment of the purported "gap" in civil-military relations, as described in both media and academic circles in the 1990s. THOMAS S. SZYANA ET AL., THE CIVIL-MILITARY GAP IN THE UNITED STATES: DOES IT EXIST, WHY, AND DOES IT MATTER? 15 (2007), http://www.rand.org/content/dam/rand/pubs/monographs/2007/RAND_MG379.pdf.

76. DESCH, CHANGING SECURITY ENVIRONMENT, at 3; *see also* Marybeth Peterson Ulrich, *Infusing Normative Civil-Military Relations Principles in the Officer Corps, in* THE FUTURE OF THE ARMY PROFESSION 655, 658 (Lloyd Matthews ed., 2005) ("there is no commonly accepted theoretical framework upon which to evaluate various civil-military behaviors").
77. Bacevich, *The Paradox of Professionalism*, at 304.
78. Morris Janowitz noted the same more than fifty years ago in his seminal sociological study of the military establishment. Janowitz, THE PROFESSIONAL SOLDIER, at 138–39 (observing that the military has "never sought to establish principles for limiting the political activities of the military profession as a pressure group on its own behalf"). There is, however, a Department of Defense policy that reminds service-members that service itself does not deny them opportunity to engage in their duties as a citizen (e.g., voting, joining and participating in political organizations out of uniform), but does impose various restrictions on individual partisan behavior (e.g., participate in partisan political fundraising activities, and publically advocating for a political candidate, cause, or party). This policy does not address the strategic civil-military relationships discussed here. *See* Dep't of Defense Directive (DODD) 1344.10, subject: Political Acitivites by Members of the Armed Forces, Feb. 19, 2008, http://www.dod.mil/dodgc/defense_ethics/ethics_regulation/1344-10.html.
79. BLACK'S LAW DICTIONARY 545 (8th ed. 2004) (definition of "fiduciary duty").
80. *Id.* at 1315 (definition of "fiduciary relationship").
81. RESTATEMENT (THIRD) OF AGENCY: DEFINITIONS AND TERMINOLOGY § 1.01 (2006) [hereinafter AGENCY RESTATEMENT]. The "Restatement" is an authoritative "formulation of common law and statutory elements" to summarize the "law as it currently stands," and is published by the American Law Institute (ALI), an independent and non-profit group of lawyers, legal scholars, and judges. *See* AMERICAN LAW Institute.org, http://www.ali.org/index.cfm?fuseaction=publications.faq. The employment of agency theory in this book, however, is really an adaptation. Unlike in business scenarios in which legal agency theory governs, there is no "hiring" of a general or admiral, or payment of Services by contract, by a civilian elected or appointed official acting as the principal. Nevertheless, the expectations and behaviors of those parties inside these relationships imply that they have implicitly adopted fiduciary principles, making agency theory a reasonable framework through which to describe how the parties relate to one another.
82. JAMES M. DUBIK, JUST WAR RECONSIDERED: STRATEGY, ETHICS, AND THEORY 22 (2016).
83. MOTEN, PRESIDENTS & THEIR GENERALS, at 5.

CHAPTER 3

The Case-In-Chief: What the Law Does (Not) Say

If any of the parties to a strategic civil-military relationship were to search the stacks of leather-bound tomes in a law library for standards or rules for judging the health of their interactions in context, they would end their hunt tired and disappointed. This chapter will examine the Constitution, legislation, case law, administrative regulations, and military doctrine. These sources demonstrate the irony that the law provides both a cause of strategic civil-military friction, and a missed opportunity to establish norms and expectations for the conduct of these relationships.

The Constitution Structures Civil-Military Relations

The U.S. Constitution's relevance to civil-military relations is worth exploring because, at the very least, it is referenced reverently by those in uniform as a benchmark for their subordination to civilians under the Rule of Law. However, generic military subordination to civilian control is as explicit as the Constitution gets, for its distinctive contribution to national security rests in dividing federal power between the executive branch and the legislative.[1] The branches' respective spheres of influence and control within the defense establishment were designed to be equally powerful, but not equally efficient.[2]

This constitutional structure was intended to strengthen the country's ability to respond militarily to both domestic insurrection and foreign enemies. However, constitutional law scholar Akhil Reed Amar argues

D. Maurer, *Crisis, Agency, and Law in US Civil-Military Relations*,
DOI 10.1007/978-3-319-53526-5_3

that the "awesomeness of these new military powers, and their evident susceptibility to abuse if not properly constrained," also drove the Framers toward this simultaneous division and blurring of defense-related authority.[3] In crafting the federal government's war powers, the Framers were strongly influenced by Locke and Montesquieu. James Madison, for instance, argued that Montesquieu's theory on the separation of powers counseled against setting the "whole power" of multiple departments (branches of government) in a single organ of government.[4] This division of labor has, in effect, complicated the administration of national security, but not without justification. Supreme Court Justice Frankfurter wrote:

> [b]efore the cares of the White House were his own, President Harding is reported to have said that government after all is a very simple thing. He must have said that, if he said it, as a fleeting inhabitant of fairyland. The opposite is the truth. A constitutional democracy like ours is perhaps the most difficult of man's social arrangements to manage successfully... [the Framers of the Constitution] rested the structure of our central government on the system of checks and balances. For them the doctrine of separation of powers was not mere theory; it was a felt necessity.[5]

Most of Article I, the longest section of the Constitution, establishes general administrative qualifications and minutia for Congress.[6] However, Clause 8 begins to identify the specific affirmative powers of Congress, including "to provide for the common Defence [sic]," to "declare War... and make Rules concerning Captures on Land and Water," to "raise and support Armies," to "provide and maintain a Navy," and to "make Rules for the Government and Regulation of the land and naval Forces."[7] These "common defense" clauses, obviously, say nothing expressly about *how* the national government should wield the Army or Navy that the Congress raises, supports, and provides.

As a result, the power-sharing and deliberate inefficiency Madison and Montesquieu preached as a necessary check on tyranny becomes manifestly necessary.[8] Article II, while mostly concerned with how a President is elected,[9] grants the President the title of "Commander in Chief" of the nation's armed forces[10] and implies that this executive function encompasses the authority to oversee the employment of the armed forces in combat.[11] However, the full extent of this power is not defined or capped[12]; the specific functions demanded by such a role are not listed.[13]

Even though the Framers devoted more words to the President's oath of office clause[14] (fifty-four) than to the President's national security powers (only thirty-four), the text still establishes rough parameters for a division of labor in the field of defense.[15] For instance, the President is best equipped to unilaterally speak for the republic in affairs of state and command its military force.[16] But the President cannot, by constitutional authority alone, lead the country in prolonged war, or fund the Services to prepare, equip, or train them to fight without the knowledge, consent, or express action of Congress.[17] Congress, for its power under the Constitution's text, has no complementary authority to make war plans, or establish national security strategy based on military force, or command campaigns, or to direct specific military targets.[18] This has not stopped Congress from occasionally intervening with direct oversight of tactical and operational matters during an on-going war. After an early Union failure at Ball's Bluff in late 1861, for example, Congress established a "Joint Committee on the Conduct of War," consisting largely of virulently anti-slavery Republicans, who repeatedly called commanding generals and other officers to testify (often about the performance of their superiors), beseeched President Lincoln to more dramatically involve himself with the tactical planning of his Army, and ardently criticized the slow-to-move General McClellan.[19]

Both Articles I and II are silent about which branch must dominate in nuanced circumstances involving the combat deployment of the nation's military. This question of how much power the President has to unilaterally employ the military without consulting Congress first, let along get approval from that branch, remains debatable—even within an administration. In 2011, President Obama unilaterally deployed forces to fight with NATO partners in Libya, and did not seek congressional authority, arguing that the use of air strikes and missile launches in support of NATO allies and a United Nations Security Council Resolution was not the kind of hostility envisioned by the 1973 War Powers Resolution, and thus required no approval from Congress to continue. However, in 2013, President Obama sought congressional authorization to deploy forces to fight in Syria.[20] Silence has led to further analysis by the courts and management of this shared power through legislation.[21] Neither of these Articles, moreover, suggests what expectations, norms, or standards of behavior should guide the relationship between civilian and military authorities in the national government. The document is also silent as to which branch of government makes defense strategy. As a foundational charter for the new republic, the Constitution concerned only *inter*-branch authority, not the relationships inside those branches that haggle and compromise over that authority.[22] To describe or define such relationships would have been wholly out of character and without great need, especially given the Framers' intent to deliberately burden the federal government by forced balancing and sharing of power.[23]

Further, the complex web of bureaucracies and agencies that play roles in modern national defense would have been unforeseeable to the Framers. Even if they had predicted that international events, domestic pressures, and personalities[24] of those in public office would likely expand expectations that both civilians and military performing duties related to national security will work in concert or collaboratively,[25] the Framers would have regarded the resulting tensions as inherently inseparable from their desired partition of power. As Henry Kissinger has written, "[t]he purpose of the separation of powers was to avoid despotism, not to achieve harmonious government."[26]

Nevertheless, even if the Constitution is silent in these matters, practice can perfect and validate the exercise of executive authority in the domain of national security. A long-standing practice by the Executive Branch, known of by Congress and never questioned, creates a "gloss" on the President's authority.[27] This "gloss" that transforms systemic practice into binding precedent is important because, as the Supreme Court recognizes, the Constitution:

> contemplates that practice will integrate the dispersed powers into a workable government... [because it] does not disclose the measure of the actual controls wielded by the modern presidential office... [but rather] [s]ubtle shifts take place in the centers of real power that do not show on the face of the Constitution."[28]

The same logic of precedent is true for Congress.[29] Strategic theorist Bernard Brodie noted that the upper level of government where this strategizing and "practice" occurs necessarily includes civilians and military elites.[30] Therefore, both groups must understand the "basic and prevailing conception of what any war existing or impending is really about and what it is attempting to accomplish,"[31] especially if they attempt to rationalize their conduct with the implied gloss argument rather than a reference to explicit statutory authority or a Constitutional grant of power.

For these reasons, the Constitution might be said to be the root cause of American civil-military conflict. For sound reasons, both pragmatic and philosophical, it erects formal barriers to decision-making efficiency. Further, the Constitution forces compromise among the pluralistic parties and interests that make policy and engage in subtle manipulation of each other's behavior and choices by affecting or creating options—the practice called Choice Architecture described in Chapter 1. This implies, and possibly encourages, a degree of power-sharing without an objective set of expectations or standards to govern those ambiguous and often unpredictable relationships. Legislation, as described later, fails to fill this gap inadvertently created under Articles I and II.

Legislation Organizes Civil-Military Relations

When legislators have approached the subject of national, strategic-level policy-making by civilians and military leaders, their purpose has generally been aimed at improving the efficiency of systems and reducing redundancy among departments and agencies. The reach of those acts has been limited to roles and authorities. These acts have not addressed mutual or unilateral obligations and duties owed by one strategic party to the other. The opportunities and desirability for legislation to establish such duties are clear, but have been repeatedly missed. Amy Zegart has attributed this to the dominant role in national security assumed by the president and bureaucratic actors in the Executive Branch, whose individual interests and motives drive the "evolution" of particular national security institutions. This leaves, Zegart contends, Congress with only "sporadic, largely ineffectual oversight."[32]

In a rather recent example, Congress passed the Iraq Liberation Act of 1998, a statement of policy advocating for regime change in Iraq, signed into law by President Clinton.[33] As a result, General Anthony Zinni, the Commander of Central Command (USCENTCOM) at the time, sponsored an interagency war game to envision what would likely occur after a hypothetical American invasion of Iraq to depose Saddam Hussein.[34] Called "Desert Crossing," the war game's disquieting results suggested several undesirable strategic themes that would prove prophetic.[35] First, the war game concluded that there was a need for hundreds of thousands of troops for an extended presence. Second, it observed that regime change would not necessarily guarantee regional stability. Third, it recommended relying almost exclusively on existing tribal and political structures to establish post-Saddam stability.[36] This war game was not only ignored three years later by the Bush Administration, convinced of the ability to democratize the country from the "outside-in," but Zinni himself was prevented from advising his successor at USCENTCOM, General Tommy Franks, during the planning phase of Operation Iraqi Freedom where Franks' mission included regime change.[37] Instead, Secretary of Defense Rumsfeld continously encouraged the adoption of a campaign plan that avoided a lengthy troop build-up in the Middle East, and was heavily reliant on "shock and awe" delivered by high-precision munitions into the heart of Baghdad and a rapid advance by a limited number of ground troops and special operations forces.[38]

This legislative act demonstrated national commitment to replace a foreign government with one that reflected democratic values; it specifically envisioned whole-of-government assistance to the new democratic regime; and it spurred interagency assessment of the multifaceted economic, political, and security problems that would likely flow from regime change. To impose a requirement that the executive branch engage in substantial, concerted civil-military strategy-making among American policy elites would have been appropriate and consistent with the Act's purpose. Nothing, however, in the Iraq Liberation Act directly imposed or even suggested such coordination requirements. Nothing, therefore, spoke to the quality or nature of the relationships that would engage in such coordination, and tacitly confirms Zegart's proposition.

This legislative problem follows a historical pattern. For instance, the National Security Act of 1947[39] formally institutionalized a "Joint Chiefs" organization, one whose origin sprang from a desire to contain the improvisational "juggling" that characterized President Roosevelt's decision-making methodology in World War II.[40] This Act not only established a central committee of the highest ranking officers from each of the individual Services, it gave the Army Air Corps its own status along with the Navy and Army, created the Office of the Secretary of Defense and the "National Military Establishment."[41] For President Truman, unification of the Services was a device that elevated his power by interposing a "supersecretary" over all the Services, creating a way to meld the often disparate views of "strategy, supply, and operations."[42] This tentative step toward efficiency and unification, however, left the Secretary of Defense weak relative to the Service Secretaries, who retained their Cabinet posts.[43] Amended in 1949, the revised National Security Act[44] created the slightly more unified Department of Defense and an Office of the Chairman of the Joint Chiefs of Staff. However, it granted that office no more authority than that of liaison to the President and Secretary of Defense and of spokesman for the other four-star generals and admirals at the helm of their Services. The Service chiefs, in turn, remained empowered as principal military advisors to the President, each of whom remained in the operational chain-of-command.[45]

Over the next decade, similar attempts to reduce redundancy and improve efficiency within the national security establishment were debated. The 1953 Defense Reorganization Plan,[46] issued by the newly elected Eisenhower Administration, was based on growing pains within the Department of Defense spurred by the National Security Act of 1947 and lessons learned during the Korean War. The Plan clarified the responsibilities of the Services relative to the unified commands in the field, gave the Chairman of the Joint Chiefs of Staff more control over the direction and membership of the Joint Staff, redistributed senior civilian staff functions among the Service secretariats, and reinforced ultimate civilian responsibility for the Department of Defense as a whole.[47] President Eisenhower wrote: "[t]here must be a clear and unchallenged civilian responsibility in the defense establishment…[which] is essential not only to maintain democratic institutions, but also to protect the integrity of the military profession."[48] The Plan, while aiming to strengthen various political offices overseeing national security, did not aim to create an objective set of standards that would, in effect, guide the civilian and military leaders by fostering norms and expectations of that strategic relationship, given the principle of military subordination to civilian control.

Similarly, the Defense Reorganization Act of 1958[49] more clearly placed field commands under the direct operational authority of the Secretary of Defense, and submerged the military department civilian secretaries under the "direction, authority, and control" of the Secretary of Defense. The Act's primary motivations were to "provide more effective, efficient, and economical administration" in the Defense Department, "eliminate unnecessary duplication," and "provide for unified strategic direction of the combatant forces."[50] Unity and efficiency were the dominant themes in this legislation; establishing norms and expectations among the civilian and military parties working (theoretically) in concert was not.

Three decades later, the Goldwater-Nichols Act of 1986 was the next, and most recent, substantial legislative effort to reform the American national security establishment. Not long before he retired in 1982, then-Chairman of the Joint Chiefs of Staff, Air Force General David Jones, testified before a House subcommittee: "[t]he corporate advice provided by the Joint Chiefs of Staff [JCS] is not crisp, timely, very useful, or very influential."[51] Congress wished to avoid the systemic planning faults that contributed to the aborted Iran hostage rescue operation in 1981.[52] Congress was also influenced by the military's response to the bombing of the Marine Corps barracks in Beirut, the Grenada mission, and the hands-off, dissociative relationship between Secretary of Defense Casper Weinberger and military planners.[53] The ultimate objective of the Goldwater-Nichols Act, then, was to aid national political authority with better military advice, and rescue the JCS from its own limitations and failures. After more than four years of drafting bills in both the House and Senate and initial resistance to the JCS reform from inside the Pentagon, was again to "strengthen civilian authority" inside the Defense Department, but also to "improve the military advice provided to the President, the National Security Council, and the Secretary of Defense."[54]

Recognizing that the separate Services had separate cultures, institutional identities driven by their particular historical roles and routine missions, and disjointed approaches to planning and weapons acquisition, the Act placed more responsibility and clearer lines of direct authority on the field commanders to train, plan, and fund for contingencies in a more "joint" fashion. The Chairman was elevated to a position of primacy over the other members of the JCS to make him the senior officer in the United States military and principal military advisor to the President and Secretary of Defense.[55] The Act tasked the Chairman to assist the President and Secretary of Defense in "providing for the strategic direction of the armed forces."[56] Not only was the Chairman to relay requirements from the combatant commanders, he was no longer left to negotiate with the Service chiefs to seek a unified corporate decision or recommendation.[57] This left the Chairman holding at least three pots: independent, principal military advisor to the President, advisor and confidant to the Secretary of Defense, and primary advocate for the remainder of the JCS and combatant commands.[58]

However, precariously balancing three pots often leads to unforeseen consequences, one of which is that the Act did not expressly elevate the Chairman's position to the most powerful or influential military officer in the strategic-civil military relationship and as a result did nothing to clarify which pot was most important if the three were in tension with each other. The Act also created the position of Vice Chairman, of equal grade, who is also appointed by the President and confirmed by the Senate.[59] It also required the Chairman to present dissenting views of the Service chiefs alongside his own recommendations.[60] The President and Secretary of Defense could still seek independent advice and recommendations from the Service chiefs.[61] Furthermore, the Act established a strict operational chain-of-command running from President to Secretary of Defense to commander of a "combatant command [COCOM],"[62] removing the Service chiefs, the Chairman, and individual military department secretaries from the operational loop,[63] but allowed the President or Secretary of Defense the option of inserting the Chairman into the line of communications between National Command Authority and the combatant commanders, or to "oversee the activities of" those commands.[64] The Act gave the commanders of the combatant commands the authority to direct and employ subordinate forces in operations, training, and logistics, and gave them veto authority over officers nominated by the Services to serve as subordinate commanders.[65]

The Gulf War tested this reorganization in 1990–91.[66] That conflict revealed that the Department of Defense's new structure, dominated by commanders in the field rather than the individual Services in wartime, was able to better coordinate the command of Service-component forces in flexible ways, and demonstrated that this reorganization could increase the likelihood of operational success with the Chairman as the principal military advisor.[67] In effect, by rearranging the division of labor among the senior-most military elite and giving more power to the Chairman, the Act opened possibilities for new voices to work as influential agents. It transformed the Joint Staff from a rank-heavy but low-impact "think tank" to a well-publicized and high-impact "action staff."[68]

While this new seating arrangement advanced the cause of improving the quality of professional advice that the Service chiefs and combatant commanders gave to policy-makers, that was the extent of the Act's role in shaping the behaviors of the military and civilian elite relative to each other. Even though the Act established an educational "capstone course" required for newly promoted flag officers, "designed specifically to prepare [them] to work with the other armed services," the Act did not include a similar requirement to prepare for working with senior civilian policy-makers—in or out of the Defense Department.[69] The Act even refers to the Service chiefs as the "agent" of the superior civilian Service secretary.[70] But the Act is silent about how those agency relationships ought to normatively look. No standard, expectation, or norm is codified with respect to the overlapping or mutual duties and responsibilities in these principal–agent relationships. A powerful personality in the position of Chairman of the JCS, for instance, remained subject only to his general understanding of the Constitution's subordination of the military to the President, his oath of office, and any self-imposed limits beyond those established in Goldwater-Nichols.[71]

As a consequence, subsequent Chairmen of the Joint Chiefs of Staff, and their subordinate Joint Staffs, may in practice be relegated to quasi-informed and quasi-influential "onlookers" to wartime strategy.[72] As was the case with the General Tommy Franks, Commander of USCENTCOM from 2000–2003, the purposes of Goldwater-Nichols Act can become frustrated because the Act does not adequately establish norms for the behavior and interaction of these key strategic elites. The early months and years of the Global War on Terror reveal that circumstances may offer a potent combination of a combatant commander who distrusts and ignores the JCS but who subordinates his military experience to the will of a civilian political appointee with an "indomitable bureaucratic presence" like Donald Rumsfeld.[73]

"Disciplined and ambitious"[74] but also "loyal and diligent,"[75] General Franks was a believer that the early Afghanistan campaign was a successful proof of concept for Rumsfeld's ideas on military transformation, and was "uninterested" in post-war stabilization planning.[76] As a result, Franks insufficiently questioned the Secretary of Defense's underlying assumptions or goals leading to the invasion of Iraq in 2003.

Despite the most sweeping legislative attempt to make the upper echelon of military command work more effectively and more efficiently under civilian control since World War II, the Act says nothing of accountability. The Act does not give the strategic civil-military elites or the American public any way to objective diagnose whether that arrangement in practice is "healthy"—the relationship simply *is*. In terms of affecting American strategic civil-military relationships, the Goldwater-Nichols Act (like the legislative efforts before it) was a missed opportunity.

The oath that new military officers swear upon receiving their commissions is also provided by federal statute and is similarly unhelpful. The oath does not specify particular duties in the strategic civil-military relationship. This oath of office obligates the officer to work loyally and diligently in support of the Constitution, but also enjoins the officer to "faithfully discharge the duties of the office" in which they serve—two responsibilities that could be mutually exclusive.[77] One such principle is that of civilian dominance over the military This suggests that the officer does not obligate himself to work loyally, faithfully, or diligently on behalf of a particular civilian—political—superior. As this oath is generic (given to all officers, regardless of their rank, duty position, or branch of Service), such a specified duty would be out of place. Indeed, such an affirmative duty to a specific office-holder would practically be an oath of personal fidelity and would obviate any sense of a separate, apolitical military.[78]

As an unintended consequence of the oath's emphasis on protecting the Constitution "against all enemies, foreign and domestic,"[79] it implies that the senior strategic military officer's prime duty is to support and defend the Constitution, but leaves out any nuanced application at the strategic policy-making level of government where the Constitution leaves its mark on the separation of powers and the principle of civilian control. Further, there is a widely held belief—at least among Army (and possibly Marine Corps) officers—that the absence of any specific duty to "obey the orders of the President of the United States" (as is required of enlisted Soldiers) implies a moral obligation to *disobey* when the order, policy, rule, or standard is "not in the best interest of the Army at that moment" and that officers are trusted by the American people to exercise such judgment.[80] Consequently, the oath offers little guidance to a strategic military leader, in the position of "choice architect," caught between faithfully implementing the political decisions of a civilian elected official which he believes to be contrary to principles articulated or implied by the Constitution, and a personal opinion based on military experience and expertise.[81]

Implying that this generic oath of office was insufficient alone, the National Defense Authorization Act for Fiscal Year 1998, Congress amended Title 10 of the U.S. Code with a short provision assigning specific duties to "commanding officers and others in authority" in the Army and Air Force.[82] However, this legislative provision, like the oath, offers no definitive (or even implied) guidance to participants in the strategic civil-military relationship. The amendment did not target the strategic relationship between senior military and civilian decision-makers. Rather, it sought to impose stricter accountability for commanders overseeing their subordinates, likely spurred by the basic trainee sex abuse and harassment scandal and subsequent courts-martial at Maryland's Aberdeen Proving Ground in 1997.[83]

Moreover, the text of the statute also clearly aims down and in, not up and out. It imposes a set of obligations on commanders only with respect to those service members junior in rank and subordinate to their direct command authority, and says nothing about relations with superiors, or those outside the span of the commander's authority. It was formally incorporated into, *inter alia*, Army Regulations[84] and several features of that regulation provide further evidence of an understanding that the general duties Congress mandated were not envisioned as guides for senior officers *qua* agents in the civil-military unequal dialogue. First, the Regulation only applies to the responsibilities of officers assigned to positions of "command."[85] Second, the Regulation only references the commander's relationship with the unit he or she commands and the Soldiers under his or her command authority.[86] Most military participants in the strategic civil-military relationship are not commanders as defined earlier, but advisory "choice architects" relative to the civilian officials and elected leadership. In those roles, such as the Chairman of the Joint Chiefs of Staff, the officer has no command authority. Therefore, the moral requirements intended by this code provision apply only through a self-imposed force of personal discipline, not by force of law, on those strategic military leaders over any subordinates they directly supervise and manage.

Legislation dealing with military officers, therefore, tends to address only two issues. As the National Security Act and the Goldwater-Nichols Act illustrate, one issue is the organization of the armed forces and Congress's effort to reduce redundancy and improve efficiency. The other issue pressing upon the minds of legislators is reflected by the oath of office provision and the "requirement of exemplary conduct" provision, which address a generic officer's supreme duty to the Constitution and a generic commander's responsibility for guiding the moral, ethical conduct of his or her subordinates. Neither type of legislation, however, offers a prescriptive guide for the members of the strategic civil-military relationships. Consequently, they offer no way to objectively assess the health of those relationships. The same inadequacies mar case law, as described in the following text.

Case Law Remains Silent on Civil-Military Relations

Just as the Constitution and legislation remain silent regarding the norms and expectations of behavior that affect the quality of a strategic civil-military relationship, U.S. case law fails to offer precedent by which to create or infer such standards. Silence from the courts in this matter is not surprising. The nature of a strategic civil-military relationship is such that the parties must coordinate, discuss, and compromise on sensitive national security and war-making decisions for which there are no "judicially discoverable and manageable standards for resolving" the conflict.[87] Because neither the Constitution nor statutes specify legal duties owed by these parties to each other, such problems are likely to be interpreted as non-justiciable "political questions" by the courts.[88]

Moreover, the identity of the relevant cast of characters involved in such crises likely inhibit "victims" from raising claims against the "offenders" even if the courts provided a forum for such debate. These strategic relationships, for instance, are highly personnel and are largely shielded from public view and scrutiny.[89] The parties have no incentive to openly complain about an unhealthy or pathological relationship while still in their assignments, and certainly are incentivized to shy away from disclosing evidence of poor decision-making in which they played some part.[90] It is no great surprise, then, that when courts do get involved, it is in the much clearer context of criminal misconduct. Superficially, these criminal cases appear ready-made for establishing definitive boundaries on permissible conduct in civil-military relations. However, a closer look reveals them to be as unhelpful as statutes currently are. The "offender" is usually a military officer *below* the strategic policy-making level, and the offense is typically brash and obvious disrespect toward a civilian leader well above the level of any civil-military relationship in which the offender actually participates.

Illustrating the point is perhaps the best-publicized court-martial involving egregious insubordination and disrespect: the 1925 prosecution of the infamous, highly decorated, William "Billy" Mitchell, then a Colonel and the leading advocate for an independent Air Force in the wake of the First World War.[91] In early September 1925, two naval air disasters consumed the public's attention, as well as the military's. Three Navy seaplanes crashed into the Pacific en route to Hawaii, and a dirigible, the Navy's U.S.S. *Shenandoah*, killed fourteen when it split into two during a thunderstorm over Ohio, falling out of the sky during its public relations flight.[92] As the leading proponent of military air power, reporters quickly sought Colonel Mitchell's opinion about the incidents. Though not involved in the planning or design of the aircraft, nor was he involved in the events themselves, Mitchell publically rebuked the Navy and War departments for what he called their "incompetency, criminal negligence and almost treasonable administration of our national defense."[93] Within days of saying that "official stupidity" was the proximate cause of the disasters,[94] he was charged with bringing "discredit upon the military service" for comments that were "prejudicial to good order and discipline," under Article 96 of the Articles of War.[95] Mitchell was convicted and sentenced to a suspension from command and rank for five years. He resigned shortly thereafter, but remained publically adored and was considered a "martyr" for the cause of an independent Air Force.[96]

However, even Mitchell's sensational seven-week trial, in which then-Major General Douglas MacArthur sat as a panel member, lacks substantive relevance to the question of strategic civil-military relationships.[97] Mitchell was a national figure, well known throughout the military for his wartime heroics in the novel tactic of aerial bombardment and later advocating for a unified Air Force contrary to War Department policy as the Assistant Chief of the Army Air Service.[98] But his notoriety stemmed from opinion, rather than station, as he was only a Corps-level staff officer in San Antonio, Texas, at the time he made his criminal remarks and not in a position to officially counsel senior civilian policy-makers in the national government.[99] Moreover, his comments were aimed not a specific policy-maker or senior military leader, but rather the policies of the institutions of defense generally—the Navy and War Departments. As a military bureaucratic "insurgent," fighting corporate policy and doctrine he viewed as dated or dangerous, Mitchell is historically important: his advocacy before and during the court-martial influenced Congress to pass the Air Corps Act in 1926.[100] But as a model for how military justice can or should guide public or strategic civil-military relations, Mitchell's trial offers no relevant lessons.

In the two-thirds of a century since the Uniform Code of Military Justice (UCMJ) was first enacted, the *only* criminal case involving an officer's contempt toward civilian officials, for which there is binding precedent on any relevant subsequent cases, was the 1965 court-martial of Second Lieutenant Henry Howe. Howe was charged with violating Article 88, UCMJ,[101] for carrying a protest sign that, in part, read "Let's have more than a choice between petty ignorant facists [sic] in 1968" on one side, and on the other side of the sign, the words "End Johnson's Facist [sic] aggression in Viet Nam."[102] Lieutenant Howe was certainly not engaged in a strategic argument with senior civilian officials when he wrote these words, nor was he privy to the planning, debate, and arguments of the military and civilian leaders he implicitly denounced in his protest sign.

The purpose of the punitive UCMJ article with which Howe was charged was to prohibit military officers from engaging in "contemptuous speech" against certain high-ranking civilian officials, thereby implicitly strengthening the principle of subordination to civilian constitutional authority over the military.[103] Yet, the crime's definition itself comes with caveats that leave application to the *strategic* civil-military relationship highly improbable. Unlike comments that may be personally contemptuous, an officer's *adverse criticism of the President, Congress, or the Secretary of Defense in the course of political discussion and debate* is not a criminal offense.[104] Further, "expressions of opinion made in a purely private conversation should not ordinarily be charged" under this crime.[105] Politically oriented criticism, or the perception of it among the parties, is obviously a source of continuous strain and tension that often leads to what appear to be civil-military "crises" and may substantively affect national security decision-making. As a consequence, the UCMJ's focus on preventing contemptuous and public disrespect aimed at the civilian official *qua* their individual person, rather than their policy decision, makes Article 88 an irrelevant stick by which to prod the military members into appropriate behavior relative to their civilian partners in the strategic civil-military relationship.

The nature of more common cases involving officers implicating this article of the UCMJ are illustrated by the investigation, fine, and forced retirement of an Air Force Major General in 1993, who publically referred to President Clinton as "gay-loving," "womanizing," "draft-dodging," and "pot-smoking" at an Air Force banquet speech.[106] Just as with Lieutenant Howe, this general officer intended to disparage the personal conduct and history of his commander-in-chief, not engage in an academic policy debate. All other criminal investigations and prosecutions of senior military officers tend to deal not with their relationships across the civil-military divide related to strategic decision-making and policy, but rather with their improper personal or sexual relationships with subordinates or their financial misconduct.[107]

Other avenues of UCMJ prosecution include charges of Dereliction of Duty,[108] Conduct Unbecoming an Officer and Gentleman,[109] or Conduct Prejudicial to Good Order and Discipline.[110] In practice, however, these appear as unlikely deterrents to pathological civil-military relationships as the Contempt offense under Article 88 of the UCMJ. No such charges, or even the hint that they might be employed, were made during the two most public and controversial episodes in which a President has relieved a senior officer of command in wartime in the last sixty years. President Truman relieved General Douglas MacArthur for exceeding his operational mandate, and for MacArthur's impolitic public statements about doing so, in Korea.[111] General Stanley McChrystal resigned after being recalled to Washington, D.C., by President Obama, from his command headquarters in Afghanistan. McChrystal and his staff had been interviewed by an embedded magazine journalist in which candid, disparaging remarks aimed at the President Obama's administration, inner circle of advisors, and war-fighting strategy were voiced, suggested, or otherwise countenanced.[112] Both cases involved patent insubordination and unvarnished disrespect.[113] However, neither case was seriously considered a crime for which these popular and competent generals would have been court-martialed or disciplined.

The reluctance to prosecute these striking examples of public conflict at the highest political-military level of policy-making suggests that punitive criminal law has little bearing on the question of deterring or punishing such breaches of the civil-military relationship, let alone diagnosing the health of such strategic relationships. As journalist Thomas Ricks wrote, to equate such failure to a criminal offense would likely chill any motive to innovate—that is, to risk failure or breach a status quo or doctrine.[114] Moreover, in General McChrystal's case, any proposal to consider admonishment or discipline under the UCMJ would have been weakened by the fact that nobody believed tension with the Administration was borne of personal disgust or animosity with President Obama, or even the result of a substantive policy disagreement.[115]

Ultimately, President Obama's decision to accept General McChrystal's tendered resignation was likely a calculation prompted by several factors, none of which included the relevance of a potential criminal prosecution.[116] First, underlying President Obama's decision was his aides' deep distrust of the Pentagon, at least with respect to its support for the administration's strategic review of the Afghanistan mission.[117] Second, an earlier McChrystal public gaffe, in which he implicitly criticized both Vice President Biden's preferred strategy and the amount of time these strategy review sessions were taking in Washington, served as the trigger for his first "warning."[118] Finally, President Obama's decision would inevitably be viewed in historic terms: inspired by the history of American general officer tension with the Oval Office during a war, in which the latter's authority seems challenged, the presidential precedent has been to relieve the offending officer, laud his long and skilled service and honorable sacrifice, but force him into retirement.[119] Public opinion approved of President Obama's decision by a wide margin.[120]

In sum, punitive criminal law does not envision addressing civil-military conflict at the strategic level either as a deterrent or as a guide for promulgating or imputing norms or expectations of conduct. The cases that *have* gone to trial feature relatively low-ranking officers contemptuously attacking the personal attributes of one or more civilians (Howe's case), or the organization as a whole (Mitchell's case). The manner in which courts have punished the offender, the rank of the offender relative to the civilian "victim," and the dearth of legal precedent on the subject, all illustrate that neither the UCMJ itself nor criminal case law offers any direct or implied norms to guide the relationship between senior strategic civilian and military leaders. Finally, the cases that *could have* been prosecuted but were not (as with MacArthur and McChrystal) remind all parties to the strategic civil-military relationship that conspicuous controversy will likely be addressed via political, not legal, means. Ultimately, the result has been a periodic reassertion of civilian control over a "runaway" military by removing the offending military agent from the relationship altogether.[121] In the absence of relevant Constitutional guideposts, statutory requirements, or case precedent, the next most relevant potential source of criteria ought to be found within regulatory provisions, or the tools through which the Executive Branch administers itself. Unfortunately, as described later, these sources again offer missed opportunities.

Administrative Regulations Focus on Undue Personal Gain, not Civil-Military Relations

Regulations issued within the Executive Branch, either by the President or subordinate agencies, appear suited as means by which to prescribe norms of behavior for those parties engaged in strategic civil-military relationships. As illustrated later, however, regulations miss this opportunity, just as Congressional legislation does. Where statutes impose organization, aiming to reduce redundancies, internal executive branch directives that implement ethics policy focus largely on personal financial responsibilities and prohibiting conflicts of interest that affect the public's perception of, or actual impact on, an impartial government workforce. These sources are silent, like case law, on the unique fiduciary responsibilities that are created and managed by the parties to civil-military relationships.

For example, President George H.W. Bush issued an Executive Order in 1989, titled "Principles of Ethical Conduct for Government Officers and Employees."[122] This Order was intended to "establish fair and exacting standards of ethical conduct for all executive branch employees" thereby "intend[ing] only to improve the internal management of the executive branch."[123] This Order is largely relevant for establishing the now well-known fourteen principles of ethical conduct.[124] At first glance, it is ripe for articulating a set of norms that might guide members of a strategic civil-military relationship, and therefore create an objective means to diagnosis suspected pathologies in that relationship:

> Public service is a public trust. Each employee has a responsibility to the United States Government and its citizens to place loyalty to the Constitution, laws and ethical principles above private gain.[125]

Reviewing the subsequent principles, however, the President clearly wished to reinforce a basic commitment to running a government that was (and was perceived to be) impartial, honest, and fair. But each principle is narrowly tailored: Other than the general expectation to "place loyalty to the Constitution, the laws and ethical principles above private gain,"[126] six of the fourteen principles relate exclusively to an employee's financial decision-making and are prohibitions[127] on unethical "private gain" at the expense of government (public) interests.[128] The remaining affirmative duty principles[129] simply direct the employee to engage in "honest effort," to act impartially, to "protect and conserve Federal property," to "disclose waste, fraud, abuse, and corruption," to pay their taxes, to obey equal opportunity laws, and to avoid creating the appearance that they are violating an ethical precept.[130] Not one of the fourteen principles relate to the advice and counsel that military officers must provide to the civilian policy-makers and elected officials in whom the Constitution grants ultimate national security authority. The remainder of the implementing regulation simply discusses these duties in greater detail.[131]

The Joint Ethics Regulation [JER],[132] a Department of Defense [DoD] publication, is also nearly silent on the subject. Other than referencing the fourteen principles of ethical conduct,[133] its "political activities" chapter[134] is focused exclusively on reminding employees that they are not prevented from exercising basic obligations of "citizenship," and is concerned with preventing undue influence of partisan political organizations, members of Congress, or political parties in personnel management decisions.[135] The closest the JER comes to providing a helpful diagnostic tool to the participants in strategic civil-military relationships is in the final chapter, which describes "ethical values" and "ethical decision-making." Here, the DoD lists nine "primary ethical values," including honesty, accountability, fairness, caring, promise-keeping, and responsible citizenship.[136] Only two of these values appear to have applicability to the strategic civil-military relationship. The JER defines "honesty" by listing its various attributes, one of which is "candor," defined as the "forthright offering of unrequested information... [which is] necessary in accordance with the gravity of the situation and the nature of the relationships."[137] Given the strategic policy-making level at which these parties interact, with decisions ultimately affecting how wars are waged and the lives of those Americans who wage them, it would not be surprising that candor is a virtue highly touted by senior officials in these civil-military relationships.[138]

Furthermore, the JER describes "responsible citizenship" as the "civic duty of every citizen" to "exercise discretion [in] personal judgment in the performance of official duties within the limits of their authority so that the will of the people is respected in accordance with democratic principles."[139] This definition begs for clarification. It leaves at least four questions unanswered, including what the government employee should do if "promise-keeping" means being deferential toward a partisan position that the employee believes is in the best interest of the country; how the employee should act if his or her office has no explicit "limit on authority;" whether the "will of the people" is best captured by the Presidential administration or by Congress; finally, it fails to answer what should guide one's discretion.[140]

Failing to address these questions, let alone answer them, reflects poorly on the JER's capacity to serve as a functioning administrative guide for participants in strategic civil-military relationships, or as tool to diagnose their relative health. As the JER and other administrative regulations do not create viable norms, expectations, and standards for the complex interpersonal interactions among the nation's elite policy-makers and military leaders, the final source of possible authority left to examine is military doctrine. Like the higher orders of law and precedent describe earlier, however, this source has no definitive answer either.

Military Doctrine Looks Down and In, not Up and Out

The American military defines "doctrine" as the set of "fundamental principles by which the military forces or elements thereof guide their actions in support of national objectives."[141] Doctrine represents the military's preferences for what "means" to employ and how to employ them, in context of a given "end" or national policy, and explains why those means will be successful.[142] Douglas Macgregor wrote that doctrine is generally "collective body of thinking and writing that…exerts a unifying influence and supports the coordination of operations, tactics, training, and modernization"[143] But as "collective body of thinking and writing," doctrine is not proclaimed in a vacuum. Instead, doctrine evolves much like scientific paradigms.[144] The how, what, and why described by doctrine are questions answered partly by the organization's historical experience, specialized technical knowledge, geography, traditions, the capabilities of likely enemies, and assumptions about how civilian policy-makers will employ the organization.[145]

This final factor can be quite influential. The military's sense of how it is to remain objectively aloof or professionally apolitical, based on Constitutional principles, will determine the extent to which it will necessarily defer to civilian control.[146] Military doctrine, ultimately, is a collection of related approaches which guide and justify future decision-making, built upon appreciation of external circumstances and internal capabilities, generally agreed upon and followed by a specific population.

Thus, like the Constitution, legislation, case law, and regulations, military doctrine appears to be a possible resource for identifying, or at least imputing, specific objective criteria that guide strategic civil-military relationships.[147] In several ways, however, doctrine remains a missed opportunity despite its ability to evolve over time as a function of the proponent organizations' self-criticism, external political influence, or the organization's interpretation of how it will answer policy demands.

First, the Department of Defense's capstone joint doctrine[148] is not purposed to provide such a tool. Rather, it describes in great detail the complicated structure of U.S. national security, including key organizations like the National Security Council relative to the Department of Defense, and the planning and resourcing processes that shape routine and contingency decision-making.[149] However, any reference to "unity of effort" and "coordination" is limited to coordination among the executive branch departments and agencies, non-governmental organizations, the private sector, and other nations.[150] As its focus is the enabling of joint planning and operations among the separate Services, this doctrine is not oriented on the subtleties or nuances of particular relationships among civilian and military strategic policy-makers.

Second, doctrine promulgated by the various Services falls short in the same way. The Army's senior institutional leader, its Chief of Staff, publishes his "vision" of what the Army is, does, how it does it, and its future, in a capstone doctrine document simply called, "The Army."[151] In its most recent form, this doctrine is aimed at all uniformed service members and civilian employees of the Department of Army, and espouses "four essential characteristics" of the Army professional: military expertise, honorable service, *esprit de corps*, and stewardship.[152] Like the JER, the doctrine emphasizes the virtue of "trust," and the commensurate requirement of candor that enables trust to form. However, the doctrine's subsequent discussion of trust relates generically to the relationship between Soldiers fighting for each other on the battlefield and between Soldiers and their uniformed chain-of-command.[153]

While this doctrine does specifically mention "civil-military relations" and highlights military subordination as a key "cornerstone," it applies vaguely to all service members regardless of rank and position, and only requires that a military professional "understand" the role of the civilian leader and "understand" their responsibilities to the civilian leadership.[154] The general observation that military "input is vital" to the policy-making process is the extent to which this doctrine details those responsibilities. It says nothing of the specific relationship between senior participants in the strategic civil-military relationship, notwithstanding a recent history of apparent and public conflict, tension, and resignations.

The closest this doctrine comes to relating practical standards is in its "reference publication," the document that expounds on the principles identified in the original doctrine.[155] Here, the Army specifically mentions "senior Army leaders," but in context of their maintaining the trust "with the American people."[156] Certainly, it is possible to impute that "the American people" is meant here to encompass their elected representatives in Congress and with the President.[157] However, the remaining three paragraphs in all of Army doctrine devoted to "civil-military relations" do not explain how to pragmatically maintain this trust, except through, by inference, "understand[ing] and appreciat[ing] the critical role that civilian control of the military has played throughout our history."[158] The only hint at what could be interpreted as general prescriptive criteria for strategic civil-military relationships is the "duty to ensure that the military perspective is candidly and professionally presented in all appropriate forums."[159] Readers are left to speculate what "professionally" means *if* it is something distinct from "candid" and what an "appropriate forum" would be under given circumstances. This duty, then, would be unhelpful if assessing General Shineski's testimony before Congress in 2003 about the number of troops required in post-war Iraq, widely interpreted as contrary to known civilian leadership preferences. Was it a valid trigger for civil-military strife or was it instead a valid articulation of a candid, "professional" opinion borne of military judgment as the Goldwater Nichols Act authorizes?

Though it does not help answer that question, the doctrine attempts to further explain that a "key condition" of proper civil-military relations" is the "mutual respect and trust between civilian and military leaders," which is fulfilled "by strictly adhering to a set of norms established by law and past practice."[160] However, several features render this prescription too indefinite to be of any great assistance. As discussed previously, there is no definitive "set of norms established by law." Moreover, if Betts is correct that only one's political perspective offers a way to judge the behaviors of these parties,[161] then "past practice" is often an inconsistent or irrelevant guide, serving as weak precedent.

Indeed, by reminding Army professionals that their advisory role is "confined . . . to the policy-making process [but not] to engage publically in policy advocacy or dissent," the doctrine does not address formidable, but foreseeable, situations. For example, it does not define "advocacy," nor suggest any, let alone proper, course of action when a senior military professional believes answering a question would reflect personal judgment without the intent to advocate or the reasonable expectation that the statement could be interpreted as "boxing in" the civilian leadership.[162] This prohibition on "dissent" and "advocacy" is so nonspecific that it appears, at least, contrary to the common interpretation of the officer's oath, which implies a higher duty to Constitutional principles, than to any specific policy or practice.[163]

Additionally, the doctrine does not put the military professional on notice that the demands, expectations, and norms associated with advising civilians at the strategic level can and will shift between one political administration and the next, nor that they may change dramatically within the same administration based on civilian leaders' experiences and exposure to military advice. Third, it only generically addresses all "military professionals," and imprecisely refers to "elected and appointed officials," and the civilians in "other federal and states entities."[164] This leaves the question of how civilian control is to be observed in the context of a senior military official's relationship with another agency or department, other than the Department of Defense, unanswerable. If there is a difference in the degree, extent, or nature of the candid advice to be offered in those circumstances, this doctrine does not describe it or justify it.

In July 2014, the Army recognized an "omission in [its] doctrine" and issued a white paper to "glean [the] fundamental nature" of, and to express, the "Army Ethic."[165] According to the Army's leadership, this Ethic is designed to explain "why we conduct ourselves morally and ethically... [and it] provides motivation and inspiration for each of us to perform our Duty in a manner worthy of the Trust of the American people and each other."[166] Despite the potential to encompass within this Ethic a nuanced description of the duties, expectations, and norms in the strategic civil-military relationship, the white paper reads like training material provided to the Army as a corrective measure, responding to uncomfortable history of well-publicized moral lapses, "double standards, evidence of unfaithfulness, [and] disregard for the law" since military combat operations began in October, 2001.[167] The histories of the Abu Ghraib prison torture scandal,[168] the Afghanistan mass murder conviction of Staff Sergeant Robert Bales,[169] and the infidelity and abuse by Brigadier General Jeffrey Sinclair,[170] among other crimes, need not be recounted here, but seem to have inspired the Army's self-searching inquiry to define and publish an understandable code that will "serve as the foundation for developing the moral identity of Army Professionals."[171] As the white paper demands, "unethical practices must not be tolerated."[172]

Evidently, the white paper was not concerned, just like the doctrine it sought to update, with the particulars of stressed, strained, or fractured strategic civil-military relationships, which are often not ethical dilemmas at all and rarely criminal. Rather, civil-military strain is usually based on misconceptions, failed communications between parties, intemperate overstatements, or attempts by one body of professionals to expand the "jurisdiction" of their influence, intruding into another group's domain of assumed expertise or legitimate authority.[173] The Army, in contrast, seeks to establish an Ethic that will "prevent misconduct... [and] to stop unethical practices."[174]

The other Services suffer the same faults. Their doctrine also aims "down and in" to manage their service members' generic relationships and duties with each other, promoting values like integrity and selfless service, with vague expressions of general respect for the chain-of-command, and reminders that civilians control the military. The Air Force has a punitive directive that "provides specific guidance on required standards of conduct, performance, and discipline."[175] This directive discusses everything from legal use of social media by airmen, to religious accommodation, political activities, and personal grooming. It also restates the Air Force core values of "integrity first, service before self, [and] excellence in all we do."[176] The foreseeable strain and tension in civil-military relationships is nowhere addressed. The Air Force's capstone doctrine similarly is silent. The only reference to policy or politics is a curt warning that military doctrine should be free from the fashionable political fads that too quickly change, free from the influence of "budget battles" and the cult of personalities placing their stamp on what should be solely based on the "lessons of warfare."[177] Navy doctrine is not any more explicit with regard to strategic civil-military relationships than the Army or Air Force. It has no explicit doctrine *per se* concerning foundational moral guidelines. However, like the Air Force, the Navy does publish a "core values charter" listing three attributes expected of all sailors, regardless of rank and including civilian employees of the Department: honor, courage, and commitment.[178] Under "honor," the Navy reminds its professionals to "make honest recommendations to [their] seniors" and to "deliver bad news forthrightly"—clearly implied tasks if candor is a valued attribute.[179] The Navy recognized the doctrinal gap, as the Army did, in a recent report from the U.S. Naval War College.[180] This report called for institution-wide reassessment of the Navy Ethic, seeking to make it proactive and preventive across the organizational culture. However, it too seems more concerned with stemming illegal and unethical choices of its sailors, arguing they undermine war-fighting capabilities.[181] Nothing expressly relates to the senior flag officer and the relationship with strategic policy-makers; instead, obvious truisms and generalizations are commonplace.[182]

In sum, Doctrine does not describe critical reasons for friction in these relationships, at what echelon they occur, how to avoid or relieve tensions, or provide historical vignettes as illustrations.

Notes

1. *See generally* U.S. Const. art. I and art. II.
2. Youngstown Sheet & Tube Co. v. Sawyer, 343 U.S. 579, 629 (1952) (Douglas, J., concurring) (noting the differences in the speed with which the executive branch can act, contrasted against the "cumbersome, time-consuming, and apparently inefficient" legislative branch).
3. Akhil Reed Amar, America's Constitution: a Biography 114–15 (2005).
4. The Federalist No. 47 (Madison).
5. *Youngstown Sheet & Tube Co.*, 343 U.S. at 593 (Frankfurter, J., concurring).

6. To wit: age requirements for election as a Senator or Representative; the effect of an impeachment; the time, place, and manner of elections; financial compensation; and determining internal "rules of its proceedings." U.S. Const. art I, §§ 2–7.
7. U.S. Const. art. I, § 8, cl. 1, 11–14.
8. Youngstown Sheet & Tube Co. v. Sawyer, 343 U.S. 579, 587–88 (1952) (holding that President Truman's Executive Order 10340 to the Secretary of Commerce to seize private steel mills and keep them operating, in order to avoid a "catastrophic" national strike by employees in the midst of the Korean War, was unconstitutional: Article II grants the president power to see that the laws are faithfully executed, and the directive in question was precisely the kind of order that would have been constitutional if enacted by Congress under its Article I powers).
9. U.S. Const. art II, § 1.
10. U.S. Const. art II, § 2, cl. 1.
11. Amar, America's Constitution, at 115; *see also* The Federalist No. 69 (Hamilton).
12. *Youngstown Sheet & Tube Co.*, 343 U.S. at 610 (Frankfurter, J., concurring) ("[t]he powers of the President are not as particularized as those of Congress").
13. David Luban, *On the Commander in Chief Power*, 81 S. Cal. L. Rev. 477, 483 (2008) ("[t]he Commander in Chief Clause is a sphinx, and specifying its powers and the theory generating them is its riddle").
14. U.S. Const. art II., § 1, cl. 8.
15. Noah Feldman & Samuel Issacharoff, *Declarative Sentences*, Slate.com (Mar. 5, 2007), http://www.slate.com/articles/news_and_politics/jurisprudence/2007/03/declarative_sentences.html.
16. *See, e.g.*, Letters of Pacificus, No. 1 (Alexander Hamilton); *see also* Haig v. Agee, 453 U.S. 280, 291–92 (1981).
17. The president can deploy combat forces to hostile areas to engage in armed fighting without the consent of Congress for limited periods of time, but with explicit notification to Congress of the executive action and purpose. *See* 50 U.S.C. 1541 *et seq.* (1973).
18. *See* Hamdan v. Rumsfeld, 548 U.S. 557, 591–92 (2006) (*quoting* Ex Parte Milligan, 71 U.S. 2 (1866)).
19. *See* U.S. Cong., 37th Cong., Report of the Joint Committee on the Conduct of the War (1863), *available at* https://archive.org/details/reportjointcomm08war. Another example of congressional investigation into specific choices made by civil-military elites, in the midst of the war being waged by those elites, is the MacArthur Inquiry, established to investigate the circumstances of President Truman's dismissal of General MacArthur from combat command in Korea in 1951. *Military Situation in*

the Far East, Hearings Before The Committee On Armed Services and The Committee On Foreign Relations United States Senate, 82nd Cong. (1951) [hereinafter *MacArthur Senate Statement*].

20. Scott Wilson, *Obama Administration: Libya Action Does Not Require Congressional Approval*, WASH. POST, June 15, 2011, http://www.washingtonpost.com/politics/obama-administration-libya-action-does-not-require-congressional-approval/2011/06/15/AGLttOWH_story.html; Peter Baker & Jonathan Weisman, *Obama Seeks Approval by Congress for Strike in Syria*, N.Y. TIMES, Aug. 31, 2013, http://www.nytimes.com/2013/09/01/world/middleeast/syria.html?pagewanted=all&_r=0.
21. Other than a conflict-specific "Authorization for the Use of Force" from Congress, the War Powers Resolution of 1973 is the prime example. This Joint Resolution remains highly controversial and easily avoided by presidents unwilling to subject their execution of commander-in-chief responsibilities to congressional review. *See* Authority to Use Military Force in Libya, 35 Op. O.L.C. at 8–13 (2011), http://www.justice.gov/sites/default/files/olc/opinions/2011/04/31/authority-military-use-in-libya_0.pdf. Among other things, this Joint Resolution asserted a reminder that the "constitutional powers of the President as Commander-in-Chief" to put U.S. forces into hostilities abroad was not unlimited. *See* War Powers Resolution, 50 U.S.C. 1541 *et seq.* (1973).
22. The debate over how "unitary" the Executive Branch is, for instance, still finds passionate arguments on both sides. *See, e.g.*, Lawrence Lessig & Cass Sunstein, *The President and the Administration*, 94 Colum. L. REV. 1 (1994) (arguing that the President does not have sole authority over all administration agencies and powers that flow from his executive authority). *But see* Steven G. Calabresi & Saikrishna B. Prakash, *The President's Power to Execute the Laws*, 104 YALE L. J. 541 (1994) (arguing that Constitution's text and original meaning created only a "trinity" of powers, and anything not legislative or judicial in nature implicitly fell under the president's authority to "execute the laws").
23. Myers v. United States, 272 U.S. 52, 293 (1926) (Brandeis, J., dissenting):

    > [t]he doctrine of the separation of powers was adopted by the Convention ... not to promote efficiency but to preclude the exercise of arbitrary power. The purpose was, not to avoid friction, but, by means of the inevitable friction incident to the distribution of the governmental powers among three departments, to save the people from autocracy.

24. As President, Theodore Roosevelt was largely regarded as an expansionist, greatly swelling the role of the Chief Executive in foreign relations and expressions of military authority abroad, claiming such power vested in his office as

the sovereign and needed no express constitutional basis (the "residuum of power" argument). His successor, William Howard Taft, took the opposite approach to executive authority, and limited his office to that which was explicitly authorized by the Constitution or Congress or was necessarily implied by either. PETER M. SHANE & HAROLD H. BRUFF, SEPARATION OF POWERS LAW 22–23 (2005); EDMUND MORRIS, THEODORE REX 23–24, 386–416 (2001) (wherein Morris quotes Henry Adams's famous description of Roosevelt's power after concluding the peace talks he hosted between Russia and Japan, calling him the "best herder of Emperors since Napoleon," *id.* at 414).

25. Millett et al., *The Effectiveness of Military Organizations*, at 44.
26. HENRY KISSINGER, DIPLOMACY 21 (1994).
27. Youngstown Sheet & Tube Co. v. Sawyer, 343 U.S. 579, 610–11 (1952) (Frankfurter, J., concurring); *see id.* at 635 (Jackson, J., concurring) ("[w] hile the Constitution diffuses power the better to secure liberty, it also contemplates that practice will integrate the dispersed powers into a workable government"); *see also* Dames & Moore v. Regan, 453 U.S. 654, 686 (1981) (*citing* Frankfurter's concurrence in *Youngstown*).
28. *Youngstown Sheet & Tube Co.*, 343 U.S. at 653 (Jackson, J., concurring).
29. Myers v. United States, 272 U.S. 52, 283 (1926) (Brandeis, J., dissenting) ("[a] persistent legislative practice which involves a delimitation of the respective powers of Congress and the President, and which has been so established and maintained, should be deemed tantamount to judicial construction, in the absence of any decision by any court to the contrary") (*citing United States v. Midwest Oil Co.*, 236 U.S. 459, 469).
30. BERNARD BRODIE, WAR AND POLITICS 439 (1973).
31. *Id.*
32. AMY B. ZEGART, FLAWED BY DESIGN: THE EVOLUTION OF THE CIA, JCS, AND NSC 39–41, 107 (1999).
33. Iraq Liberation Act of 1998, Pub. L. 105–338, 112 Stat. 3178 (1998) (stating, *inter alia*, "[i]t is the sense of Congress that once the Saddam Hussein regime is removed from power in Iraq, the United States should support Iraq's transition to democracy by providing immediate and substantial humanitarian assistance to the Iraqi people, by providing democracy transition assistance to Iraqi parties and movements with democratic goals").
34. MICHAEL R. GORDON & GENERAL BERNARD E. TRAINOR, THE ENDGAME: THE INSIDE STRUGGLE FOR IRAQ, FROM GEORGE W. BUSH TO BARACK OBAMA 6–7 (2013).
35. For the unclassified executive summary of "Desert Crossing," *see* GORDON & TRAINOR, COBRA II, at 668–73 (2007).
36. *Id. See also* United States Central Command, *Desert Crossing Seminar: After Action Report*, http://www2.gwu.edu/~nsarchiv/NSAEBB/NSAEBB207/Desert%20Crossing%20After%20Action%20Report_1999-06-28.pdf.

37. GORDON & TRAINOR, ENDGAME, at 9.
38. GORDON & TRAINOR, COBRA II, 38–40.
39. National Security Act of 1947, Pub. L. No. 80–253, 61 Stat. 495 (1947).
40. RODMAN at 16, ZEGART at 109–110.
41. James R. Locher III, *Has it Worked? The Goldwater-Nichols Reorganization Act*, NAVAL WAR C. REV. (Autumn 2001), at 95, 98.
42. ZEGART, at 62.
43. James R. Locher III, *Has it Worked? The Goldwater-Nichols Reorganization Act*, NAVAL WAR C. REV. (Autumn 2001), at 95, 98; ZEGART, at 111.
44. National Security Act Amendments of 1949, Pub. L. No. 81–216, 63 Stat. 578 (1949).
45. Thomas L. McNaugher & Roger L. Sperry, *Improving Military Coordination: The Goldwater-Nichols Reorganization of the Department of Defense, in* WHO MAKES PUBLIC POLICY: THE STRUGGLE FOR CONTROL BETWEEN CONGRESS AND THE EXECUTIVE 219, 223 (Robert S. Gilmour & Alexis A. Halley eds., 1994).
46. Defense Reorganization Plan No. 6 of 1953, *reprinted in* 67 Stat. 638 (1953), http://www.gpo.gov/fdsys/pkg/STATUTE-67/pdf/STATUTE-67-Pg638.pdf.
47. Dwight D. Eisenhower, *Special Message to the Congress Transmitting Reorganization Plan No. 6 of 1953 Concerning the Department of Defense*, April 30, 1953, http://www.presidency.ucsb.edu/ws/?pid=9831.
48. *Id.*
49. Department of Defense Reorganization Act of 1958, Pub. L. No. 85–599, 72 Stat. 514 (1958).
50. *Id.* (amending Section 2 of the National Security Act of 1947).
51. *Reorganization Proposals for the Joint Chiefs of Staff: Hearings Before the Investigations Subcomm.*, H. Comm. on Armed Services, 97th Cong. 54 (1982) (statement of General David Jones, Chairman of the Chiefs of Staff).
52. James R. Locher III, *Has it Worked? The Goldwater-Nichols Reorganization Act*, at 100.
53. Thomas L. McNaugher & Roger L. Sperry, *Improving Military Coordination: The Goldwater-Nichols Reorganization of the Department of Defense*, at 229.
54. Goldwater-Nichols Act, at pmbl.
55. 10 U.S.C. § 163(b)(2).
56. 10 U.S.C. § 153(a)(1).
57. 10 U.S.C. § 151(b)(1).
58. Peter D. Feaver, *The Right to Be Right*, at 113 (commenting on General Peter Pace's role during the deliberation over the 2007 surge strategy in Iraq).
59. 10 U.S.C § 154.

60. 10 U.S.C § 151(d)(1).
61. 10 U.S.C § 151(e).
62. There are nine COCOMs, divided between "functional" and "geographic" responsibilities: U.S. Strategic Command (USSTRATCOM), U.S. Special Operations Command (USSOCOM), and U.S. Transportation Command (USTRANSCOM) have global responsibilities based on their respective technical or tactical focus; whereas, U.S. Pacific Command (USPACOM), U.S. European Command (USEUCOM), U.S. Central Command (USCENTCOM), U.S. Southern Command (USSOUTHCOM), U.S. Northern Command (USNORTHCOM), and U.S. Africa Command (USAFRICOM) have geographic areas of responsibility. *See* Department of Defense, UNIFIED COMMAND PLAN, http://www.defense.gov/ucc/.
63. 10 U.S.C § 162(b).
64. 10 U.S.C § 163(a) and (b).
65. 10 U.S.C § 164.
66. According to Colin Powell, the first Chairman under the new law for a full tenure, the Act's organizational transformations were first tested by U.S. engagement in Panama (Operation Just Cause) in 1989 and in dealing with the aftermath of the fall of the Berlin Wall—crises that demonstrated the Chairman's ability to speak for himself rather than seek a composite or consensus view from the individual Services. COLIN POWELL, MY AMERICAN JOURNEY 422, 438–39, 447 (1995).
67. Thomas L. McNaugher & Roger L. Sperry, *Improving Military Coordination: The Goldwater-Nichols Reorganization of the Department of Defense*, at 243–44.
68. Eliot Cohen, *In DoD We Trust*, NEW REPUBLIC (June 17, 1991) at 29, 31.
69. 10 U.S.C § 663(a).
70. 10 U.S.C §§ 3033(d), 5033(d), 8033(d) (perform ... military duties ... as are assigned to him by the President, the Secretary of Defense, or the [Service] Secretary [including] "keep[ing] the Secretary ... fully informed of significant military operations affecting the duties and responsibilities of the Secretary [while always remaining] "[s]ubject to the authority, direction, and control of the Secretary of Defense).
71. Such was the case with General Powell. His long association with the Reagan and first Bush Administrations, his White House Fellowship, and his time National Security Advisor gave him unprecedented credibility with the civilian leadership. Many pundits and scholars expressed concern about his singular voice of military strategy in Washington during the Panama invasion in 1989 and the Gulf War in 1990–91, which seemed (at least to those observing from outside his inner circle) to effectively silence the Service chiefs and field commanders with their alternative views. Cohen, *In DoD We Trust*, at 34–35.

72. GORDON & TRAINOR, COBRA II, at 5.
73. *Id.* at 3–4, 53–54 ("Franks worked for Rumsfeld and only barely tolerated the JCS . . . [Franks] tended to view the chiefs [of the Services, members of the JCS] as meddlesome military bureaucrats . . . [and] resented their input").
74. *Id.* at 28.
75. *Id.* at 27 (quoting General Anthony Zinni, Franks' former superior at CENTCOM).
76. ROSE, HOW WARS END, at 267–68.
77. The officer affirms:

 I, [name of officer], do solemnly swear (or affirm) that I will support and defend the Constitution of the United States against all enemies, foreign and domestic; that I will bear true faith and allegiance to the same; that I take this obligation freely, without any mental reservation or purpose of evasion; and that I will well and faithfully discharge the duties of the office on which I am about to enter. So help me God.

 5 U.S.C. § 3331; *see also* U.S. DEP'T OF ARMY, DA Form 71 (The Oath of Office – Military Personnel) (July 1999).
78. *See, e.g.*, Major General (retired) Paul D. Eaton, *A Top-Down Review for the Pentagon*, N.Y. TIMES, Mar. 19, 2006, (calling for Donald Rumsfeld's resignation), http://www.nytimes.com/2006/03/19/opinion/19eaton.html?pagewanted=print&_r=0.
79. 5 U.S.C. § 3331.
80. ROBERT J. DALESSANDRO, ARMY OFFICER'S GUIDE 7 (2009); *see also* Lieutenant Colonel Andrew Milburn, *Breaking Ranks: Dissent and the Military Professional*, JOINT FORCES Q. (4th Quarter, 2010), at 103; *and see* Lieutenant General (retired) Greg Newbold, *Why Iraq was a Mistake*, TIME, Apr. 9, 2006, http://content.time.com/time/magazine/article/0,9171,1181629,00.html.
81. The contexts of the apparent dilemmas are important, as is the recognition that humans will often be inconsistent in their own beliefs and actions. *See, e.g.*, General Douglas MacArthur's testimony before the Senate in the wake of his relief from command by President Truman, in which he readily affirmed the President's unilateral and uncontestable authority to fire a commanding officer as inherent to "our system," *MacArthur Senate Statement*, at 26. However, when questioned as to whether a theater commander should publically express his views on the politics and policy context of the conflict in which he leads, MacArthur asserted a right of a commander to inform the public of "diverse" views on controversial issues, so that they may use the "truth" to inform their judgment and thus control the government they elect. *Id.* at 99.

82. 10 U.S.C. § 3583 [Army commanding officers]; U.S.C. § 8583 [Air Force commanding officers]. As "requirement[s] of exemplary conduct," such officers must:

 show in themselves a good example of virtue, honor, patriotism, and subordination; to be vigilant in inspecting the conduct of all persons who are placed under their command; to guard against and suppress all dissolute and immoral practices, and to correct, according to the laws and regulations of the Army, all persons who are guilty of them; and to take all necessary and proper measures, under the laws, regulations, and customs of the [Army and Air Force], to promote and safeguard the morale, the physical well-being, and the general welfare of the officers and enlisted persons under their command or charge.

 Such duties were already codified in law, dating back to 1956, in 10 U.S.C. § 5947, employing identical language, but only applied to Naval and Marine Corps officers.
83. Paul Richter, *Army Women Describe Rapes as Trial Opens*, Los Angeles Times, April 15, 1997, http://articles.latimes.com/1997-04-15/news/mn-48914_1_simpson-trial.
84. *See* U.S. Dep't of Army, Reg. 600-20, Army Command Policy para. 1-5*c*.(4)(*d*) (2014).
85. *Id.* at para. 1–1 and 1–5a.
86. *Id.* at para. 1–5*c*.
87. Baker v. Carr, 369 U.S. 186, 217 (1962) (establishing several possible reasons why a case or controversy would be considered "nonjusticiable").
88. Alternatively, some scholars argue that the "political question doctrine" only applies to questions involving the separation of powers between the judicial branch and one of the political branches. Chris Michel, *Comment: There's No Such Thing as a Political Question of Statutory Interpretation: The Implications of* Zivotofsky v. Clinton, 123 Yale L. J. 253, 259, 261 (2013) (arguing that this case implies that a "claim to a federal statutory right can never present a political question"). This suggests that disputes between the two political branches are not "political" as defined by *Baker*, but rather the very kind of cases that implicate constiutional division of labor and thus require judicial interpretation. Nevertheless, the field of national security and foreign affairs tends to shuffle cases involving these domains into the bin of nonjusticiable "political questions" because they invoke questions committed to the discretion of the executive and legislative branches. *See, e.g.*, Haig v. Agee, 453 U.S. 280, 292 (1981) ("matters intimately relating to foreign policy and national security are rarely proper subjects for judicial intervention"). *But cf.*, Zivotofsky ex rel. Zivotofsky v. Clinton, 132 S.Ct.

1421, 1436 (2012) (Alito, J., concurring) ("determining the constitutionality of an Act of Congress may present a political question in some cases"). Neither the Goldwater-Nichols Act, nor any of its predecessor legislation (*e.g.*, the National Security Act of 1947) have been addressed by the Supreme Court; these acts do not create statutory rights for any individual party.

89. DESCH, CHANGING SECURITY ENVIRONMENT, at 2.
90. *Id.*
91. Fred L. Borch III, *Lore of the Corps: The Trial by Court-Martial of Colonel William "Billy" Mitchell*, ARMY LAW., Jan. 2012, at 1.
92. *Id. See also The "Shenandoah" Disaster*, FLIGHT, Sept. 10, 1925, at 580, *available at* http://www.flightglobal.com/pdfarchive/view/1925/1925%20-%200580.html.
93. Borch, *Court-Martial of Billy Mitchell*, at 1.
94. Rebecca Maksel, *The Billy Mitchell Court-Martial*, AIR & SPACE MAG., July 2009, at 46, available at http://www.airspacemag.com/history-of-flight/the-billy-mitchell-court-martial-136828592/?no-ist.
95. Article 96 was the forerunner to the modern Article 134 offense in the UCMJ. Borch, *Court-Martial of Billy Mitchell, supra* note 212, at 3. The "commander" who exercised court-martial jurisdiction over the case, and charged Mitchell, was President Calvin Coolidge. *See* DAVID E. JOHNSON, FAST TANKS AND HEAVY BOMBERS 87 (2003).
96. DAVID E. JOHNSON, FAST TANKS AND HEAVY BOMBERS 89 (2003).
97. There is little historical record suggesting General MacArthur's later controversial views, expressing a political opinion contrary to his civilian superiors, was influenced by his participation in Mitchell's court-martial. We are left to speculate. *See* WILLIAM MANCHESTER, AMERICAN CAESAR 149–51 (1978). Not only did the two men consider themselves friends, but among the ironies of this court-martial that brought MacArthur and Mitchell together was that—a quarter century earlier—nineteen-year-old MacArthur vainly attempted to court Mitchell's sister in Wisconsin. *Id.* at 61. The association of these two, both known for their confrontations with civilian and military authority they viewed as ignorant and shortsighted, goes back even further. As a young lieutenant in the Signal Corps, Mitchell served under General *Arthur* MacArthur in the Philippines in 1898. Mitchell's own father, by then a Senator, had also served with then-Lieutenant Arthur MacArthur when he served in with the 24th Wisconsin Infantry during the Civil War. *Id.* at 43.
98. JOHNSON, FAST TANKS, at 87.
99. Borch, *Court-Martial of Billy Mitchell*, at 1–2.
100. Pub. L. No. 69–446, 44 Stat. 780 (1926). This Act officially established the Army "Air Corps" and, *inter alia*, increased the number of personnel assigned or detailed to support it, ordered it to maintain 1,800 serviceable

aircraft, and established a new "air section" in each War Department General Staff division. *See* JOHNSON, FAST TANKS, at 89–90.

101. Article 88, Uniform Code of Military Justice (UCMJ), 10 U.S.C. § 888:

> Any commissioned officer who uses contemptuous words against the President, the Vice President, Congress, the Secretary of Defense, the Secretary of a military department, the Secretary of Transportation, or the Governor or legislature of any State, Territory, Commonwealth, or possession in which he is on duty or present shall be punished as a court-martial may direct.

102. United States v. Howe, 37 C.M.R. 429, 432 (1967).
103. Lieutenant Colonel Michael J. Davidson, *Contemptuous Speech Against the President*, ARMY LAW. 1 (July 1999); *see also Hearing Before the House Comm. On Military Affairs on H.R. 23628* (Statement of Brigadier General Enoch H. Crowder, the Judge Advocate General of the Army), May 23, 1912 (discussing proposed revisions to the United State Articles of War, the forerunner to the Uniform Code of Military Justice), at 55, *available at* http://www.loc.gov/rr/frd/Military_Law/pdf/hearing_comm.pdf.
104. MANUAL FOR COURTS-MARTIAL, UNITED STATES pt. IV, 12c (2012) [hereinafter MCM].
105. *Id.*
106. John Lancaster, *General Who Mocked Clinton Set to Retire, Punishment Follows Remarks at Banquet*, WASH. POST, June 19, 1993, http://www.highbeam.com/doc/1P2-951902.html.
107. *See, e.g.*, Craig Whitlock, *Military brass, behaving badly: files detail a spate of misconduct dogging armed forces*, WASH. POST, Jan. 26, 2014, http://www.washingtonpost.com/world/national-security/military-brass-behaving-badly-files-detail-a-spate-of-misconduct-dogging-armed-forces/2014/01/26/4d06c770-843d-11e3-bbe5-6a2a3141e3a9_story.html.
108. Article 92, UCMJ; *see also* MCM, *supra* note 225, at pt. IV, 16c(3).
109. Article 133, UCMJ; *see also* MCM, *supra* note 225, at pt. IV, 59c.
110. Article 134, UCMJ, *see also* MCM, *supra* note 225, at pt. IV, 60.
111. *MacArthur Senate Statement, supra* note 140; *see also* W.H. Lawrence, *Truman Relieves M'Arthur of All His Posts; Finds Him Unable to Back U.S.-U.N. Policies; Ridgway Named to Far Eastern Commands*, N.Y. TIMES (April 11, 1951), http://www.nytimes.com/learning/general/onthisday/big/0411.html#article.
112. Michael Hastings, *The Runaway General*, ROLLING STONE, June 22, 2010, http://www.rollingstone.com/politics/news/the-runaway-general-20100622; for background on the journalist and his personal views on

General McCrystal, as well as speculation on the latter's motivation to be interviewed by the popular magazine, *see* BOLGER, WHY WE LOST, at 339–42.

113. Marybeth P. Ulrich, *The General Stanley McChrystal Affair: A Case Study in Civil-Military Relations*, PARAMETERS (Spring 2011), 86–100.
114. RICKS, THE GENERALS, at 451–53.
115. ADMIRAL JAMES STAVRIDIS, THE ACCIDENTAL ADMIRAL: A SAILOR TAKES COMMAND AT NATO 109–13 (2015) (Stavridis was McChrystal's superior, serving as the North Atlantic Treaty Organization [NATO] Supreme Allied Commander for Operations [SACEUR] at the time). *See also* Ulrich, *The General Stanley McChrystal Affair*, at 86. Indeed, in the immediate aftermath of the offending article's publication in *Rolling Stone*, the debate over whether President Obama should relieve McChrystal, or simply recall and censure him, was widespread—both in public editorials and inside the White House. *Id.* at 90. Arguments for and against relief were premised on whether the general's presumed ability (according to Eliot Cohen, a "selfless, fearless, and inspiring… military genius") to accomplish the strategic mission before him was more important than his staff's imprudent comments. Eliot A. Cohen, *Why McChrystal Has to Go*, WALL STREET J., June 23, 2010, http://www.wsj.com/articles/SB10001424052748704853404575322800914018876 (arguing that he should be relieved); Greg Jaffe & Ernesto Londono, *Is General Stanley McChrystal Someone the President Can Afford to Fire?*, WASH. POST, June 22, 2010 (quoting both Eliot Cohen and Peter Feaver as saying this was a "firing offense"), http://www.washingtonpost.com/wpdyn/content/article/2010/06/22/AR2010062202069.html; *see also* Max Fisher, *7 Cases for Keeping McChrystal*, THE ATLANTIC, June 22, 2010, http://www.thewire.com/politics/2010/06/7-cases-for-keeping-mcchrystal/23976/.
116. In fact, the Department of Defense [DoD] Inspector General conducted an investigation into the episodes captured in the *Rolling Stone* article and did not release its findings until nine months after McChrystal's forced resignation, and concluded that there was insufficient evidence to prove any violation of the UCMJ or DoD policy or rules. *See* Memorandum from Michael S. Child, Jr., Acting Deputy Inspector General, Department of Defense, for Inspector General, Department of the Army, subject: Review of Army Inspector General Agency Report of Investigation (Case 10-024) (8 April 2011), http://www.dodig.mil/fo/Foia/PDFs/ROI-508.pdf.
117. Ulrich, *The General Stanley McChrystal Affair*, at 89; *see also* WOODWARD, OBAMA'S WARS, at 371–74.
118. Ulrich, *The General Stanley McChrystal Affair*, at 88–89; *see also* GATES, DUTY MEMOIRS, at 491, *and* LEON PANETTA, WORTHY FIGHTS 253 (2014) (calling General McChrystal's remarks at a London think tank as probably right, but "ill-advised" for appearing to "box in" the administration).

119. *See* GATES, DUTY MEMOIRS, at 487–91 (Secretary of Defense Robert Gates' memory of the White House response to the *Rolling Stone* article). *See also* President Harry Truman, Statement by the President, April 10, 1951, http://www.pbs.org/wgbh/amex/macarthur/filmmore/reference/primary/officialdocs02.html; *compare* President Barack Obama, Statement by the President in the Rose Garden, June 23, 2010, *available at* http://www.whitehouse.gov/the-press-office/statement-president-rose-garden.
120. Jeffrey M. Jones, *Most Approve of Obama's Decision to Remove Gen. McChrystal*, GALLUP.COM, http://www.gallup.com/poll/141041/approve-obama-decision-remove-gen-mcchrystal.aspx (reporting on a June 25, 2010 USA Today/Gallup poll).
121. GATES, DUTY MEMOIRS, *supra* note 56, at 491; *see also* BARRY POSEN, THE SOURCES OF MILITARY DOCTRINE 45 (1984).
122. Exec. Order No. 12,674, 5 C.F.R. 2635 (1989), *modified by* Exec. Order No. 12,731, 5 C.F.R. 2635 (1990).
123. *Id.* at pmbl. and § 504.
124. 5 C.F.R. 2635.101(b)(1)-(14) (Standards of Ethical Conduct for Employees of the Executive Branch).
125. *Id.* at 2635.101(a).
126. *Id.* at 2635.101(b)(1).
127. Identified by "shall not."
128. 5 C.F.R. 2635.101(b)(2), (3), (4), (6), (7), and (10).
129. Identified by "shall."
130. 5 C.F.R. 2635.101(b)(5), (8), (9), (11), (12), (13), and (14).
131. *See, e.g.*, 5 C.F.R. 2635, subparts B – H. The later supplementing regulation was specifically aimed at employees of the Department of Defense, but it too lacks any relevance to the strategic civil-military relationship. 5 C.F.R. 3601 (Supplemental Standards of Ethical Conduct for Employees of the Department of Defense). This regulation identifies "additional exceptions for gifts from outside sources," "limitations on gifts between DoD employees," "limitations on solicited sales," and restrictions on "outside employment and business activities" of defense employees. *Id.* at 3601.102, 103, 104, 106, and 107. Nothing addresses any larger principle beyond those prohibiting unethical private (financial) gain.
132. U.S. DEP'T OF DEFENSE, DIR. 5500.07-R, JOINT ETHICS REGULATION, CHANGES 1–7 (11 Nov 2011) [herinafter JER].
133. *Id.* at Chapter 12.
134. *Id.* at Chapter 6.
135. *Id.* at para. 6–203.
136. *Id.* at para 12–400.
137. *Id.* at para. 12–400a.(3).

138. *See, e.g.*, LEON PANETTA, WORTHY FIGHTS, at 195, 213, 226, 349–51; *see also* GATES, DUTY MEMOIRS, at 22, 84 (recounting his first meeting as Secretary of Defense with the Joint Chiefs of Staff), 87, 91 (espousing the virtue of candor toward Congress), 95 (recounting President George W. Bush's expectation for candor from his senior flag officers), 134 (quoting Gates' 2008 speech to cadets at the United States Military Academy), 188, and 576; *see also* COLIN POWELL, IT WORKED FOR ME 97, 113, 121–23 (2012); *and* COLIN POWELL, MY AMERICAN JOURNEY, at 448.
139. JER, at para 12–400j.
140. Moreover, these values are generically applied to every DoD employee from the civilian paralegal specialist working in the Fort Polk, Louisiana, Office of the Staff Judge Advocate to the Secretary of Defense. In sum, these internal Executive Branch regulations and directives appear relevant to the subject of strategic civil-military relations, but do little to establish a diagnostic mechanism for assessing their vitality or pathology.
141. DEP'T OF DEFENSE, JOINT PUB. 1–02, DEP'T OF DEFENSE DICTIONARY OF MILITARY AND ASSOCIATED TERMS, 73 (8 Nov. 2010). The individual Services' definitions are identical. ***Compare***, NAVAL DOCTRINE PUB. 1, NAVAL WARFARE, 48 (March 2010), ***and*** ARMY DOCTRINE PUB. 1–02, OPERATIONAL TERMS AND MILITARY SYMBOLS, Glossary-1, (31 Aug. 2012).
142. POSEN, SOURCES OF MILITARY DOCTRINE, at 7, 13.
143. DOUGLAS A. MACGREGOR, BREAKING THE PHALANX: A NEW DESIGN FOR LANDPOWER IN THE TWENTY-FIRST CENTURY 143–44 (1997).
144. DAVID E. JOHNSON, MODERN U.S. CIVIL-MILITARY RELATIONS: WIELDING THE TERRIBLE SWIFT SWORD vi–viii (1997).
145. POSEN, SOURCES OF MILITARY DOCTRINE, at 14; JANOWITZ, THE PROFESSIONAL SOLDIER, at 257.
146. JANOWITZ, THE PROFESSIONAL SOLDIER, at 257.
147. POSEN, THE SOURCES OF MILITARY DOCTRINE, at 16.
148. DEP'T OF DEFENSE, JOINT PUB. 1, DOCTRINE FOR THE ARMED FORCES OF THE UNITED STATES (25 March 2013).
149. *Id.* at Chapter II, especially Figures II-1 and II-3.
150. *Id.* at i, and para. V-14.
151. ARMY DOCTRINE PUB. 1, THE ARMY iii (Sept. 17, 2012).
152. *Id.* at para, 2–1.
153. *Id.* at paras. 2–2, 2–3, and 2–4.
154. *Id.* at para. 2–26.
155. ARMY DOCTRINE REFERENCE PUBLICATION [hereinafter ADRP] 1, THE ARMY PROFESSION, Preface (14 June 2013).
156. *Id.* at para. 6–9.
157. *Id.* at para. 6–10.
158. *Id.*

159. *Id.* at para. 6–11.
160. ADRP 1, at para. 6–12.
161. BETTS, COLD WAR CRISES, at xv.
162. *See, e.g.*, Suzanne C. Nielson, *Rules of the Game? The Weinberger Doctrine and the American Use of Force, in* THE FUTURE OF THE ARMY PROFESSION 627, 627 (Lloyd Matthews ed., 2005) (commenting on General John Shalikashvili's 1995 remarks at George Washington University, as Chairman of the Joint Chiefs of Staff, clearing advocating for a policy that disassociated the U.S. from "nation-building").
163. DALESSANDRO, ARMY OFFICER'S GUIDE, at 7.
164. ADRP 1, at para. 6–10.
165. CENTER FOR THE ARMY PROFESSION AND ETHIC [hereinafter CAPE], U.S. ARMY TRAINING AND DOCTRINE COMMAND, *The Army Ethic*, at i (11 July 2014) [hereinafter *Army Ethic*].
166. *Id.* at 1.
167. *Id.* at 2.
168. *See, e.g., Final Report of the Independent Panel to Review DoD Detention Operations* (August 2004), *available at* http://www.defense.gov/news/Aug2004/d20040824finalreport.pdf.
169. Kirk Johnson, *Guilty Plea by Sergeant in Killing of Civilians*, N.Y. TIMES, June 5, 2013, http://www.nytimes.com/2013/06/06/us/sergeant-robert-bales-testimony.html?_r=0.
170. Craig Whitlock, *Disgraced army general, Jeffrey A. Sinclair, receives fine, no jail time*, WASH. POST, March 20, 2014, http://www.washingtonpost.com/world/national-security/disgraced-army-general-jeffrey-a-sinclair-receives-fine-no-jail-time/2014/03/20/c555b650-b039-11e3-95e8-39bef8e9a48b_story.html.
171. CAPE, *Army Ethic*, at 2.
172. *Id.*
173. According to Don Snider, professional groups such as the collective body of military officers—usually at the strategic level of rank and authority—"engage in competition and negotiation for legitimate jurisdictions within which to apply their expertise . . . [so] the task of the profession's strategic leaders is to identify its competitors, carefully analyze the competition, renegotiate jurisdictions, and create and maintain professional legitimacy." Don M. Snider, *The U.S. Army as Profession, in* THE FUTURE OF THE ARMY PROFESSION 3, 26 (Lloyd Matthews ed., 2005).
174. CAPE, *Army Ethic*, at 7.
175. DEP'T OF AIR FORCE, INSTRUCTION 1–1, AIR FORCE STANDARDS (7 Aug 2012), http://www.180fw.ang.af.mil/shared/media/document/AFD-120820-005.pdf.
176. *Id.* at 4.

177. Dep't of Air Force, Doctrine Document 1 (AFDD 1), Air Force Basic Doctrine, Organization, and Command 6–7 (14 October 2011).
178. *Available at* http://ethics.navy.mil/content/corevaluescharter.aspx (the same three values are espoused by the Marine Corps, http://www.hqmc.marines.mil/hrom/NewEmployees/AbouttheMarineCorps/Values.aspx).
179. *Id.*
180. *Ethics in the Navy* (24 March 2014), https://www.usnwc.edu/getattachment/4fdc7dfe-2b5b-46da-aad8-670628c6fbe2/Ethics-in-the-US-Navy-24-March-2014.aspx.
181. *Id.* at 5.
182. *See, e.g.*, Thomas J. Cutler, The Bluejacket's Manual 555 (2009) (observing that "one of our governing principles is civilian control of the military" is a matter that makes the Navy a "more complicated organization than we might wish for").

CHAPTER 4

The Expert Witnesses: A Cross-Examination

Huntington, Professionalism, and Two Forms of Control

Professor Samuel Huntington's relevance to the subject of civil-military relations, and political science more generally, is unquestioned.[1] His seminal work, *The Soldier and the State*,[2] remains the field's common point of departure, even though published in 1957.[3] Given that a nation's security is affected by the quality of its internal military institutions, Huntington argued that national security was shaped by two basic forces that molded these institutions: a "functional imperative" (the threats to a state's security) and a "societal imperative" (the mix of social dynamics, "ideologies, and institutions dominant within the society").[4] These two forces "come[ ] to a head" in the "relation of the officer corps to the state" and therefore provided the focus of his study.[5]

Huntington's view of the military officer's professionalism is critical to understanding his Cold War-era theory, and his ultimate relevance and contribution to the field decades later. For Huntington, a professional was a "peculiar type of functional group with highly specialized characteristics," distinct from a trade, craft, or vocation.[6] Huntington chose to illustrate this with the example of lawyers and doctors, both of whom "pursue a 'higher calling' in service of society."[7] Three characteristics elevated a profession above a vocation: expertise, responsibility, and corporateness. Expertise was in a "significant field of human endeavor" and based on a combination of education and experience, and evaluated by "objective standards of professional competence."[8] Responsibility meant

D. Maurer, *Crisis, Agency, and Law in US Civil-Military Relations*,
DOI 10.1007/978-3-319-53526-5_4

unselfishly "performing a service" that was "essential to the functioning of society."[9] Finally, members of that profession illustrate corporateness by sharing a sense that they were a "group apart from laymen" guided by self-created standards and able to enforce those standards on one another.[10] For Huntington, officership was "strongest and most effective when it closely approaches" this professional "ideal."[11]

Meeting this ideal, he conceded, was not easy for military officers over much of history and was not dominant in the United States until the late-nineteenth century.[12] To be an expert military officer, one had to be proficient in the "management of violence."[13] This necessarily included duties of organizing, equipping, and training a force, planning its actions, and directing it during combat—a suite of abilities that became an "extraordinarily complex intellectual skill requiring comprehensive study and training."[14] This was an additional skill that was heaped upon that timeless baseline ability to withstand, physically and emotionally, the toil and torment that characterizes "soldiering." Barbara Tuchman's rendering of the confusion and discomfort of a fourteenth century Spanish knight is familiar to any modern veteran of American counterinsurgency campaigns, no matter the technological sophistication of weapons or the *raison de la guerre* that have separated the two epochs.

> [B]ad quarters, the shelter of a tent or branches, a bad bed, poor sleep with their armor still on their backs, burdened with iron, the enemy an arrow-shot off... To arms! To arms! With the first drowsiness, an alarm; at dawn, the trumpet... As lookouts, as sentinels, keeping watch by day and by night, fighting without cover, as foragers, as scouts, guard afterguard, duty after duty. 'Here they come! Here! They are so many—No, not as many as that—This way—that—Come this side—Press them there—News! News! They come back hurt, they have prisoners—no, they bring back none. Let us go! Let us go! Give no ground! On!' Such is their calling.[15]

To be a responsible military officer meant using his knowledge and ability only for "socially-approved purposes" and never in a way that would "wreck the fabric of society."[16] To be part of the corporate body, a military officer must segregate, at least to a degree, from society in terms of where he lives and other visual signals, like their uniforms, autonomously applying his expertise in a responsible manner for the benefit of those he guards.[17]

As a natural consequence of these characteristics of the modern professional officer, Huntington concluded that the professional military ethic was an attitude of "conservative realism."[18] This attitude was contrary to the liberalism of the political elites for whom the military worked, and prevailed as the way in which officers approached and defined challenges they faced. For example, conflict was a universal part of human nature according the military mindset; the future was never realistically foreseeable; the disciplined, cohesive organization was greater than individual ability and accomplishment; policy should be premised on the worst-case scenario, erring on the side of caution by emphasizing the immediacy and strength of potential threats.[19] Most importantly, Huntington noted that this ethic depended on being passively apolitical.[20]

"Politics," he wrote, was "beyond the scope of military competence."[21] But as the personalized instrument of policy, Huntington suggested that the military officer shouldered three "responsibilities" or functions: representative, advisory, and executive.[22] First, the officer had the right to present expert views of the military needs and objectives to Congress and the administration. Second, the officer had a duty to analyze and discuss alternative courses of action with civilian leaders, offering a risk assessment in military terms. Third, the officer was duty-bound to implement policy decisions even if they deviate or counter his expert military judgment. [23]

The crux of the civil-military relationship problem, for Huntington, was discovering how to set the conditions necessary to achieve effective military operations externally against an adversarial state or military while diminishing the military as a politically powerful actor internally, bounding its ability to compete for political power domestically with elected civilians. This implied the military, despite a role in representing, advising, and executing, has no comparable "Veto Function." In his view, the only way to achieve that goal given the fundamental military ethic of conservative realism and the inherent differences between civilian policy-making and military action was to maximize the sense of professionalism. To "box in" the military, Huntington advocated a combination of extreme professional autonomy to carry out activities within a defined military sphere of expertise, responsibility, and corporateness while enforcing rigid subordination to civilian control. This state of affairs he labeled as "objective control"[24] and it has outlasted all other theoretical competitors. It remains firmly fixed as the prevailing view in the United States among national security practitioners.[25]

Janowitz, Civil-Military Fusion, and the Military as a Pressure Group

Morris Janowitz, a sociologist, had a different objective in mind. His 1960 work, *The Professional Soldier: A Social and Political Portrait*, studied the military as a social organism to "describe the professional life, organizational setting, and leadership of the American military."[26] Like Huntington, though, Janowitz also analogized military professionals to other specialized professionals like lawyers and doctors.[27] As Huntington suggested by his explanation of professional expertise, responsibility, and corporateness, Janowitz too suggested that professional groups of officers develop self-identity and a "system of internal administration . . . [leading to] the growth of a body of ethics and standards of performance."[28]

Unlike Huntington, however, Janowitz argued for a less rigid and explicit division of labor, observing that some officers are positioned to blur the Huntingtonian ideal of distinctly separate spheres. "[W]hile every military task ultimately impinges on international politics, some senior officers have tasks which involve direct political planning and political negotiation."[29] He explicitly points to "every field commander stationed abroad" and the members of the Joint Chiefs of Staff who, "as principal military advisors, are thoroughly enmeshed in the political estimates as they prepare their strategic plans."[30] Despite this inevitable "fusion" of roles, Janowitz noted the wide-spread military cultural "mechanical acceptance of civilian supremacy" without establishing "principles for limiting the political activities of the military profession as a pressure group on its own behalf."[31]

Three trends seemed, at the time, to encourage the military's behavior as a pressure group, which dimmed unequivocal civilian authority. Janowitz suggested that these were inter-service rivalries,[32] the limited role of Congress in overseeing the day-to-day affairs of the Armed Forces, and the "intensified struggle [by military elites] to gain access to the pinnacle—to the Chief Executive and to the National Security Council."[33] Countering these trends, he observes, are various "mechanisms" that civilian leadership can employ to dampen military assertiveness.[34] Janowitz wrote that they can and will allocate funds between and among the various Services; they can and will allocate missions and responsibilities between and among the Services; and they retain the ultimate constitutional trump card: the responsibility for advising the President and Cabinet on military aspects of international relations.

However, Janowitz did not seem to acknowledge that these control devices may serve less ably as checks and more as triggers for tension. First, they do not expressly prohibit the means by which the military can "exercise considerable initiative."[35] For example, extensive relationship building though military-to-military engagements abroad. Second, these devices amplify strains on the relationship when there are unresolved personality differences and policy disagreements between military elites and political leadership. For example, internal executive branch disagreements, as when a Secretary of Defense is "outmaneuvered" by policy advisors in the National Security Council, preventing the former's views from proper articulation during cabinet-level discussion.[36]

This required accepting the notion of civil supremacy and an agency-like subordination to it.[37] For Janowitz, this implied that military education must change so that its students develop not just a general commitment to the American democratic system but also as a forum for discussing the "standards that should govern the behavior of officers vis-à-vis civilian appointees and Congress."[38] Janowitz himself left these standards unarticulated.

Cohen and Unequal Partnerships

Eliot Cohen departs from Huntington and Janowitz in several ways. First, he is skeptical of the analogy of military officers to professional lawyers and physicians: "[u]nlike law [and] medicine... [the military profession] binds its members to one employer, the state, and has only one fundamental form, the large Service branch."[39] This assertion, however, is debatable. A private lawyer also has arguably only one employer at a time for each particular case. His or her particular client, for which codified rules of professional responsibility exert control on the lawyer's ability to deviate from that client's strategic objectives and prevent representation of conflicting interests simultaneously.[40] Under normal circumstances, a lawyer—like the military officer—is also bound to one principal client. There are contexts in which attorneys serve and represent clients without specific individual identities, such as general counsel for corporations or other organizations. Military lawyers represent the interests of the command or unit to which they are assigned unless specifically detailed as a defense counsel in a military justice capacity or represent the interests of qualified recipients of basic legal assistance services.

Cohen also claims that officers have "hazier" ultimate purposes.[41] Not all roles, responsibilities, and missions assigned to the Soldier are as clear-cut as "win the battle and go home," he suggests.[42] According to Cohen, they also "anticipate [war's] requirements, they study past uses of violence, they practice simulations, but very rarely engage in the *central activity* that defines their profession."[43] This conclusion about "hazier" purposes, too, is debatable on two grounds. First, military professionals' central *purpose* may be to engage in combat on behalf of the nation and at the direction of civilians, but their "central activity" is usually not serving in harm's way. Given the amount of time officers spend in training, initial and continuing education, and various garrison duties other than direct combat, the *central* activity of the profession may just be the opposite of Cohen's description: to prepare for combat, not to execute it.[44] Second, contrasting officers against other professionals in this way is too unsophisticated a distinction. Lawyers and doctors have roles that demand preventative actions or treatment, imply education of the client or patient, and require varying degrees of subject matter expertise across a broad range of knowledge under myriad conditions created by, or affecting, the client or patient. Just as military officers do not simply "fight, win, and go home," all lawyers are not litigators (and litigators do more than just go to trial) and all doctors are not surgeons.

In another relevant way, however, Cohen convincingly departs from the forefathers of American civil-military relations theory. He argues that the classical or "normal" theory, which treats Huntingtonian "objective control" as the ideal, is both unrealistic and ineffective.[45] Instead, Cohen portrays the elites as if they were in a limited partnership.[46] Civilian leaders, generally expected to set policy goals, identify long-term objectives and provide resources, are like senior partners in a firm. They have general liability for profit, obligations, and debts, but are ostensibly superior to the military elites, who are akin to junior partners with limited liability, and little management accountability. In this analogy, there are blurred, not impermeable, lines dividing civilian and military respective spheres of work. Politicians do not simply "fire and forget," selecting a policy objective in wartime and then allowing maximum discretion to the field commanders. They also coax, negotiate, and sustain alliances with foreign powers, decide what "acceptable risk" is for a given campaign or operation, communicate their decisions to the public, and "arbitrate" tactical differences that arise among their operational military advisors.[47]

However, Cohen suggests that this overlap in roles imposes a moderate burden on the military too. Military strategic leaders must understand the political context in which policy decisions are made or debated in order to properly frame options and advise the civilian leadership about risk.[48] For Cohen, a realistic strategic civil-military relationship should be described as an "unequal dialogue:"

> the ultimate domination of a civilian leader is contingent, often fragile, and always haunted by his own lack of experience at high command . . . [f]or a politician to dictate military action is almost always folly. Civil-military relations must thus be a dialogue of unequals and the degree of civilian intervention in military matters a question of prudence, not principle.[49]

Cohen concludes that the most effective leaders knowingly crossed the objective line separating civilian from military responsibility when the circumstances[50] required more than simply "ratifying" a military course of action.[51] By this style of management, some politicians behaved much the way a senior law firm partner might intrude into the handling of a particular litigation or client when the firm's larger goals for profit or keeping a long-term client are threatened by the action or inaction of a junior partner or associate.[52]

According to Cohen's "unequal dialogue" framework, the "challenge of a supreme [civilian] leader lies not in choosing at which level of guidance or abstraction to function, but rather in . . . understanding the forest by examining certain copses and even individual trees with great care."[53] But even this framework, where the subordination of military to civilian is presumed to be an inviolable tenet, does little to define conditions in which displays of distrust or insubordination are symptomatic of an unhealthy and ill-functioning relationship.

Further complicating efforts to define the quality of a particular strategic civil-military dialogue is what could be called the public relations "sunscreen." As explained by Michael Desch, scholarly interest in these crises remains high while public interest remains unaffected for two reasons. First, civilian leaders have "little interest in publicizing their ongoing problems with the American military because these problems make the civilian leader look weak."[54] Second, the military is reluctant to signal strife with politicians because the "notion of subordination to civilian authority is so deeply embedded in its professional culture that it is difficult for most military officers to admit publically" their concerns or grievances.[55] As a result, two of the parties to the relationship liberally screen the public from information that would place them under the unwanted glare of attention, preventing the parties in the relationship from being burned by adverse publicity.

Though tempting to simply say the winner of disputes between strategic civilian and military leaders is the party whose preference was eventually adopted or executed, Desch also attributes the diagnostic challenge to the *real politk* nature of the relationship itself.[56] The positions on an issue or policy debate may change frequently, or be strategic in the sense that they might not reflect true personal preferences but rather organizational preferences, or vice versa. Moreover, compromises and negotiated resolutions to various internal disagreements are common and do not necessarily signal the victory of one side over another, or whether it was the military elite's direct personal influence that changed policy.[57] Therefore, "control" as it exists between the parties is not easily defined, and only looking at disputes will distort how conflict-ridden the relationship actually is.[58]

Feaver, Agency, and Rational Actors

Peter Feaver's explicit adoption of a "principal-agent" framework comes closest to hinting that there might be a way to diagnose the health of a strategic-level civil-military relationship in an objective way and based on context clues. Focusing on episodes of tension and conflict, Feaver argues that "friction . . . reflects the kind of conflict one would expect from a certain combination of civilian choices and military responses. Civil-military relations are best understood as a game of strategic interaction."[59] While that perspective is fundamentally reasonable, he unfortunately analyzes the behavior of two parties in stark, rational actor, terms. He proposes a "game-theoretic approach" that, he claims, reveals the "micro-foundational logic" and causation, even if it might lose some color of realism as a result of its methodology.[60]

In crafting his "alternative theory," intended to update certain aspects of Huntington's theory,[61] Feaver argues that civilian elites' behavior is generally focused on monitoring the military to varying degrees depending on how high an expectation the civilians have that the military will obey direction and policy faithfully.[62] Because the civilians, not the military, have a constitutionally granted superior position, and serve as representatives of the public, they can claim "the right to be wrong,"[63] something akin to parental scrutiny of a child's behavior. Feaver grants civilian officials the "privileged position" with "legitimate authority over the military" because, metaphorically, "civilians invent the military, contracting with it to protect society from enemies" in a way analogous to an employer contracting with a potential employee, delegating to that employee the power to execute business decisions on the employer's behalf.[64] Feaver does acknowledge the contextual differences that surface when trying to apply a formal principal–agent model (noting the "information asymmetries" that favor the military agent due to superior technical knowledge and proximity to the battlefield, as well the scale of harm if the civil-military relationship becomes "pathological:" a potential *coup* or battlefield defeat).[65] He compares this principal–agent relationship to that of a stockholder (principal) and board of directors (agent), employer (principal) and employee (agent), and voter (principal) and politician (agent).[66]

Using terms from microeconomic principal–agent theory, Feaver categorizes military officer corps behavior as a choice between "working" and "shirking," a decision dependent on the military's expectation of being detected shirking and whether it will be punished by civilian leadership for doing so.[67] Under this view of civil-military relations, Feaver argues that a "working" military is one that performs according to how the principal (civilian leadership) would ideally desire, assuming that principal had complete knowledge of what the agent could do and was, in fact, doing.[68] On the other hand, "shirking," under this view, did not imply laziness or non-industriousness. Rather, he defined it as deliberate conduct other than as directed or authorized by the principal when the military agent disagrees with how, when, where, or why to best provide for national security in a specific instance.[69] For example, a combatant commander would be "shirking" if he knowingly provided the President or Secretary of Defense with an inflated estimate of what a military operation would cost (in dollars or lives) in order to shape the forthcoming policy choice along lines preferred by the military.[70] Perhaps more egregiously, shirking would include unauthorized public protests or appeals to other political actors, or "bureaucratic foot-dragging" in order to delay implementation of a policy deemed unfavorable by the military.[71]

Though Feaver acknowledges that this model does not predict whether, or explain why, "good" or "bad" national security outcomes will occur,[72] he does propose that the model describes the quality of this "strategic interaction" on a spectrum in terms of consequences or effects. For example, "unsavory options" like failing to carry out a policy directive, or inflating budget requirements occur would tilt toward the more benign side of the spectrum. At the extreme end of the shirking spectrum, Feaver argues that the ultimate form of shirking would manifest as either a battlefield defeat or a coup.[73]

The rational civilian principal, though, has a spectrum of scalable options through which to monitor and punish the military agent's behavior to offset the risk of, or damage caused by, by shirking. Such options range from complete dominion over budgets and doctrine, unilaterally changing wages and benefits, and modifying accessions policy, to case-by-case restrictions on how much power it delegates to the military,[74] to actual "punishment."[75] For example, holding up or denying a promotion, cutting the defense budget, administrative discharge, or criminal sanction for violating the Uniform Code of Military Justice. Such restrictions might come in the form of formal restraints on military autonomy—imparting policy preferences into rules of engagement and other standing orders, or even shifting responsibility for a particular mission to other agencies.[76] Or, restraints may be more subtle. Civilians may cause or exploit inter-service rivalries, providing civilians the opportunity to arbitrate in what Feaver calls an "institutional check." Alternatively, he suggests that imposing regular and intrusive reporting requirements and audits, or bloating the size of the civilian secretariats in the Department of Defense relative to the uniformed staffs, have the same restraining effect.[77]

Feaver's principal–agent framework, nevertheless, remains problematic for the generation of objective criteria in five ways. First, his model assumes rational actors and aggregates the conduct and decisions of many individuals on both sides of the civil-military divide. Consequently, it ignores irrational behavior, subsumes personal motives and competence, and only looks to choices of working, shirking, monitoring, and punishing.[78] It does not take into account the less-than-fully educated biases and heuristics or the personal relationships often formed by participants in the professional civil-military relationship, generating actions less informed by self-interest and more spurred by a "sense of fairness and concern about reputation…[that would be critical for establishing and maintaining] 'social networks' and 'group cohesion'."[79] His model does not seem to account for choices of actors, like geographic combatant commanders, who straddle the civil-military divide and are neither a pure principal nor a pure agent.[80] Nor does his model seem to accept that supposedly rational decisions by the civilian principal to monitor or punish the military agent may backfire, inciting the military to shirk in ways the monitoring and punishment was meant to deter, as Janowitz noted as early as 1960.[81] Moreover, his model offers no apparent way to evaluate the underlying contextual reasons, whether rational or not, behind the choices and voices expressed in what Cohen called the "unequal dialogue" between the civilian and military elites.

Finally, though asserting that his theory adopts and extends Huntington in a way that avoids Huntington's outdated assumptions, Feaver does not address the more nuanced and realistic contexts where there is dispute or tension among senior military advisors, as between a combatant commander and a Service Chief of Staff, about long-term objectives and the number of troops needed to meet those objectives[82]; or in which agents and principals work, shirk, monitor, and punish with respect to the three broad functions of advising, representing, and executing that these agents perform.[83] James Dubik, a recent critic of Feaver's application of Agency Theory, argues that it is "radically incomplete." Because of an overdrawn emphasis on just two key factors—who holds power and how control is effected—Dubik holds that the theory ignores who, how, and why plans and strategies are generated, studied, negotiated, fought over, replaced, managed, and publicized.[84] For this reason, Dubik holds in contempt Feaver's conclusion that the Vietnam War was a positive illustration of civilian control over the military.[85] While his theory is potentially predictive of civilian control over the subordinate military, Feaver comes close to, but not quite, being able to provide all three parties a way to gauge the health of that strategic relationship in context against objective criteria.

Dubik, himself a decorated combat general, makes a compelling case for moving beyond an overly contrived and analytical reduction of these complex relationships to a simple issue of "power, control, obedience, compliance, and the right to be wrong."[86] His study and laudable effort to modernize Just War Theory, by pulling in the strategic decision-making of senior civilian and military leaders into the discussion of *jus in bello*, is long overdue. He adds some much-needed realism to this theory by reminding us that war (preparing for it, planning it, waging it across myriad levels of bureaucracy throughout government) is not a simple handoff from a political leader to the generals and admirals.[87] His critique of Feaver's principal–agent framework is a sound one, for it identifies that "the *right* in the *right to be wrong* cannot be a universal right, a right that any civilian, on any topic, and under any conditions can claim against any member of the military. Rather, it is limited to some civilians, on some topics, and at some times . . . and says nothing about when the right to be wrong can be used responsibly."[88]

Unfortunately, just as Feaver's aim was too narrowly focused, Dubik's full-throated attack on Agency Theory is *also* ignoring a larger picture. Dubik's analysis seems unalterably concerned with a very restrictive version of the theory or meaning of "agency"—the microeconomic version relied upon by Feaver, and one which Dubik oversimplifies as an "employer-employee relationship."[89] For Dubik, Agency is explained as "how the senior political leader principals get their military subordinate agents to do what they want done, how they want it done."[90] With that tight, limited, definition of Agency, it is no wonder he finds fault with reducing these relationships to a study of working and shirking; it is also no wonder that the he does not see a way to adduce standards or norms for holding those same leaders accountable, or for diagnosing the health of those relationships in context. As we will come to see later, Agency can mean far more when explained in terms we might find far more familiar—that of the patient and doctor, or attorney and client. *Those* principal–agent relationships are defined not terms of obedience, compliance, and control, but on the same grounds Dubik seems to be searching for: shades of overlapping (but not entirely) authority, a mutually agreeable and defined scope of responsibility, and duties of candor and loyalty. Indeed, where Dubik believes Agency theory (as described by Feaver) is only about doing what the leadership wants, in the manner in which the leadership wants it done, a more expansive understanding of Agency demonstrates that "what" is to be done is usually a conversation, not a dictate, and "how" that is to be done is nearly always a decision for the subject matter expert *agent* to make, not the principal. Without subscribing to it or acknowledging he's doing it, he approaches an argument that makes this point:

> both civilian and military leaders have a duty to provide their best advice, make their best case, challenge assumptions and predictions, and present evidence and counterevidence as the debate ebbs and flows... [and] the right to be wrong requires some form of mutuality between senior political and military leaders greater than is found in direct, monitory, and obey-or-be-punished framework. These leaders have correlative duties: military leaders pledge loyal subordination, and civilian leaders exercise their responsibility wisely.[91]

Dubik rightly notices that Feaver's theory ignores the consequences or effects of strategic decision-making—it appears to be a morals-free zone that lacks any relation to the real-world emotional and physical drama that leads to and defines war-making.[92] He finds great value in Cohen's conceit of the "unequal dialogue"—one that is anything but morals-free.

> [T]he reality is that good war-waging decisions are most likely to emerge from a set of political and military leaders bluntly and continuously arguing with one another in an attempt to identify strategy, policy, campaign, and organizational solutions . . . [i]n the principal-agent framework, obedience is what matters most, not the content of orders and directives; in Cohen's account, content matters significantly.[93]

By ignoring other meaningful approaches to Agency, Dubik misses an opportunity to extend his argument while sustaining the basic components of the principal–agent theory that *do* define the essential structure of these strategic relationships. He suggests that Cohen's unequal dialogue "demands that senior political and military leaders hold each other accountable for outcomes, for decisions and actions they take together that affect the life of the political community."[94] Yet, he still leaves much on the table. Dubik proposes that the unequal dialogue must morph into action or execution of the plans and decisions made, but gives us no terms for grading the way it morphed.[95]

Nevertheless, he offers hints that again suggest a much deeper view of Agency: "respect and candor . . . make the dialogue work."[96] To the extent, Dubik highlights the importance of shared responsibilities and collaboration; he is on track to eventually arrive at more a realistic and meaningful description of the kind of Agency that defines these relationships in practice.[97] To the extent, he fails to define *how* they are to hold each other "accountable"—by what standards or norms—Dubik leaves the discussion unfinished.

Mackubin Thomas Owens, in contrast, offers three "criteria for judging the health of civil-military relations:" the "relative harmony between civilians and the military," the "effectiveness of the armed forces in executing missions," and "constitutional balance" between the executive and legislative branches. These criteria are a step forward. They are not directly tied to a crisis or overt dispute between civilian and military elites, thus avoiding the ambiguous signals such events often portray. They also incorporate Owens's observation that this relationship is a bargain among three parties—the people of the state, the government, and the military. Though one step forward, Owens' criteria are also a few steps back. These criteria, for instance, are too ambiguous to be of any additional practical help in objectively diagnosing the health of a strategic civil-military relationship. The "harmony" of the relationship is not defined, qualitatively or quantitatively, and Owens does not say against what standard that harmony is "relative"—historically similar episodes? Some known objective benchmark of "good" or "harmonious" relations? Furthermore, the "effectiveness" of a military completing its mission is notoriously complex and contentious, with little agreement about how is it to be measured. This leaves Owens' three-part test for civil-military relationships important because it recognizes a need to judge their health, but largely impotent because the judging criteria are too vague, leaving the participants and the public not much wiser or capable of diagnosing ill-health.

These academic approaches to the behavior within these strategic civil-military relationships are helpful in a theoretical sense, for their efforts bring certain issues into sharp relief[98] and suggest two important and enduring attributes of this subject. First, the main scholarly voices from Huntington and Janowitz during the Cold War, to Cohen, Feaver, and Owens in a more recent era, recognize two autonomous classes with distinct core competencies, comparative advantages, and socially expected functions. Where these scholars appear to diverge is the extent to which these autonomous classes do, in practice, merge or blend, under what conditions they merge, and whether those mergers have short- or long-term benefits and costs. The second enduring attribute evidenced by the scholarship is that many extant theories hint at the possibility of, but do not overtly establish, a mechanism by which to assess the health of these relationships in their circumstantial contexts, against an objective standard.[99]

*****

Civil-military relations scholarship, from Huntington to Owens, does not provide a consistent diagnostic framework. Not only does the literature not fully answer these questions but also there is no clear answer to be found in the law or other forms of written authority either. The Constitution, as discussed earlier, provides a shell or structure for the federal government, and assigns roles related to national security that are divided between executive and legislative authorities in power-sharing scheme designed to be turbulent, uncomfortable, and inefficient. Statutes, like the National Security Act and the Goldwater-Nichols Act, provide no clarity either as they tend to reorganize executive branch agencies and departments for the greater purpose of finding efficiencies, streamlining processes and systems in order to achieve greater transparency in decision-making, or to reduce costly redundancies that complicate joint operations and planning.

Case law that does address civil-military strife focuses only on criminal insubordination and disrespect, ignores episodes of strategic civil-military tension, and therefore offers no precedent as a guide to the participants of those relationships. Administrative regulations are oriented on eliminating conduct that appears like unjust enrichment and personal gain at government expense among *all* service members regardless of rank or position. Finally, military doctrine aims "down and in" not "up and out," proposing to express moral codes of generic virtues to guide service members' ethical decision-making.

As well-established and accepted rules, standards, and codified norms of behavior, all of these sources of authority offer potential venues for articulating an objective means for diagnosing unhealthy strategic civil-military relationships. Unfortunately, all remain missed opportunities and the academic literature does not overtly suggest a diagnostic tool. In the next chapter, I will present evidence from the Armed Services and politicians themselves that strongly suggest the American military establishment already views itself in agency terms. Therefore, the "agency theory" of civil-military relationships might be approached like that of the legal agency model, rather than the current microeconomic agency model, or as an unequal dialogue, or as fraternal twins with distinct professional autonomy. From that perspective, I will suggest that codified and transparent norms of conduct akin to rules of professional conduct or professional responsibility for attorneys can aid principal–agent participants and the public in diagnosing ailments in the health of a strategic civil-military relationship. Objective criteria, like duties of candor, competence, communication, scope of responsibility, and conflict of interest provisions could be included within an amended Goldwater-Nichols Act, reflecting the professional nature of strategic military agents and deflecting their opportunity to engage in negative and controversial "pressure group" activities for their own benefit.

Notes

1. Desch, Changing Security Environment, at xi.
2. Huntington, The Soldier and the State.
3. Don M. Snider, *Strategic Insights: Should General Dempsey Resign? Army Professionals and the Moral Space for Military Dissent*, Strategic Insights

(Strategic Studies Institute) (October 21, 2014), http://www.strategicstudiesinstitute.army.mil/index.cfm/articles/Should-General-Dempsey-Resign/2014/10/21; *see also* FEAVER, ARMED SERVANTS, at 7; ***and see*** EMILE SIMPSON, WAR FROM THE GROUND UP: TWENTY-FIRST-CENTURY COMBAT AS POLITICS 112–13 (2013).

4. HUNTINGTON, THE SOLDIER AND THE STATE, at 2.
5. *Id.* at 3 (for instance, the strata of society from which officers are drawn and what philosophy seems to drive their perspective on the use of force).
6. *Id.* at 7.
7. *Id.* at 7–8.
8. *Id.* at 8.
9. *Id.* at 9.
10. *Id.* at 10.
11. *Id.* at 11.
12. *Id.* at 22–58 (describing the evolution of the officer from mercenary to aristocrat to professional, across the modern history of France, Prussia, and Great Britain).
13. *Id.* at 11 (quoting Harold Lasswell).
14. *Id.* at 13.
15. BARBARA W. TUCHMAN, A DISTANT MIRROR: THE CALAMITOUS 14TH CENTURY, 63 (1978) (quoting Díaz de Goméz, contemporary and biographer of Don Pero Niño).
16. *Id.* at 13–14.
17. *Id.* at 16–17.
18. *Id.* at 61. *But see* SIMPSON, WAR FROM THE GROUND UP, at 113 (arguing that Huntington's approach was both "unrealistic" and "seriously out of date" and wrongfully "elevates" the military ethic to that of a "cult").
19. HUNTINGTON, THE SOLDIER AND THE STATE, at 63–66.
20. *Id.* at 68–69.
21. *Id.* at 71.
22. *Id.* at 72.
23. *Id.*
24. *Id.* at 83–85. For some observers, the planning and operations of the air and ground offensive campaigns in the 1990–91 Gulf War examplified Huntington's ideal of "objective control." ROSE, HOW WARS END, at 220, 267; ***and see*** COHEN, SUPREME COMMAND, at 7–8 (observing the popular perception that the Gulf War was a "model of beign tactical neglect by an enlightened civilian leadership").
25. COHEN, SUPREME COMMAND, at 229.
26. JANOWITZ, THE PROFESSIONAL SOLDIER, at liv.
27. *Id.* at 5, 135, 228–31.
28. *Id.* at 6.

29. *Id.* at 70.
30. *Id.*
31. *Id.* at 138–39.
32. For example, competition over missions, roles, and budget shares between the Department of the Army and the Department of the Navy.
33. Janowitz, The Professional Soldier, at 349–50.
34. *Id.* at 363–65.
35. *Id.* at 367.
36. *See, e.g.*, Kiron Skinner, *A Secretary of Defense With a Doctrine Could Help Obama*, N.Y. Times, November 30, 2014, *and* John Nagl, *The President Needs a Secretary of War*, N.Y. Times, November 30, 2014 (discussing, *inter alia*, the relationship between President Obama and his first three Secretaries of Defense: Robert Gates, Leon Panetta, and Chuck Hagel), http://www.nytimes.com/roomfordebate/2014/11/30/what-kind-of-pentagon-chief-does-obama-need/the-president-needs-a-secretary-of-war.
37. Janowitz, The Professional Soldier, at 426.
38. *Id.* at 429.
39. Eliot A. Cohen, *The Unequal Dialogue*, at 448.
40. *See, e.g.*, American Bar Association Model Rule of Professional Conduct, Rule 1.6 and Rule 1.7 (prohibiting, *inter alia*, an attorney from representing conflicting interests of two separate clients in the same litigation or proceeding), http://www.americanbar.org/groups/professional_responsi bility/html.
41. Cohen, *The Unequal Dialogue*, at 448.
42. *Id.* at 452.
43. *Id.* at 452 (emphasis added).
44. U.S. Dep't of Army, Pam. 600–3, Commissioned Officer Professional Development And Career Management Chapter 4 (1 Feb. 2010) (describing the Army officer's professional military education over the course of a career, from branch basic courses to the Senior Service Colleges).
45. Cohen, Supreme Command, at 7–8; Cohen, *Unequal Dialogue*, at 447.
46. This conceit is the author's, not Cohen's.
47. Cohen, Supreme Command, at 10.
48. *Id.* at 7–8 (quoting Clausewitz, and noting that "there is no field of military action that might not be touched by political considerations").
49. *Id.* at 12.
50. For example, the nature and scope of the conflict, personalities of subordinates, and relationships with other civilian elites.
51. *Id.* at 208–12.
52. His view reflects themes in Clausewitz's admonition.
53. Cohen, Supreme Command, at 212.
54. Desch, Changing Security Environment, at 2.

55. *Id.*
56. Desch, Changing Security Environment, at 5 (identifying this as an obstacle to assessing civil-military relations based on "who prevails when [their] preferences diverge").
57. Betts, Cold War Crises, at 250, n. 3. *See also* Moten, Presidents & Their Generals, at 349 (describing the 2011 Quadrennial Defense Review, in which the Army was able to avoid cutting four combat divisions, despite Secretary of Defense Rumsfeld's preference for the cut; the "save" only served to exacerbate Rumsfeld's frustration with the individual Services and provoked his vocal ire).
58. Cohen, Supreme Command, at 2–5.
59. Peter D. Feaver, *Crisis as Shirking: An Agency Theory Explanation of the Souring of American Civil-Military Relations*, 24 Armed Forces & Soc'y 407, 407 (Spring 1998).
60. *Id. and see* Feaver, Armed Servants, at 13.
61. Feaver, Armed Servants,, at 3, 9.
62. *Id.* at 2–3.
63. *Id.* at 9.
64. *Id.* at 54–55, 57.
65. *Id.* at 69–72.
66. *Id.* at 12–13.
67. *Id.* at 3.
68. *Id.* at 61.
69. *Id.* at 59–60.
70. *Id.* at 68. If the senior military officer made repeated comparisons of current facts to earlier, negative, images from recent history of ill-fated operations or serious and unexpected losses, that officer is attempting to influence the lawmakers to view the current situation less than objectively, inviting them to rely subconsciously on what is familiar, even if irrational to do so. *See* Richard H. Thaler & Cass R. Sunstein, Nudge: Improving Decisions About Health, Wealth, And Happiness 25 (2009).
71. Feaver, Armed Servants, at 68.
72. *Id.* at 66.
73. *Id.* at 58–59.
74. *Id.* at 75–77.
75. *Id.* at 91–94, and Table 3.2.
76. *Id.* at 75–77.
77. *Id.* at 81–84.
78. What is "rational" is often formally defined as that decision which exhibits internal coherence, maximizing utility, and ignoring "irrelevant" alternatives. But this excludes decisions logically made based on personal preferences and the actor's long-term objectives—aims that might trigger the

actor to act "irrationally" in the short-term, or logical decisions based on limited information about what choices can be made by the actor. Kahneman suggests that "substantive" criteria should expand the meaning of "rational actor" to include the actor's evolving expectations as they experience positive and negative consequences of their actions, not just their expectations before making a decision. Daniel Kahneman, *New Challenges to the Rationality Assumption*, J. INSTITUTIONAL & THEORETICAL ECONOMICS 150/1 (1994), at 18, 19–21 (distinguishing between *experienced utility* and *decision utility*).

79. *See* FREEDMAN, STRATEGY: A HISTORY, at 593–95 (reviewing scholarship from behavioral economics on "bounded rationality" that criticized the false realism of "rational actor" theories in the social sciences); *see generally* Amos Tversky & Daniel Kahneman, *Judgment Under Uncertainty: Heuristics and Biases*, SCIENCE, Sept. 1974, at 1124 (explaining various cognitive factors influencing how people generally come to believe certain forecasts, probabilities, and other uncertainties) ("people rely on a limited number of heuristic principles which reduce the complex tasks of assessing probabilities and predicting values to simpler judgmental operations . . . these heuristics are quite useful, but . . . they lead to severe and systematic errors").
80. *For example*, the Under Secretary of Defense for Policy or the members of the Joint Chiefs of Staff. *See* JANOWITZ, THE PROFESSIONAL SOLDIER, at 70; COHEN, SUPREME COMMAND, at 10. Even the Secretary of Defense could be considered in a hybrid position, appointed and serving at the pleasure of the president, but also in the operational chain-of-command and directly responsible for overseeing the entire defense establishment as the "agent" of the president. *See, e.g.*, Ashton Carter's comments upon his nomination as Secretary of Defense, *quoted in* Craig Whitlock, *Ashton Carter, passed over before, gets picked by Obama to be defense secretary*, WASH. POST, Dec. 5, 2014, http://www.washingtonpost.com/world/national-security/ash-carter-passed-over-before-gets-picked-by-obama-to-lead-pentagon/2014/12/05/33a2429a-7c95-11e4-9a27-6fdbc612bff8_story.html ("If confirmed in this job, I pledge to you my most candid strategic advice . . . and I pledge also that you will receive equally candid military advice.").
81. JANOWITZ, THE PROFESSIONAL SOLDIER, at 349–50, 367.
82. WOODWARD, OBAMA'S WARS, at 241–43, 257–60 (revealing apparent tension between then-commander of Central Command, General Petraeus and the Chairman of the Joint Chiefs of Staff, Admiral Mullen, during a strategy session with President Obama, describing various proposals for a troop "surge" in Afghanistan; describing President Obama's meeting with the Service Chiefs—without the presence of the USCENTCOM Commander or his subordinate theater commander, General Stanley McChrystal—to elicit their candid opinions about strategy in Afghanistan).

83. Huntington, The Soldier and the State, at 72.
84. Dubik, Just War Reconsidered, at 64–65.
85. *Id.*, at 66.
86. *Id.*, at 66–67.
87. *Id.*, at 24, 36.
88. *Id.*, at 81–82 (emphasis in the original).
89. *Id.*, at 62.
90. Dubik condenses the principal-agent relationship to this oversimplified description many times. *Id.*, at 71, 79, 111, 123, 144.
91. *Id.*, at 85–87.
92. *Id.*, at 64–67.
93. *Id.*, at 91.
94. *Id.*, at 92.
95. Instead, he describes the mechanics of what he calls the "decision-execution regime": multiple scales of dialogue among various key civilian and military personnel engaged in executing, monitoring, and adapting in a continuous cycle of activity. *Id.*, at 124.
96. *Id.*, at 111–12.
97. *Id.*, at 144 ("Waging war . . . requires senior political and military leaders to work together in a cooperative leadership space, which includes, but is separate from, each participant's individual, role-defined scope of authority").
98. Michael Walzer, Just And Unjust Wars: A Moral Argument with Historical Illustrations xi (1992).
99. Owens, Renegotiating the Bargain,, at 15. *See, e.g*, Major Shon McCormick, *A Primer on Developing Measures of Effectiveness*, Mil. Rev. (July-August 2010), at 60–66 (discussing challenges of "measuring problematic variables" in military contexts, like stability operations). Moreover, what is "victory" and who decides when it has arrived? *See* J. Boone Bartholomees, *Theory of Victory*, Parameters, Summer 2008, at 25–36; *and see* Eric Schmitt, *Threats and Responses: Military Spending; Pentagon Contradicts General On Iraq Occupation Force's Size*, N.Y. Times, Feb. 28, 2003, http://www.nytimes.com/2003/02/28/us/threats-responses-military-spending-pentagon-contradicts-general-iraq-occupation.html. Is "victory" even possible in modern armed conflict? Former Secretary of Defense Robert M. Gates asks this very question. Gates, Duty Memoirs, at 567.

CHAPTER 5

The Expert Witnesses: The Fingerprints of Agency

The military's reluctance to encode in its doctrine a set of criteria or norms that would both guide the participants in strategic civil-military relationships and offer all three populations (military, civilian leadership, and the public) a means for objectively assessing the health of those relationships is understandable. With nothing in the Constitution, statutes, regulations, or case law to guide it, doctrine has no commonly accepted or consistent policy from which to derive an applicable standard. Nevertheless, there is circumstantial evidence from the civilian and uniformed strategic leaders of the military that strongly suggests a wide-spread, tacit, acceptance of fiduciary duties and an "agency" role, much the way that the Supreme Court has interpreted "systematic, unbroken" conduct by the President, and to which Congress acquiesces, forms a precedential "gloss" on the expressed constitutional and statutory authority of the Chief Executive.

Two civilian national security leaders provide starting points. In his memoirs, Robert Gates distilled lessons from his four years serving as Secretary of Defense for two Presidents. "Widely considered the best defense secretary of the post-World War II era,"[1] he described as his unique position as a broker between the President and the Pentagon, designing a process by which candid military opinions would be offered and heard.[2] To Gates, the President is "ultimately accountable for success or failure" of military operations and decisions as the Commander-in-Chief.[3] That view reflects basic agency law: a "principal" is legally bound by actions taken by his agent, provided those actions

D. Maurer, *Crisis, Agency, and Law in US Civil-Military Relations*,
DOI 10.1007/978-3-319-53526-5_5

were in furtherance of the agent's responsibilities, within the scope of his authority to act on behalf of the principal, or were directed by the principal.

TSAVESecretary Gates' further prescriptions for the conduct between a President and senior military officers reinforce the image of the "principal-agent" dynamic. For example, the President must give his senior military advisors a reception for their opinions, even if contrary to his preference; senior officers must provide their "best and most candid advice" to the President; the senior officer must "obey loyally, especially when they are overruled;" senior officers should not make, even if asked, public statements to third parties like the media or directly to a pubic audience that actually, or appear to a reasonable observer to, impose limits on the President's freedom of choice, or freedom of action; finally, senior officers should never "speak out" on "politically sensitive issues" or "matters beyond their area of responsibility" or "expertise."[4] These expressions of candor, responsibility, and lanes of authority between a recognized superior and a subordinate with technical or specialized knowledge, are fundamentally fiduciary concepts reflecting the dynamic between a principal and agent.

Interviewed by Bob Woodward of *The Washington Post*, President Obama implicitly concurred with Gates' observations as he reflected on his relationship with his senior officers:

> I also had a lot of confidence . . . that the way our system of government works [is that] civilians have to make policy decisions. And then the military carries them out. You know, I don't see this as a civilian versus military situation the way I think a lot of people coming out of Vietnam do . . . a lot of the political frames through which these debates are being viewed don't really connect with me generationally. I'm neither intimidated by our military, nor am I thinking that they are somehow trying to undermine my role as commander in chief.[5]

When publically commenting on General McChrystal's resignation in 2010, President Obama noted themes of complete military subordination to civilian policy and the implied principal-agent virtue of "trust," as well as implying that an unwritten code of conduct established the objective basis for his decision.[6]

This perspective is shared widely across the senior military leadership, assuming the words of various combatant commanders and Chairmen of the

Joint Chiefs of Staff are representative of the larger population of senior uniformed leaders. After President Truman relieved General Douglas MacArthur from command in Korea in 1951, MacArthur testified before a joint committee of Congress during which he described a general duty to obey a lawful order, regardless of its merit or "wisdom."[7] The next general to be relieved by a President from combat command for an apparent breach of civilian control, General McChrystal, also noted themes of subordination to the civilian decision-maker, as well as the confidentiality of the communications between these "unequal" partners:

> I wanted to stay ... but I wanted to do what was best for the mission ... I felt whatever that the president felt was best for the mission was what I needed to do, so I was happy to go with whatever decision that he made.[8]

He refused to disclose, even three years after his forced resignation, the conversation in the White House that led to the ultimate decision and public announcement: "what is said between the president and I in the Oval Office really needs to be between us."[9]

Several recent Chairmen of the Joint Chiefs of Staff have echoed themes of candor and unequivocal responsibility to act within the confines (or "scope") of legitimate military authority and expertise. General Martin Dempsey, Chairman since 2011, said "[a]ll of my predecessors ... when they came to educate me about my job, the single consistent, persistent theme was candor ... relationships are based on candor."[10] In several white papers he produced earlier, when Commander of the Army's Training and Doctrine Command, he believed the same but implicitly acknowledged the inherent tension between candor and respect for the scope of one's authority: "In all aspects of its existence and operations the American Profession of Arms advises with disciplined candor and is willingly subordinate to, and a servant of, civilian authorities."[11] He noted:

> [c]ivilian leaders, duly elected by the people, Congress and the Executive branch, have ultimate authority over the Army ... at the same time, owing to their moral obligation to speak truth and bear true witness to all their fellow citizens, Army professionals and particularly its leaders must always exercise disciplined candor and avoid political alignments when advising the leaders that they serve under, both political and military.[12]

General Dempsey acknowledged that in the strategic civil-military relationship, the "agent's" subject-matter expertise can conflict with the desires of the superior "principal," but must still be articulated:

> [m]ilitary professionals hold unique expertise and their input is vital to formulating and executing effective policy. This requires that the military's unique perspective and advice be heard in the formulation of laws and policies that create, support, and employ our armed forces, or its effectiveness can be reduced to the detriment of the Republic.[13]

General Dempsey's predecessor as Chairman, Admiral Michael Mullen, was similarly predisposed. "The more you personally disagree with a policy, the harder you have to absolutely advocate for it once the decision is made."[14] Pre-decision, however, Mullen was also concerned with military actions that reduced, or at least appeared to reduce, the number of available options or "decision-space"[15] open to the civilian principal, thereby limiting his or her ability to make fully informed policy within the civilian's legitimate prerogative.

Gates, Obama, MacArthur, McChrystal, Dempsey, and Mullen all imply that the strategic civil-military relationship is one that closely resembles jurisprudential concepts of agency, whether it is between a Secretary of Defense and the Chairman of the Joint Chiefs of Staff, or between a President and a theater combatant commander. The expert's subordination to the non-expert; the desirability for confidentiality; loyalty to both the policy and policy-maker once the decision has been cast, even if the expert's advice was not heeded or heard; and the military leader's duty to refrain from speaking beyond his or her capacity, authority, or responsibility are recurring themes. With this evidence in hand, jurisprudential agency is a proper basis upon which to look for objective criteria that may help all the parties diagnose whether a particular episode signals conflict, whether that conflict is symptomatic of an unhealthy relationship, or if it, instead, exemplifies solid and sound democratic politics.

Notes

1. Greg Jaffe, *Book Review: 'Duty: Memoirs of a Secretary at War,'* The Washington Post, Jan. 7, 2014, http://www.washingtonpost.com/opinions/book-review-duty-memoirs-of-a-secretary-at-war-by-robert-m-gates/2014/01/07/0d8acad0-634d-11e3-a373-0f9f2d1c2b61_story.html?hpid=z1.

2. GATES, DUTY MEMOIRS, at 70–71, 82–83 (describing how the Secretary of Defense straddles two teams: as a member of the hand-picked cabinet, "serving only at the pleasure of the President," and on the "broader national security team").
3. *Id.* at 574–75.
4. *Id.*
5. WOODWARD, OBAMA'S WARS, at 377.
6. Statement by the President in the Rose Garden, 23 June 2010, http://www.whitehouse.gov/the-press-office/statement-president-rose-garden.
7. *MacArthur Senate Statement*, at 27–28.
8. Eun Kyung Kim, *McChrystal on resignation: 'I wanted to stay in the job,'* TODAY.COM, http://www.today.com/news/mcchrystal-resignation-i-wanted-stay-job-1B7854301.
9. *Id.*
10. Jim Garamone, *Dempsey Speaks on Experiences in Civil-Military Relations*, DoD NEWS, DEFENSE MEDIA ACTIVITY, 20 Nov 2014, http://www.defense.gov/news/newsarticle.aspx?id=123693.
11. CENTER FOR THE ARMY PROFESSION AND ETHIC, ARMY: PROFESSION OF ARMS 15 (7 Oct 2010), http://www.cape.army.mil.
12. *Id.*
13. U.S. ARMY TRAINING AND DOCTRINE COMMAND, *The Profession of Arms: An Army White Paper*, at 26 (8 Dec 2010), *available at* http://www.benning.army.mil/armor/content/PDF/Profession%20of%20Arms%20White%20Paper%208%20Dec%2010.pdf.
14. Julian Barnes & Adam Entous, *Interview Excerpts: Adm. Mike Mullen*, WALL STREET J. (September 28, 2011), http://www.wsj.com/articles/SB10001424052970204831304576597291196115556.
15. *Id.*

CHAPTER 6

The Rebuttal Witnesses: From Agency to Norms to Diagnosis

In the aftermath of the failed Bay of Pigs invasion by Cuban exiles trained by the Central Intelligence Agency, President Kennedy felt compelled to reassert his expectations of the senior-ranking uniformed officers:

> I expect the Joint Chiefs of Staff to present the military viewpoint in governmental councils in such a way as to assure that the military factors are clearly understood before decisions are reached… *While I look to the Chiefs to represent the military factor without reserve or hesitation, I regard them to be more than military men and expect their help in fitting military requirements into the over-all context of any situation*, recognizing that the most difficult problem in Government is to combine all assets in a unified, effective pattern.[1]

Notwithstanding this invitation to the Service chiefs to actively express their "more than military" strategic views, Kennedy assertively closed the door to such views during the Cuban Missile Crisis in October 1962.[2] The chiefs, already immersed in planning for a large-scale U.S. invasion of Cuba to remove Castro from power while simultaneously signaling strength to the Soviet Union, advocated for armed confrontation. They preferred direct air strikes on the missile launch sites, coupled with a blockade and ground troops. Believing that these views ignored relevant political, diplomatic, and military constraints that would likely escalate armed tension with the Soviet Union, Kennedy instead relied solely on Chairman of the Joint Chiefs of Staff, General Maxwell Taylor, for military advice. At the precipice of a major war, he was the only member of the

D. Maurer, *Crisis, Agency, and Law in US Civil-Military Relations*,
DOI 10.1007/978-3-319-53526-5_6

secret Executive Committee ("ExComm") of the National Security Council meeting during those tense thirteen days wearing a uniform, for he was the only military officer Kennedy trusted.[3]

It is neither intuitively nor objectively clear that this was *unhealthy* civil-military tension. If we look at the outcome from the much clearer vantage of historical hindsight, relying on advice from the expert Joint Chiefs very well could have triggered World War III.[4] On the other hand, the Kennedy Administration's distrust of its senior flag officers may have bled into Lyndon Johnson's subsequent administration, affecting the outsize influence of Robert McNamara during the gradual escalation in Vietnam.[5] From the various participants' perspectives, Kennedy's invitation to the Chiefs to actively consider political contexts in rendering their counsel would probably have breached tenets of Huntington's "objective control" theory in the same way that the civilian-led Defense Department was perceived to negatively micromanage the operational aspects of combat in Southeast Asia later that decade. If the Joint Chiefs had been more outspoken in their counsel during the beginning moves of the Vietnam War, it is not clear at what point their dissent, debate, or disagreement would have crossed the line into outright insubordination or obstruction.[6] Nor is it clear whether their public statements implicitly criticizing the Administration would have been viewed, in the light of history, as *remedies* for a pathologically unhealthy civil-military relationship, or as *symptoms* of the unhealthy relationship.

As argued earlier, neither scholarly theory nor the law adequately provide the means to diagnose strategic civil-military tensions and apparent conflict. Nevertheless, there is evidence outside of doctrine that suggests that the Armed Services themselves intrinsically adopt a role in these relationships that is akin to a "principal-agent" dynamic. First, this chapter will broadly describe a framework on which to view the evidence: agency under the law. Second, it will present that evidence. Third, it will argue by analogy that elements of the former, including fiduciary concepts like actual and apparent authority, and duties like candor, loyalty, and good conduct, can be applied explicitly by the participants in the strategic civil-military relationships.

Jurisprudential Agency

"Agency," as applied in the argument in the following text, is not the "agency" modeled by the work of scholars like Peter Feaver. Feaver's theory of civil-military relations, is limited by assuming and portraying the participants as rational actors, ignoring their motives, competence, information asymmetry, and foreseeable irrational decision-making. Feaver's theory also aggregates the participants into broad civilian and military categories, without consideration for nuanced personalities or positions that might behave as both principal *and* agent simultaneously. Finally, it does not explain behavior that superficially appears irrational but is driven by unpublicized ulterior motives, like the agent's understanding of what a particular duty suggests he or she should do in a given situation. I do not contend that Feaver's rational actor model fails to accurately predict or explain civil-military elites' *behavior*; rather, it bears noting explicitly that the agency theory he has portrayed has no intent of, or capacity for, diagnosing the *health* of a strategic civil-military relationship against objective criteria.

In contrast, the legal concept of agency *does* offer a basis on which to build such criteria. Unlike Feaver's model that depicts agency as "strategic interaction," agency as understood by lawyers is a defining *characteristic, attribute,* or *trait* of a relationship between two or more parties, acting in their best interest, and which consequently imposes obligations on those parties relative to each other.[7] This form of agency is not *premised* on rational behavior, nor does it need to aggregate the personalities into categorical groups, nor does it propose a narrow band of possible actions and reactions by the participants (like working, shirking, monitoring, and punishing). Rather, agency under the law is

> the fiduciary relationship that arises when one person (a "principal") manifests assent to another person (an "agent") that the agent shall act on the principal's behalf and subject to the principal's control, and the agent manifests assent or otherwise consents so to act.[8]

There is a "meeting of the minds" or mutual agreement that the principal shall be in the legitimate and superior decision-making or decision-approving position relative to the agent; the agent, in turn, shall engage in activities on behalf of the guiding interests and objectives of the principal.[9] By legally binding the principal to obligations and actions of the agent, who has undertaken those obligations or acted for the principal, the principal augments his or her native capacity and expands the scope of his or her capabilities.[10]

Under this view of agency, the roles of principal and agent have certain technical, but rather simple, meanings. A principal is "one who authorizes another to act on his her behalf" and is usually liable for conduct of the agent he or she employs.[11] An agent, therefore, is "one who is authorized to act for or in place of another; a representative."[12] As one classic treatment of the subject noted: "lunatics and idiots cannot acts as agents."[13] The bond that exists between these two participants is "fiduciary"—that is, a "relationship in which one person is under a duty to act for the benefit of another on matters within the scope of the relationship."[14] As expressed by the terms of the agreement between them, this duty arises in circumstances in which a principal seeks to rely on the expertise or advice of the agent in order to accomplish some goal that the principal cannot or will not achieve on its own.[15] This leaves the principal partially dependent on the skill and conduct of the agent.[16]

These generic definitions capture an enormous range of transactions, leading one scholar to call agency "indispensible to even the simplest functions of modern life."[17] For example, the trustee-beneficiary, guardian-ward, and attorney–client relationships are fiduciary in nature and fit the principal-agent mold.[18]

Such relationships necessarily impose duties on the agent: faithful integrity and loyalty, "good faith, trust, confidence, and candor" among them.[19] The duty of candor is further defined as "duty to disclose material facts."[20] The duty of good faith requires fair dealing such that neither party is prevented from "realizing the agreement's benefits."[21] The duty of loyalty requires that the agent abstain from "self-dealing" or using their position to further his or her own interests, rather than the principal's interests.[22]

Furthermore, the law of agency generally imposes other objectively determined duties of "care, competence, and diligence" to assure the principal that certain basic expectations will be met when delegating authority to the agent.[23] Notwithstanding their own special skill, knowledge, competence, and diligence, the agent is not permitted to freelance. Rather, agents have a duty to "take action only within the scope of the agent's actual authority" and to "comply with all lawful instructions received from the principal."[24] Moreover, such actions must be "reasonable" and "refrain from conduct that is likely to damage the principal's enterprise."[25] This raises the obvious question. What happens when the agent's actions conflict with those of the principal because they are not reasonable from the perspective of the principal, or exceed the scope of authority granted, or hinder the principal's objectives? This "Agency Problem" is well known in the literature[26] and implies that the agent behaves according to precepts or *internalized* ethical rules that diverge from the standards or boundaries set by the principal—called an exercise of *moral agency*.[27]

Because these duties legally bind the principal, and will determine the extent to which an agent has breached the terms of the agreement, the definition of "authority" is critical.[28] Authority vested in an agent can be *actual*. That is, the agent has acted reasonably based on manifestations made by the principal to the agent that the principal "wishes the agent so to act."[29] Those manifestations may be express or implied by the principal, but in either case the agent is limited to conduct that is reasonably believed to be "necessary or incidental to achieving the principle's objectives."[30] Alternatively, authority may be only *apparent*. That is, power to act on behalf of the principal in relation to a third party, but only based on that *third party's* reasonable belief that the actor has the authority, and the belief is "traceable to the principal's manifestations."[31] Such acts bind the principal, even if that authority was not intended to be vested in the agent.[32] Finally, the agent's authority to act may be *implied*. Such "authority [is] intentionally given by the principal to the agent as a result of the principal's conduct, such as the principal's earlier acquiescence to the agent's actions."[33]

In the next three chapters, we will see how these concepts from the law of agency, especially the fiduciary duties and types of authority, can be inferred as *tacit* elements of strategic civil-military relationships from the way in which key participants have acted out their roles and responsibilities relative to one another.

Notes

1. National Security Action Memorandum 55 from President John F. Kennedy, to The Chairman, Joint Chiefs of Staff, subject: Relations of the Joint Chiefs of Staff to the President in Cold War Operations (28 June 1961), http://www.ratical.org/ratville/JFK/USO/appE.html#NSAM55 (emphasis added). According to historian and Kennedy advisor Arthur Schlesinger, J.r., Kennedy was deeply "disappointed" in his senior military advisors for what he viewed as a "cursory review" of the CIA's plan leading the Bay of Pigs debacle. Arthur M. Schlesinger, Jr., A Thousand Days xvi, 295 (2002) ("after the Bay of Pigs, Kennedy had little regard for the JCS and their recommendations"). According to historian Matthew Moten, General Maxwell Taylor was the primary author of this memorandum, as a recommendation to President Kennedy following Taylor's personal investigation of the Bay of Pigs debacle. Moten, Presidents & Their Generals, at 279–80.
2. McMaster, Dereliction of Duty, at 24–29.

3. *Id.*
4. *See* Craig, *The Political Leader as Strategist*, at 482 ("inability or unwillingness on [the part of civilian leaders] to exercise critical control over such plans and decisions runs the risk of placing in military hands powers that can jeopardize the national security for which the political leadership has ultimate responsibility").
5. MOTEN, PRESIDENTS & THEIR GENERALS, at 292–93 (as an exmaple, Moten notes that President Lyndon Johnson's first meeting as President on the subject of Vietnam did not include any member of the JCS).
6. MCMASTER, DERELICTION OF DUTY, at 332–33.
7. Deborah A. DeMott, *The Lawyer as Agent*, 67 FORDHAM L. REV. 301, 301–02 (1995) (distinguishing the common law of agency from the "agency" employed in other fields, such as economics, based in part on the assertion that lawyers are also officers of the court and members of a self-regulating profession).
8. AGENCY RESTATEMENT, at § 1.01.
9. *See* DeMott, *The Lawyer as Agent, supra* note 409, at 302–03 ("the defining elements of the relationship are mutual manifestation of consent, the agent's undertaking to act on behalf of the principal, and the principal's right to control the agent... [where 'control' means] prescribing on an ongoing basis what the agent shall or shall not do").
10. BLACK'S, at 67 (definition of "fiduciary duty").
11. AGENCY RESTATEMENT at 1230 (definition of "principal").
12. BLACK'S at 68 (definition of "agent").
13. ROGER GRESELY WOODYATT, THE LAW OF AGENCY 3 (1900).
14. AGENCY RESTATEMENT at 1315 (definition of "fiduciary relationship").
15. *Id.* at 1315 (definition of "fiduciary relationship"). In this sense, the agent is an "instrument" or "technology" that "enhances a person's ability to act." Paula J. Dalley, *A Theory of Agency*, 72 U. PITT. L. REV. 495, 498 (2011).
16. Tamar Frankel, *Fiduciary Law*, 71 CALIF. L. REV. 795, 800 (1983).
17. Dalley, *A Theory of Agency*, at 497 ("[t]he foundational principle of agency law is that the principal, who has chosen to conduct her business through an agent, must bear the foreseeable consequences created by that choice. Conversely, as the bearer of the risks, the principal is entitled to receive the benefits created by the agency relationship"). *See also* Frankel, *Fiduciary Law*, at 798 ("our society is evolving into one based predominantly on fiduciary relations").
18. BLACK'S, at 1315 (definition of "fiduciary relationship"). *See* RESTATEMENT (THIRD) OF THE LAW GOVERNING LAWYERS § 26 cmt. b (2000) ("[l]egal representation saves the client's time and effort and enables legal work to be delegated to an expert. Lawyers therefore are recognized as agents for their clients in litigation and other legal matters.") *See also* James A. Cohen,

Lawyer Role, Agency Law, and the Characterization "Officer of the Court," 48 BUFF. L. REV. 349 (2000);

19. BLACK'S, at 545 (definition of "fiduciary duty").
20. *Id.*, at 544.
21. *Id.*, at 544–45. *See also* AGENCY RESTATEMENT, at § 8.15 ("Principal's Duty To Deal Fairly And In Good Faith").
22. BLACK'S, at 545. *See also* AGENCY RESTATEMENT, at § 8.01 ("General Fiduciary Principle"). *See also* Grace M. Geisel, *Client Responsibility for Lawyer Conduct: Examining the Agency Nature of the Lawyer-Client Relationship*, 86 Neb. L. Rev. 346, 351–52 (2007) (suggesting that independent contractors are sometimes agents when they work on behalf of a principal's interests, as—for example—an attorney, and distinguishing them from a "master-servant" form of agency (now called "employer-employee" in common law) in which the principal retains the right to positively control the physical "attributes" of the agent's conduct).
23. AGENCY RESTATEMENT, at § 8.08.
24. *Id.* at § 8.09 ("Duty to Act Only Within Scope of Actual Authority . . . ").
25. *Id.* at § 8.10 ("Duty of Good Conduct"). *But see* W. Bradley Wendel, *Public Values and Professional Responsibility*, 75 Notre Dame L. Rev. 1, 53 (1999) (discussing the challenge of applying pure agency theory to the attorney-client relationship in light of situations in which the attorney—holding to their role as an independent professional with a code of responsibility and as officer of the court system—must depart from or confront an illegal or morally disagreeable choice of the client).
26. Kathleen M. Eisenhardt, *Agency Theory: An Assessment and Review*, 14 ACAD. MGMT. REV. 57, 58 (1989).
27. *See generally* James Burk, *Responsible Obedience by Military Professionals: the Discretion to do What is Wrong, in* AMERICAN CIVIL-MILITARY RELATIONS: THE SOLDIER AND THE STATE IN A NEW ERA 149, 151–54 (Suzanne C. Nielson, Don M. Snider eds.) (2009) (arguing that the "discretionary application of professional knowledge cannot depend on unthinking obedience" and that there is a "protected space" of decision-making afforded to military professionals that, in effect, gives them the moral authority or legitimate grounds on which to disobey or question an order—that is, an execution of "responsible obedience" based on a duty to serve the nation's best interests during some of their interaction with and work for their civilian principals). Thanks to Dr. Don M. Snider for suggesting that aspect of the agency subject was worth noting here.
28. *See, e.g.*, Geisel, *Client Responsibility for Lawyer Conduct: Examining the Agency Nature of the Lawyer-Client Relationship*, at 353–55 (describing various forms of authority under agency law, and citing to numerous jurisdictions for cases defining the legal characteristics of these forms of authority).

29. Agency Restatement, at § 2.01 ("Actual Authority").
30. *Id.* at § 2.02 ("Scope Of Actual Authority").
31. *Id.* at § 2.03 ("Apparent Authority").
32. Black's, at 142 (definition of "Apparent Authority").
33. *Id.* at 143 (definition of "Implied Authority").

CHAPTER 7

Exhibit A: Scope of Responsibility and Authority

All fiduciary duties implied in a principal-agent relationship flow from the structure of that relationship—the specific division of labor, authority, and scope of responsibility that the parties expressly or tacitly agree upon. This chapter will look at the myriad ways in which four men approached their respective roles as civilian or military leaders and how they understood or behaved within (our outside) the expected scope of responsibility. In those four vignettes, in which we can see a *spectrum* of how the antagonists might divide themselves and their responsibilities, we can easily contrast the picture of a man who entirely *united* the roles of civil administrator and military leader in one heroic legend. These men—two from the American Civil War and two from the early decades of the Cold War—were not the Alexander stereotype, simultaneously ruling an empire and on horseback on the front line of a cavalry charge, or personally scouting enemy battle formations and positions. As "overlord" of a new alliance of Greek city-states, Alexander combined, in Keegan's words, "brains, grace, charm, skill at arms, and more self-confidence than was usual even in one deliberately raised to believe in himself."[1] His was a government of one, and the hand which grasped the sword belonged the head that governed the state. In contrast to the four men described later, Alexander's scope of responsibility was bursting, and offered no room for any other partner in what we would today call a "civil-military relationship." This contrast might illuminate just how significant it is to divide these responsibilities and authorities, and how problematic it can be when that division is misunderstood.

D. Maurer, *Crisis, Agency, and Law in US Civil-Military Relations*,
DOI 10.1007/978-3-319-53526-5_7

President-General-Soldier-in-Chief: The Case of Jefferson Davis

About a week before the Confederate artillery opened fire on the small Fort Sumter garrison in Charleston's harbor, and opened the Civil War, the senior general of the Rebel army, Braxton Bragg, received a letter from the provisional President of the Confederate States of America. The general was then in command of the defenses of another strategic southern port—the harbor at Pensacola, Florida. As Bragg read the final words of Jefferson Davis's letter, he would no doubt have been confused.

> I have written you freely and hurriedly because I wished to exchange views with you and felt assured that you would understand that there was no purpose to dictate; and under an entire confidence that your judgement would control your conduct... [t]hough you are addressed as a Genl [sic] upon official matters yet I wish you to regard this not as a letter of the President but of your old comrade in arms.[2]

Davis, General Bragg's "old comrade in arms," was apologizing for the tactical "suggestions" with which he infused his letter from its beginning. Far more dictation than suggestion, President Davis's advice on where and how to emplace units as small as mortar batteries was meant to be helpful. One imagines Davis sitting alone at his desk in Montgomery, Alabama (then the capital of the Confederacy), agitated by insomnia and boils, weakened by chronic gastrointestinal discomfort, penning his letters in a state of continuous stress, anxiety, and uncertainty at the very infancy of his confederate nation. He wished to offer four ways in which his general could achieve victory at Fort Pickens—or what Davis called four "modes of success:" surrender by the Union garrison; abandonment; "by breach of the front wall or explosion of glacis mines exposing the work to capture by assault;" fourth, evacuation after reducing the fort to rubble.[3]

*****

Jefferson Davis played a central role in the history of his two countries—the one he was born into but rebelled against and the one he tried to fashion by war. Whether he was a *good* president is a difficult question because he has no Confederate to contrast him against, his tenure was entirely enflamed by war, his nation did not survive the war he led, and he was—quite arguably—sitting in an unlawful political station created out of the crime of rebellion. His relationship with his subordinate commanding generals was, expectedly, complicated and personality driven. In hindsight, it is perhaps even more misunderstood by the public because we have no gauge for either understanding the civil-military nature of those relationships or diagnosing whether they were unhealthy under the circumstances. Because Davis's view of his own presidential authority tends to intermingle that of politician and general, his story is a case study of the idea of the principal-agent "scope of representation"—or at least how Davis, in application, may have been guilty of ignoring this precept many times and confusing his role as principal or client with that of his generals—the true agents.

In jargon well known to one class of agents, a lawyer's "scope of representation and allocation of authority" *requires* the counselor to:

> abide by a client's decision [for] the objectives of representation and . . . shall consult with the client as to the means by which they are to be pursued. A lawyer *may* take such action on behalf of the client as is impliedly authorized to carry out the representation.[4]

Importantly, this "scope" provision reminds outside observers and paying clients that the "lawyer's representation of a client . . . does not constitute an endorsement of the client's political, economic, social or moral views or activities."[5] By assuring the client's possession of ultimate authority over the purposes of the relationship, "within the limits imposed by the law,"[6] this Rule, by analogy, reflects similar principles implied by the constitutional separation of powers and the apolitical subordination of the military to a civilian commander-in-chief, as well as values—like nonpartisan military advice—reflected in the officer's oath and in doctrine. Furthermore, Eliot Cohen's description of the civil-military "unequal dialogue" can be inferred from the Rule's allocation of authority:

> [c]lients normally defer to the special knowledge and skill of their lawyer with respect to the means to be used to accomplish their objectives, particularly with respect to technical [and] tactical matters . . . [c]onversely, lawyers usually defer to the client regarding such questions as the expense to be incurred and concern for a third person who might be adversely affected.[7]

The "special knowledge and skill" of the agent-lawyer is analogous to the technical and tactical knowledge and skill of the agent-military officer. Similarly, the lawyer's deference to the client's perspective on expenses and the adverse effect on third parties is analogous to the officer's deference to the civilian policy-maker's perspective on political cost and public opinion incited by the decision. Such similarities align this particular fiduciary duty neatly with the potential principal-agent pair in a strategic civil-military relationship.

*****

As an early example of strategic civil-military relations under Jefferson Davis's wartime leadership, his letter of instruction to General Bragg reveals glimpses of the personality traits for which Davis was later loathed by his own countrymen and which would alienate his subordinate military commanders. He viewed himself not so much as the political leader, executive, or principal statesman, but as a "first-among-equals" combat leader—if not a General-in-Chief himself. U.S. Grant later wrote that Davis held an "exalted opinion of his own military genius"[8]—an opinion widely shared during the war by the Confederate press. In 1863, after the defenses of Vicksburg finally fell to a combined Union ground and naval siege and General Lee's retreat back to Virginia after Gettysburg's climactic but futile charge on Cemetery Ridge, John Moncure Daniel, editor of the Richmond Examiner, imputed these strategic disasters to Davis's "infallible egotism . . . wrapped in sublime self-complacency."[9] The brother of Davis's own vice president called him a "conceited, hypocritical, sniveling . . . dogged knave and fool."[10] A Confederate senator referred to him as an "amalgam of malice and mediocrity."[11] Mary Chestnut, resident of Fredericksburg, famed war diarist and wife of Davis's aide, readily admitted that he was "greedy for military fame."[12]

One biographer, however, notes that Davis's well-known micromanagement and distrust for many of his subordinate commanders must be considered at least partially the consequence of the unprecedented circumstances in which he was uncomfortably enveloped. James McPherson, no apologist for the Confederacy, acknowledged that the government was "inventing itself from scratch and Davis knew more about organizing and administering an army than any other southerner."[13] Indeed, Davis had more tactical experience in uniform, and knew more about the financing, mobilizing, and organizing military means than most other politicians of his day or our own. He was a graduate of the United States Military Academy, served for seven years in the Regular Army, later re-joined the Army to fight and command a regiment in the Mexican-American War, was the Secretary of War under President Pierce, and served as Chairman of the Senate Committee on Military Affairs. Moreover, in the final months before the shooting war began, he was appointed a Major General in the Army of Mississippi. His eagerness to delve into tactical and operational decision-making—noticeable throughout the war—was symptomatic of his inability to check his own natural impulse to command troops. It was an impulse borne of experience and an experience which was a key factor in the Southern Congress's original nomination of Davis as President.[14]

Davis ardently believed that, as Commander-in-Chief, the President of the Confederate States of America was also the "General-in-chief" and could, if he desired, command troops in the field. He was not alone in that belief. At the first battle of Manassas, in July 1861, many southerners expected him, *because of* his experience, to take the field command of the army.[15] At least sensing a need for his personal presence there, Davis commandeered a train from Richmond with a single aide, got to the grassy battlefield in eyesight of the Blue Ridge in mid-afternoon, borrowed a horse and "rode toward the sound of the guns." He even tried to rally straggling soldiers escaping the smoke and blood of the battle: "I am President Davis... follow me back to the field," he pleaded.[16] After the battle, with Union forces retreating north to Washington, Davis wanted to pursue and nearly dictated an order to the field commanders to do so.[17]

The belief about the proper role of a commander-in-chief, by the mid-1860s, was certainly contributing to the battlefield dalliances he would prefer. Extending beyond the announcement of grand policy aims, the president—including Lincoln in the North—would have been somewhat expected to be involved in the more mundane aspects of translating that policy into strategies, and those strategies into military operations and tactical objectives.[18] Without long-term, highly specialized and professionalized staffs supported by enormous bureaucracies, warfare in fact and in theory far was simpler to manage. This belief, over the course of the war, matured and the advent of the general staff system in Prussia later in the century would shape the American experience in post-Civil War reorganization efforts. But at the time of Bull Run, presidents—especially with Davis's martial experience—could and did merge the civil-military relationship without fear of institutional shirking or bedevilment. Critics of Davis were animated not so much by his bloated scope of responsibility, but his clumsiness in trying to do both equally well.

Davis's belief in what a general ought to be is fascinating because it simultaneously suggests what image he wished to make, and others to hold, of himself:

> The General [is] the remote commander of the individuals, of the men, rather than the internal police; he has time to visit hospitals, to enquire into supplies, to supervise what others must execute; and the men come to regard him, when so habitually seen, as the friend of the individual; but they also know him in another capacity . . . as it were placed on a pedestal, he seems the power that moves and controls the mass.[19]

As Davis understood it, the president was this kind of ideal general too, and as a general he was the ever-comforting but decidedly directive father figure. This approach carried significant risk. In May of 1862, when General Joseph Johnston twice called off an assault on a flank of George McClellan's Union army just outside the capital city of Richmond without consulting Davis, who had already approved the assault, Johnston explained that he did so "because it seemed to me that to do so would be to transfer my responsibilities to [Davis's] shoulders. I could not consult him without adopting the course he might advise, so that to ask his advice would have been, in my opinion, to ask him to command for me."[20] Johnston, in other words, knew what informing his President would entail: Davis would pack his pistols, straddle his horse, and ride through the mucky Spring-soaked clay around the James River and personally direct the campaign for him.[21]

In the future, he would at least imply that his trips to the front lines were intended to be more "presidential" than just tactical participation. To his new General of the Army of Northern Virginia, Robert E. Lee, Davis said that he planned to head west to see General Joseph Johnston's command in Tennessee: "I propose to go out there immediately," he wrote, "with the hope that something may be done to bring out men not heretofore in service, and to arouse all classes to united and desperate resistance."[22]

Davis did travel West in 1863. This visit was no battlefield circulation by a reviewing statesmen upon a pedestal, concerned over the strategic direction of the war effort. Rather, it was a strategic personnel action. Davis's purpose was to reconcile unseemly dissent among the subordinate generals of Braxton Bragg. After the stagnant standoff following the Battle of Chickamauga, ten generals and a colonel—including three of the corps commanders—signed a pleading, if not mutinous, petition to Davis calling for Bragg's removal from command of the Army of Tennessee. At Bragg's headquarters in Marietta, Georgia, President Davis summoned these senior officers, as well as Bragg, and presided over what amounted to a grand jury indictment of Bragg's leadership, ability, and decision-making. Despite the universal lack of respect Bragg engendered among his subordinates, Davis nevertheless decided to retain him in command, and allowed Bragg to reorganize his Army while removing several of the dissenters in the process.[23]

At least twice in his tenure, Davis exercised his presidential prerogative to enhance his interference with military field command decisions. In 1862, he vetoed a bill that would have created the position of General-in-Chief; in 1864, he vetoed a bill that would have created a general staff.[24] In both cases, President Davis evidenced his preference for his own counsel. Rather than shoulder the reasonability for Confederate diplomacy and economic security, he rejected attempts to interpose military subject-matter expertise that would have both distanced him from the campfire smells, the terrible sights and ungodly percussive sounds of the Napoleonic battlefield and would have saved him from the need to serve as his own "Secretary of War."[25] At least twice, he and his personal staff were ordered away from the "ragged edge of danger" at the frontline by the commander on the field directing artillery and maneuvers—first by Robert E. Lee, and later by A.P. Hill.[26]

With a strong dose of skepticism, we can then fully swallow Davis's words during his inaugural address in early 1862: "I am yet more profoundly impressed by the vast responsibility of the office, and humbly feel my own unworthiness."[27] To a modern ear, his false humility is not convincing; but even to his contemporaries, he was a self-interested villain. General Beauregard poorly regarded his commander-in-chief (just as General McClellan loathed President Lincoln) calling him a "living specimen of gall and hatred... either demented or a traitor to his high trust... If he were to die to-day, the whole country would rejoice at it."[28]

In one example of Davis's political calculation over-riding the tactical advice offered by his expert military agents, he ardently disagreed with Major General Patrick Cleburne, a division commander in Army of Tennessee, who wrote a proposal in 1863 signed by 13 other officers, advocating that the Confederacy enlist slaves into the army to offset the mounting personnel shortages, and then grant freedom to those who served.[29] Davis suppressed the memo. He ordered Joseph Johnston, Cleburne's commander, to destroy all copies of it, and the note remained unearthed until a single copy found its way into the official records of the war in 1890.[30]

Toward the end of the Civil War, though, Davis oscillated between a frank authoritarianism over of his generals and a frank suppression of his personal preferences for the sake of supporting his field commanders—in effect, granting them a new definition of their "scope of responsibility." For instance, he and Robert E. Lee disagreed over the value and need for the summary execution of deserters from the rebel Army. Davis had pardoned or commuted many death sentences, but Lee argued that lax control induced disobedience and failed to contain the growing epidemic of desertion. "The great want in our army," Lee wrote to Davis, "is firm discipline." In a "biting commentary" back to Lee, Davis scolded his favorite commander, reminding him that his merciful decisions served a political, humanitarian, and public relations goal, and "that is not the proper subject for the criticism of a military commander."[31]

Yet, as "the noose tightened around the Confederacy's neck," Jefferson Davis reluctantly shed his earlier aversions. When, in 1865, Robert E. Lee advocated for the slave enlistment proposal first launched by Cleburne, Davis acquiesced to the political winds and military necessity when he signed a bill into law and two companies of slaves began forming.[32]

> It is now becoming daily more evident to all reflecting persons that we are reduced to choosing whether the negroes shall fight for us or against us, and that all arguments as to the positive advantages or disadvantages of employing them are beside the question, which is, simply one of relative advantage between having their fighting element in our ranks or those of the enemy.[33]

Davis also shed his aversion to limits on his responsibility for overall military strategy.[34] He bowed to the Confederate Congress's desire to appoint Lee as General-in-Chief in early 1865, which gave Davis more freedom to remove from the capital city of Richmond in a hurry, and reflected the reality that his ability to communicate with the military commanders was quickly collapsing around him. In a sorrowful note to his wife in early April of 1865, just after he evacuated to the border town of Danville, he wrote:

> I have in vain sought to get into communication with Genl [sic] Lee and have postponed writing in the hope that I would soon be able to speak to you with some confidence of the future ... I do not wish to leave V[irginia], but cannot decide on my movements until those of the army are better developed.[35]

Davis's own words illustrate the expanding and shrinking "scope of responsibility and authority" that is generally the hallmark of a principal–agent relationship. In and of itself, the change is neither good nor bad; it is simply a way to describe the shift in authority implied by, assumed by, or directly granted to his subordinate general-agents in the waning days of the war.

McClellan's Megalomania and Ridgeway's Recalcitrance

Though a brilliant administrator and engineer, General George McClellan's strong personality was not tempered by a sense of humility or modesty.[36] He never lacked an enthusiastic willingness to lecture civilian superiors, whom he considered his moral and intellectual inferiors.[37] Consider his long note to President Lincoln in July of 1862, in which he expressed his "general views concerning the existing state of the rebellion ... although they do not strictly relate to the situation of this Army or strictly come within the scope of my official duties."[38] He counseled Lincoln against waging a war in which the objective was to abolish slavery by force: "[m]ilitary power should not be allowed to interfere with the relations of servitude, either by supporting or impairing the authority of the master."[39] McClellan warned his president, in not so subtle terms, that abolishing slavery would be a "declaration of radical views," and would "rapidly disintegrate our present Armies."[40] President Lincoln, of course, found McClellan's warnings unpersuasive, and two months later announced his intent to issue the Emancipation Proclamation after the Battle of Antietam.[41] Though unpersuasive, scholars of the period noted that:

> The line between policy and strategy was dimly drawn; just as Lincoln believed he was capable of making strategy, so generals thought they were qualified to form policy. McClellan differed from other officers only in his sublime conviction that the government would fall if it refused to adopt his

> ideas... he assumed that could deal with the government [i.e., Lincoln] on an equal basis as a sort of contracting party.[42]

As we have seen, the principal–agent relationship may generally be born of an agreement, or contract, or meeting of the minds, but that agreement is to the *role and function of the agent on behalf of* the principal. In no way does it forge an equal partnership of the kind implied by McClellan's views, and so Agency theory offers a way to describe the general's approach and understand why it was psuhed back against by his political masters.

Ironically, McClellan's much earlier letter from August 1861 to President Lincoln reads like a textbook illustration of military expertise advising a novice civilian politician about proposed and desired military-specific needs in order to meet political objectives.[43] McClellan made two points, in closing that letter, that are startlingly humble when contrasted against his latter frustration with politicians. First, he declined to opine definitively on the various strategic options available to Lincoln, stating this was a "question entirely political, on which I do not venture to offer any opinion."[44] Next, as if to confirm that his proposed military means would satisfy the political ends, he wrote: "I understand it to be the purpose of this great Nation to reestablish the power of the government, and restore peace to its citizens, in the shortest possible time."[45] In effect, he was asking his civilian commander-in-chief for a political orientation to the tactical map he was unfolding for his Army to follow.

*****

As one historian notes, "[a]t the summit, war and politics merge and become inextricably intertwined. A general in chief not fully attuned to the latter will not master the former."[46] After "Young Napoleon"[47] was fired twice from his position as the Union army commander by Lincoln, and subsequently lost his presidential bid against his former Commander-in-Chief, it became clear that McClellan was not properly attuned to either.[48]

Nine decades later, little in this regard had changed. In the middle of the 1950s, more than a year after President Eisenhower's administration published its New Look defense strategy of massive atomic retaliation led by the Air Force, then Army Chief of Staff General Matthew Ridgway had grown discouraged.[49] He was unable to persuade his colleagues on the

Joint Chiefs of Staff, the civilian political appointees on the National Security Council and staff, and President Eisenhower himself, that an atomic weapons-based strategy was morally bankrupt. Petulantly, General Ridgway presided over a complete revision of the Army's war fighting doctrine, Field Manual 100–5.[50] Countering the prevailing national security strategy, this doctrine adopted the *status quo ante*: fighting a conventional armed force (not strategic bombing of population centers) in order to avoid indiscriminate "[destruction of] the bases on which a peace can be built when the conflict is over."[51] Moreover, Ridgway began to speak at length, repeatedly and candidly, to other officers outside the Pentagon in the service schools. In a direct "point-by-point critique of Eisenhower's national security policies," he wrote:

> no concept could be more potentially dangerous, perhaps even fatal... [because] the only absolute weapon is man... only when we close with the enemy on the ground—as only armies can do—can we finally defeat his armed forces, and only by defeating enemy armed forces can we win victory over an enemy nation.[52]

Unlike McClellan during the Civil War, General Ridgway understood his statements implicated core tenets of military professionalism and exposed an uncomfortable maw in the Cold War American civil-military relationship.[53] Post-war President Eisenhower had rejected the counsel of his former Army colleague, and Ridgway's relationship with the Secretary of Defense Charles Wilson, was "anything but pleasant.... Mr. Wilson came in with an extensive ignorance of the military establishment and a well-established dislike for the Army... he was one of these gentlemen who have made up their minds and do not want to listen to facts."[54] Ridgeway's civilian principals pursued a national security agenda that sharply reduced the role and budget of the Army,[55] spurring Ridgway to take his case to the media, to Congress,[56] and in policy debates at the Council on Foreign Relations in New York City.[57]

The Case of the True Believer: Maxwell Taylor

If Davis was the archetype of the principal who wished to personally steer the boat for his agents, and McClellan and Ridgway reflect what happens when the agent thinks he knows better than the principal about what course that principal ought to take, then General Maxwell Taylor is the model for merging the role of principal and agent into a set of conjoined twins: two heads, two minds, two sets of animated bodies locked together, independently choosing to act in unified concert under ideal conditions—both the captain and the oarsman rowing together and navigating together. Taylor's experience in the Pentagon and White House demonstrated that an agent's scope of responsibility is often unstable, dilating wider or contracting narrowly, subject to the peculiar needs of the principal as the frictions of politics and the fog of war make decisions impossibly uncertain.

After the Bay of Pigs, President Kennedy's administration suffered a bruising blow to its optimisitc self-esteem and perception that its foreign policy choices would be level-headed, vigourously rational and enobled by idealism. In the Fall of 1961, pessimism, instead, set in as obsevers could not help but witness what appeared to be a massive geopolitical failure and military bumbling—failure that smelled like the kind of American Imperialism that preferred to act first and think second.[58] Kennedy, young in his presidency and wanting to avoid future messy entanglements in which he had not been fully engaged nor prepared to accept as his own, believed he had "soft spots" in his administration—namely, the CIA and the corporate advisory council of the Joint Chiefs of Staff. As Schlesinger put it, "he set quietly to work to make sure that nothing like the bay of Pigs could happen to him again. The first lesson was never to rely on experts…[he would] make greater use of generalists in whom he had personal confidence and remake every decision in his own terms."[59]

Kennedy as principal sought "unfettered and confidential" advice from those he brought with him into the government as agent-advisors, on whom he naturally had grounds to trust.[60] But after his first foreign policy crisis, he realized he might have to look beyond this intimate circle to those "outsiders" who publically adhered to a world view that matched his own preferences. He did not ever want to be "overawed by professional military advice again."[61]

One such outsider was a man who had spent his entire professional career on the *inside*, but whose views late in life on the appropriate use of military force in the atomic age had begun—like Ridgway before him—to strain his credibility and stain his reputation among the civilian political leadership. Maxwell Taylor, as Army Chief of Staff succeeding Ridgway, had become a self-admitted heretic for advocating the doctrine of "Flexible Response" during the latter years of the Eisenhower Adminstration, on the belief that arming, planning, and preparring for massive nuclear retaliation would only drive the world to another war—perhaps its last—and could not be a moral, militarily-prudent, or politically rational strategy.[62] The President's New Look also seemed to leave Taylor's cherished Army without a real mission or role in the securing the state or its citizens—a fear that has returned from time to time to haunt the budgets and stragetic planning of the Army.[63] Taylor's criticism was vocal—he testified before Congress in a way that Eisenhower later termed "legalized insubordination" if not "damned near treason."[64] He soon retired and wrote a popular book advocating for a strategy that accepted the probability of "limited war" and planning the military's force structure and foreign policy around the idea of both preparing for them and avoiding direct nuclear confrontation.

Fortunately for Taylor, by 1961 his military heresy was now political orthodoxy within the Kennedy White House.[65] Moreover, he was "cerebral, urbane, and skillful with a tennis racket," fluent in Spanish and French and had spent years working and studying in East Asia.[66] Impressed, Kennedy first asked him to serve on a blue-ribbon panel, the Cuba Study Group, with Robert Kennedy to assess what went wrong in the "ill-starred adventure" on the Cuban beaches, Florida training grounds, and Pentagon planning rooms.[67] A few months later, he recalled him to Active Duty as a four-star General, and after some careful negotiation of his new role, appointed him to a brand new office of Military Representative to the President, created especially or him. According to Taylor's own recollection, Kennedy wanted "someone with military experience in his immediate entourage whom he could consult readily with regard to military matters reaching his office."[68] This consultative role was officially described:

> The military representative is a staff officer to advise and assist the President with regard to those military matters that reach him as Commander-in-Chief of the Armed Forces. The Military Representative is not interposed between the President and any of his statutory advisors or advisory bodies such as the Secretary of Defense, JCS or the NSC but maintains close liaison with them and is prepared to give his personal views to assist the President in reaching decisions. He is available to represent the President when the latter desires senior military representation at home or abroad.[69]

Though "not interposed between the President" and his other Generals, Taylor was astute enough to realize hard feelings and confusion would inevitably result. “My old military colleagues, the Joint Chiefs,” he wrote, “could not be happy over the appearance on the White House scene of a competitive source of military advice.”[70] Moreover, he felt “considerable unhappiness” eminating from the Special Assistant to the President for National Security Affairs, McGeorge Bundy.[71]

However, Taylor likely provided—or appeared to provide—much more than “competitive” military advice, as that term connotes some degree of equality among the various military experts positioned to advise the President, like the Chairman of the Joint Chiefs of Staff. Derisively, Taylor referred to the Chairman as simply having the statutory authority to preside over meetings of the Chiefs and “keeping the peace” between the heads of the separate services.[72] He also recognized that his substantive views, not merely his close proximity to the Head of State, might unbalance their respective roles. Taylor noted wryly that the Pentagon would likely “fear that I would try to advance some of my heretical concepts in the White House.”[73] This fear would not have been unfounded. Taylor believed that his role as “Mil. Rep.” was to “anticipate problems of the President in the areas of my responsibility” which included not just military strategy but also intelligence and “Cold War Planning.”[74] This could not have, and did not, endear him to Bundy immediately—the former Army intelligence officer of World War II, former Council of Foreign Relations member who studied the Marshall Plan with luminaries like Allan Dulles and George Kennan, a man nicknamed “Muhatma Bundy” by classmates at Yale, and youngest dean in the history of Harvard University.[75] Taylor antiseptically described, in a way that likely scrubbed clean the dirtier and painful way in which their relationship evolved, how “we worked out a satisfactory adjustment of relations based on a continuing interchange of information regarding activities of mutual interest and the frequent attendence of staff members of our offices at the briefings and meetings of the other.”[76] As for his fellow General and Flag officers, he promised them he would not be a “roadblock to their recommendations.”[77]

Nevertheless, Taylor tried to inject himself, or using his small staff, into the pre-decisional meetings across the Potomac at the Pentagon. While certainly animating his fellow uniformed leaders to see him as an interloper, his stated benign intent was to observe—if not participate in—the formulation of the military Services’ views so that he could “develop my views concurrently and inform the Chairman in advance of any possible conflicts.”[78] While seemingly unobtrusive, this goal of Taylor’s strikes the modern reader as inconsistent with the role laid out for him by President

Kennedy. Rather than serve as a trusted liaison to the Pentagon, and councilor to the President on ideas, proposals, and decisions presented by others in uniform, Taylor's approach implied he was his *own source* of ideas, proposals, and decisions—a one-man Pentagon, nested within the West Wing.

However, Taylor's unique advocacy and inflated role clearly did not antagonize his principal. In October 1962, not long before the Cuban Missile Crisis sparked, Kennedy entrenched him as his primary military advisor—formally and officially tagging him as the new Chairman of the Joint Chiefs of Staff. Back across the Potomac full time now, Taylor focused his early effort on infusing the Chiefs with muscle and voice they had been denied or had muted. "As Chief [of Staff of the Army], I had always resented efforts by the Chairman to impose uniformity ... and I felt that any dissent should be reported to the Secretary [of Defense] or even to the President without trying to circumvent the issue."[79] His encouragement of semi-public dissent among his fellow four-stars also echoed into the ears of Secretary McNamera, telling him that Taylor "recognized his right, indeed his duty [as the political leader of the Department], to seek advice from many quarters and that he could turn to whomever he liked—to his barber or chauffer if he wished. The Joint Chiefs of Staff, however [he cautioned McNamera], had the statutory obligation to serve as the principal military advisors to him, the National Security Council, and to the President." He pleaded with McNamara to "assure that they were always given full opportunity to discharge this obligation."[80]

Taylor's expression of support for the varied views of his fellow members of the Joint Staff, along with his seemingly postive outlook on the value of hearing advice from "many quarters" even if contrary to the current norm, status quo, policy, or political preference of the administration, was magnimous and high-minded. He asserted that military officers had a parallel duty away from the current or future battlefields and "in the field of policy, particularly of foreign policy ... not merely men at arms, useful only for the dirty business of fighting wars—they had a duty also to deter wars and deterrence involves appreciation of far more than purely military matters. They should also know what military power can and cannot do and presumably recommend accordingly in invoking or withholding its use."[81] It is precisely the kind of freedom to debate he wanted as Eisenhower's Army Chief of Staff in the late 1950s. It is precisely what to expect from agent who views himself *qua* agent—that is, one who acts for the benefit of another (the principal) on matters within the scope of the relationship, because of that agent's ability to provide expert advice on a subject beyond the knowledge of the principal, or to act for the principal in a fashion beyond the competence of the principal.

Nevertheless, Taylor's views while serving as Kennedy's Chairman were more complicated, and were unavoidably colored by his having distinctively served as the President's matchless "military representivative" who shared many of the policy preferences and approaches of the administration. Taylor famously described the role of the senior military agents of the President as one that emphasizes the

> importance of an intimate, easy relationship, born of friendship and mutual regard, between the president an the Chiefs [and which] is particularly important in the case of the Chairman [of the Joint Chiefs of Staff]…the Chairman should be a true believer in the foreign policy and military strategy of the administration which he serves.[82]

A "true believer," one should note, is clearly not a skeptic, and one who probably will not whole-heartedly express or openly share a dissenting view, especially if that dissenting view comes from those other general officers he instinctively view as quarrelsome and parochially focused on their individual Services. For Taylor, it seems fair to summarize, the senior strategic military agent was a disciple, a follower, evangelical in his fulfillment of his duty to support the objectives of the political and civil leadership. At least this seemed to resonate with his approach in the final two jobs he held in uniform, though certainly does not echo his approach while serving as an agent to a principal with whom he vehemently disagreed on principle.

*****

These vignettes are not historical anomalies. None of these representations are intrinsically good or bad, healthy or unhealthy, but all present distinct variations on what each party might believe the "scope of representation" or "authority" is under the circumstance in which they find themselves working. They represent possible ways in which strategic civil-military relationships become—at least in appearance—pathologically unsound. In Jefferson Davis, we see the senior politician wanting desperately to shed the cloak of principal altogether, for his micro-management of tactical and operational details more comfortably fit the model image he held of himself as the stoic man on horseback, the commander-in-chief *qua* Alexander of Macedonia, ably conquering his political and military opponents simultaneously. Only reluctantly—and only when the end was near—did he trust just enough of his uniformed commanders to grant them the battlefield discretion they expected as within *their* scope of responsibility as military agents of the civil government. In McClellan and Ridgeway, we see the opposite archetype: The influential, popular, and expert general officer long frustrated by the resistance of his political principal to accept the military "wisdom" they offer. Couched in terms of moral suasion, both McClellan and Ridgeway took routes that indiscreetly announced their antipathy toward the politician that was, ironically, the source of their military authority and public prominence. President Kennedy, on the other hand, clearly "manifested assent" (to use the legal jargon of agency) to General Taylor in a way that fused this principal-agent duo, sharing both a philosophical approach to warfare and a belief in how military expertise ought to be employed in the White House.

All of these case studies can and should be evaluated in terms *not* just of whether they struck others as inflammatory, divisive, or encroaching on the traditional functions these two actors take on, but also on whether their performances violated or followed the "meeting of the minds"—the implicit contract of mutual expectations that glued the agent to the objectives of the principal.

If the "scope of responsibility" framework, organizing authority into a case-by-case hierarchy based on the agreed-upon preferences of those in whom this power vests, is the *sine qua non* of the principal–agent relationship, these episodes illustrate the merging or uniting of responsibility under one elite or the other. To the extent that these strategic players—whether as agent or principal—breached this wall of separation against the expectation of the others, we see a new way to label, and partly diagnose, that relationship. In the pages that follow, we will encounter other, similar, ways to diagnose these so-called crises under the rubric of agency theory and see ways in which a mantra of "fiduciary duty, honor, country" might help recast well-known civil-military relationships.

Notes

1. John Keegan, The Mask of Command 20–22 (1987).
2. Letter from Jefferson Davis to Brigadier General Braxton Bragg, April 3, 1861, in Jefferson Davis: The Essential Writings (ed. William J. Cooper, Jr.), 207–08 (2004).

3. *Id.*
4. Model Rules of Prof'l Conduct, at R. 1.2 (a) (emphasis added).
5. *Id.* at R. 1.2(b).
6. *Id.* at R.1.2 cmt.
7. *Id.*
8. Ulysses S. Grant, Personal Memoirs of U.S. Grant 344 (2001).
9. James M. McPherson, Embattled Rebel: Jefferson Davis as Commander in Chief 138, 218 (2014).
10. *Id.* at 5–6.
11. *Id.* at 218.
12. *Id.* at 43.
13. *Id.* at 19, 110–11, 191.
14. *Id.* at 15–16.
15. *Id.* at 40.
16. *Id.* at 41.
17. *Id.* at 42.
18. T. Harry Williams, Lincoln and his Generals 6 (1952).
19. Letter from Jefferson Davis to General P.G.T. Beauregard, October 16, 1861, in Jefferson Davis: The Essential Writings (ed. William J. Cooper, Jr.), 215–16 (2004).
20. McPherson, Embattled Rebel, at 85.
21. Letter to Varina Davis, May 16, 1862, in Jefferson Davis: The Essential Writings (ed. William J. Cooper, Jr.), 235 (2004).
22. Letter from Jefferson Davis to General Robert E. Lee, December 8, 1862, in Jefferson Davis: The Essential Writings (ed. William J. Cooper, Jr.), 215–16 (2004).
23. McPherson, Embattled Rebel, at 153–57.
24. Donald Stoker, The Grand Design: Strategy and the U.S. Civil War, 22–23 (2010).
25. McPherson, Embattled Rebel, at 10, 111.
26. *Id.*, at 92–94.
27. Inaugural Address as Elected President, Feb 22,, 1862, in Jefferson Davis: The Essential Writings (ed. William J. Cooper, Jr.), 215–16 (2004).
28. McPherson, Embattled Rebel, at 70.
29. *Id.* at 229–30.
30. *Id.*
31. *Id.* at 228.
32. *Id.* at 235.
33. Letter to John Forsyth, Feb. 21, 1865, in Jefferson Davis: The Essential Writings (ed. William J. Cooper, Jr.), 359–60 (2004).
34. McPherson, Embattled Rebel, at 219.

35. Letter to Varina Davis, April 5, 1865, in JEFFERSON DAVIS: THE ESSENTIAL WRITINGS (ed. William J. Cooper, Jr.), 365–66 (2004).
36. T. HARRY WILLIAMS, LINCOLN AND HIS GENERALS 24 (1952) (suggesting that the public's initial warm reception of McClellan "clouded his sense of reality" and his own abilities, and "he developed a Messianic complex.")
37. Brian Holden Reid, *General McClellan and the Politicians*, PARAMETERS, Sept. 1987, at 101, 103–04.
38. MCCLELLAN PAPERS, at 344–45.
39. *Id.* at 344–45.
40. *Id.* McClellan's political views are important for placing this recommendation in context: he was a Democrat, and supported the Union's initial and more limited aim of restoration, not the abolition of slavery. Reid, *General McClellan and the Politicians*, at 103.
41. Historian Ethan S. Rafuse suggests that the issue of emancipation had definite military implications, and this letter only evidenced the general's attempt to engage his Commander-in-Chief in a substantive dialogue, one "national security professional" to another, and did not inappropriately breach any civil-military divide. Rafuse, *General McClellan and the Politicians Revisited*, at 79.
42. T. HARRY WILLIAMS, LINCOLN AND HIS GENERALS 26 (1952).
43. Rafuse, *General McClellan and the Politicians Revisited*, at 71–75.
44. *Id.* at 74.
45. *Id.*
46. Andrew J. Bacevich, *Sycophant Savior*, THE AMERICAN CONSERVATIVE, October 8, 2007, http://www.theamericanconservative.com/articles/sycophant-savior/.
47. McClellan earned this nickname, not intended to be flattering, for his combination of intellect, apparent ego, and a willingness to pose for photographs in a classical "Napoleonic pose" with his hand slid between buttons of his jacket. Reid, *General McClellan and the Politicians*, at 104.
48. DORIS KEARNS GOODWIN, TEAM OF RIVALS: THE POLITICAL GENIUS OF ABRAHAM LINCOLN 662–666 (2005). Some scholars suggest that McClellan's reputation as a politically-oriented exemplar of broken subordination to civil government is overblown: that his (in)action, reluctance to engage the Confederate Army in battle, and deliberate shielding of information from President Lincoln were partly a symptom of his suspicion that Lincoln could not keep a secret, and provided repeated fodder for the congressional "Joint Committee on the Conduct of the War" to publically denounce McClellan's warfighting strategy and his fidelity to the cause, calling him a coward and traitor. Reid, *General McClellan and the Politicians*, at 104–08.

49. Geoffrey Perret, Eisenhower 458–462 (1999); *see also* Bacevich, *Paradox of Professionalism*, at 315–16.
50. U.S. Dep't of Army, Field Manual 100–5, Field Service Regulations: Operations 5 (27 Sep 1954), *available at* http://www.cgsc.edu/CARL/docrepository/FM100_5_1954.pdf.
51. *Id.*
52. Bacevich, *Paradox of Professionalism*, at 323.
53. *Id.* at 311–24.
54. Office of the Secretary of Defense, Oral History interview of Matthew Ridgway (April 19, 1984), final transcript dated August 28, 1984, available at http://history.defense.gov/Portals/70/Documents/oral_history/OH_Trans_RidgwayMatthew4-19-1984.pdf.
55. Moten, Presidents & Their Generals, at 274 (commenting how "surprising" Eisenhower's strategy was at the time, including his twenty percent cut to the Army's budget).
56. President Eisenhower called this "legalized insubordination." *Id.* at 275.
57. Bacevich, *Paradox of Professionalism*, at 325. Ridgeway eventually retired after his first two-year tour as the Army Chief of Staff, an unusal move and indicative of his disaffection with the political administration's handling of national defense; *see also* Moten, Presidents & Their Generals, at 274.
58. Arthur M. Schlesinger, Jr., A Thousand Days: John F. Kennedy in the White House 290–91 (2002).
59. *Id.* at 296.
60. *Id.* at 297.
61. *Id.* at 290.
62. General (retired) Maxwell Taylor, Swords and Plowshares 253 (1972); and see Russell F. Weigley, The American Way of War: A History of United States Military Strategy and Policy 421 (1977).
63. Russell F. Weigley, The American Way of War: A History of United States Military Strategy and Policy 418–20 (1977).
64. Moten, Presidents and Their Generals, 274–75, 276.
65. General (retired) Maxwell Taylor, Swords and Plowshares 253 (1972).
66. Moten, Presidents and Their Generals, 280.
67. Arthur M. Schlesinger, Jr., A Thousand Days: John F. Kennedy in the White House 292 (2002); Russell F. Weigley, The American Way of War: A History of United States Military Strategy and Policy 457–58 (1977).
68. Taylor, Swords and Plowshares 195.
69. McMaster, Dereliction of Duty, 11–12.
70. Taylor, Swords and Plowshares 197.
71. *Id.* at 198 (1972).
72. *Id.* at 195–96.

73. *Id.* at 197.
74. *Id.*
75. Gordon M. Goldstein, Lessons in Disaster: McGeorge Bundy and the Path to War in Vietnam 8 (2008).
76. Taylor, Swords and Plowshares 198.
77. *Id.* at 197.
78. *Id.*
79. *Id.* at 253.
80. *Id.* at 253–54.
81. *Id.* at 255.
82. *Id.* at 252.

CHAPTER 8

Boundaries, or a "Poverty of Useful and Unambiguous Authority"?

McClellan, Ridgeway, Davis, and Taylor occupied various spots along the spectrum of Agency's "scope of responsibility" standard. McClellan would have preferred absolute autonomy, a civil-war *generalissimo*, to wage a gentlemanly war according to his own principles and with the amount of military force he preferred, at a location and time he—and he alone—decided. His constant feuding with Lincoln on these tactical and operational issues was symptomatic of the larger, more dangerous tumor in their relationship: The disagreement and ultimate pathological incompatibility of their *strategic* view of the war they were both fighting, and a belief that the civilian leader's view represented nothing less than "embarrassingly amateurish improvisation"—the same attacks made against future presidents viewed as unexperienced in the ways of foreign policy and immature in their threatened use of military power.[1] Not until Lincoln removed the general from command for the second time did the President surgically attend to this civil-military abscess. In doing so, he revealed his tacit boundaries for the scope of responsibility he expected his generals to obey.

Jefferson Davis, on the other hand, would have also preferred absolute autonomy to wage war, though an autonomy vested in the office of the *president* as a civilian General-in-Chief, not upon the saddle of a uniformed general officer. His preference was Alexandrian—not in terms of a desire to conquest, but in terms of scope of responsibility. He occupied the far end of this spectrum, opposite that of McClellan. Somewhere in between the two poles, Generals Ridgeway and Taylor each found

D. Maurer, *Crisis, Agency, and Law in US Civil-Military Relations*,
DOI 10.1007/978-3-319-53526-5_8

themselves merging closer to their respective civilian principals. Ridgeway, out of frustration, publically vocalized his disagreement with his president's national defense strategy as if he were in a competitive political office seeking to swing votes and support toward his own anti-New Look camp. Ridgeway's stance was antithetical to his principal; in *making* that stance, he attempted to blur the boundaries between his role as expert advisor and that of Eisenhower's—an attempt that was rebuffed. Taylor, too, attempted to merge his role as agent with that of Kennedy's principal, but—unlike Ridgeway—found himself safely embraced by a White House that shared his strategic outlook, welcomed his warnings, and emplaced him knowingly and willfully as a barricading moat that distanced his fellow military experts from the inner sanctum of Camelot's walls.

With such a spectrum of potential, circumstance-specific, ways in which civilian principals and military agents might relate to one another, throwing ones hands up in the air in frustration is more likely than defining *the* right way we should expect these elites to behave. Forecasting *other* strategic elites' future behavior would be even less profitable. At this point, it becomes clear that some technique to guide the *application* of agency concepts may be useful. Correctly, or at least reasonably, identifying the principal and agent in a given context, as well as the bounds imposed on the agent's actual or implied authority and scope of responsibility, is critical to interpreting the duties of loyalty and candor in context—the duties that will be discussed in the next chapter.

One technique for identifying the bounds of the parties' relative scopes of responsibility might be found in Supreme Court Justice Robert Jackson's renowned concurring opinion in the *Youngstown* case from 1952, made famous for its interpretation of the president's executive power, relative to that of Congress, in wartime. Usually known as the "Steel Seizure case," Youngstown Sheet & Tube Co. v. Sawyer, decided in the midst of the Korean War, is a case that nearly every law school student reads, for its multiple compelling arguments would prove to have weighty implications for scoping the extent of a president's unilateral powers under the Constitution. The justices' opinions were a "stinging rebuff" (according to later Chief Justice William Rehnquist) to President Truman, limiting—at least it would appear to be so—the president's wartime power to act without the concurrence of the other popularly elected branch of government.[2]

This scoping of responsibility and authority had far-reaching influence in the decades to come as every of one of the next twelve presidents would apply military force (boots on the ground and jets in the air) overseas against and inside other nations either without the overt approval, request, or authority from Congress, or sought to interpret Congress' acquiescence or broad authorization to include implicit grants of even greater latitude. *Youngstown* became a judicial watchword for checks on inflating Executive branch military power, and served as precedential argument for curbing President George W. Bush's first attempt to create military commissions to try captured combatants being held at a U.S. naval base in Guantanamo Bay, Cuba,[3] and for finding that President Nixon's aggressive approval of FBI wiretaps on a suspected "leaker" within his own National Security Council without a court's warrant was unconstitutional, despite the leaked information's potential harm to the Administration's foreign policy and diplomacy.[4] It is a powerful explanation of the Constitution's deliberate separation of powers; it doubles as a powerful—if only accidental—explanation of Agency Theory's scope of responsibility.

What did President Truman order that was so singularly significant to the modern understanding of the American separation of powers in prosecuting armed conflict? It was a decision neither to send troops to a foreign country to engage in combat nor to escalate the dropping of bombs, nor to expand the list of enemy combatants, nor to use paramilitary assets like drones to target and kill suspected terrorists. Instead, Truman and his advisors sparked this legal controversy over wartime power-sharing with Congress with a domestic decision. They were concerned about economic price inflation as a consequence of the on-going Korean conflict—rather than enact price controls, the administration created the Wage Stabilization Board to monitor and regulate wages with a goal of avoiding costly and debilitating labor strikes. However, when the Board attempted to increase the wages of workers employed in the huge steel industry, the firms—Youngstown Sheet & Tube Company among them—rejected the plan, unless promised an opportunity to simultaneously increase the prices they could charge customers. The union representing these blue-collar employees, United Steel Workers of America, threatened a widespread national strike in response to the firms' recalcitrance. Truman rightly believed that a general strike, if long enough, would undoubtedly constrict the production of steel necessary for the military's war effort in the Far East, and would impinge domestic economic growth.

For practical reasons, the Administration chose to declare a national emergency rather than invoke known but time-consuming procedural mechanisms under existing law, like the Labor Management Relations

Act of 1947, also called the Taft-Hartley Act, which allowed for presidential intervention provided the parties gave 80 days' notice of an intent to strike. On April 8, 1952, he ordered the federal seizure of steel production facilities in order to keep them running. Ironically, attorneys in the Justice Department took a line of legal argument that actually went beyond that which President Truman himself believed. An attorney for one of the steel companies argued that the seizure was unconstitutional because it was made without the express legislative authorization from Congress. In defending the seizure against the injunction requested at the lower federal district court, government counsel hastily suggested that the text of Article II of the Constitution implied the president's inherent and residual powers during a period of national emergency—essentially, power without boundaries (provided the necessary emergency was said to exist). The district court judge rejected this fateful but flawed argument, issued the injunction against the government's possession of the mills, and the Union began its strike. Truman's administration appealed the decision to the D.C. Circuit Court of Appeals, the next rung up in the appellate system, which granted the government's request for a "stay" on the injunction, conditioned on the case being presented to the Supreme Court. Less than 10 days later—instantaneous in the appellate litigation world—the parties made oral arguments before the justices. Ultimately, the Court voted 6–3 to uphold the original injunction in favor of the steel companies and against the interests of the Administration. But getting there was a bit messy. Justice Hugo Black wrote the majority opinion, but with five published "concurring" opinions that stressed different legal grounds and arguments, the final and authoritative rule of the case was never firmly established. It would be Justice Robert Jackson's concurring opinion that would have the longest shelf-life and influence over future presidential power controversies.

Jackson observed that "comprehensive and undefined" responsibility and authority has both "practical advantages and grave dangers" with "enduring consequences" for how power is balanced or shared.[5] His was a *power corrupts; absolute power corrupts absolutely* philosophy—and so he preached that if the act of governance was to be "workable" between the two parties (the president and Congress), the governing branches must be separate but interdependent, autonomous but reciprocal.[6] Just as an agent's responsibility ought to be "scoped" by the principal, providing left and right limits on the agent's authority to act for that principal, Jackson wrote that "presidential powers are not fixed but fluctuate, depending upon their disjunction or conjunction with those of Congress." Though this logic at first seems to paint the parties as co-equal brethren with overlapping responsibilities, deciding which one will act when the other does not, Jackson's analysis of the two branches actually conformed to the logic of agency—one that emphasizes deliberate and knowing limitations imposed by one branch on another, in order to act for the benefit of the principal but "rewarding" the agent for doing so (in the political sense, acting in accordance with the will and interests of the people from whom they received an electoral mandate to govern and form whom they hope to be reelected—itself a form of agency).

Jackson concluded that the president's executive power—to wage a war, enact price controls, stabilize wages, emancipate slaves, seize steel production mills, detain enemy combatants without due process, or any other executive decision that a president chooses to implement—is at its greatest strength when the president operates with clear constitutional authority *plus* a mandate, or delegation of power, to act from Congress. Any judicial attack on an action the president takes under those circumstances would face an uphill battle, charging against a strong breastwork presumption of legality. On the other hand, he suggested that a president's power was at its "lowest ebb" when he or she acted in defiance of, or contrary to, expressed or implied Legislative will. If Congress has inherent or expressed power over the subject matter, the president's authority is stripped down and tightly corralled, legally limited to operating only to the extent he does not invade the powers of Congress.

But in the middle, what Jackson called a "zone of twilight," is when the President acts absent any implied or express direction from Congress, and must rely on his or her independent power and discretion. That discretion must consider the extent to which "congressional inertia, indifference or quiescence may sometimes, at least as a practical matter, enable, if not invite, measures on independent presidential responsibility."[7] If, by analogy, the President can be likened to an "agent" and Congress to a "principal," this three-part scale of legitimate discretion can help in determining the case-by-case extent of authority in *other* settings, *within* the executive branch, like the relationship between civilian political authority and a military commander at the national, strategic decision-making level.

Since the president obviously does not "work for" Congress, this case is not a perfect analogy. However, the strength of this resemblance is not dependent on the case's focus on presidential authority. The most relevant lesson is that Jackson's framework attempts to work out a *practical* guide for the application of *discretionary* authority between two parties that *each* have some degree of power, a distinct lane of responsibility, but who share a blurry division of labor in some contexts. Jackson was explaining how the "equilbrium" is established between the parties.[8] An equilibruim of power, responsibility, and authority to act does not imply that the parties tehmselves are in any sense equal partners. In other words, he could just as well have been writing about and explaining the generic principal-agent dynamic. Therefore, it is this *Youngstown* model that shapes how we might interpret the conduct of parties in a strategic civilain–military relationship, and it is this model that influences the recommendations for usefully and unambiguously amending the Goldwater-Nichols Act, presented a bit later in Chapter 9.

Notes

1. Jeffrey Goldberg, *The Obama Doctrine*, The Atlantic (April 2016), at 76.
2. William H. Rehnquist, The Supreme Court 273 (1987).
3. Linda Greenhouse, *Supreme Court Blocks Guantanamo Tribunals*, N.Y. Times (June 29, 2006), available at http://www.nytimes.com/2006/06/29/washington/29cnd-scotus.html?_r=0 (discussing Hamdan v. Rumsfeld).
4. *Nixon Loses Ruling in Wiretapping Case*, N.Y. Times (June 23, 1981), available at http://www.nytimes.com/1981/06/23/us/nixon-loses-ruling-in-wiretapping-case.html (discussing Kissinger v. Halperin, 452 U.S. 713 (1981). The lower appellate court opinion, relying in part on *Youngstown*'s analysis, that the Supreme Court affirmed with its 4–4 decision is at 606 F. 2d 1192 (1979)).
5. Youngstown Sheet & Tube Co. v. Sawyer, 343 U.S. 579, 634.
6. *Id.* at 635.
7. *Id.* at 637.
8. *Id.* at 638.

CHAPTER 9

Exhibit B: When Fidelity and Frankness Conflict

Loyalty and fidelity and among the more dignified, hallowed traits society cherishes among its soldiers. They are nurtured and encouraged because they fuel other primary martial goods like courage and self-sacrifice. Loyalty to one's unit, to one's brothers-in-arms, is a paramount expectation threading through military indoctrination and training. Shakespeare wrote of it: *We few, we happy few, we band of brothers;/For he today that sheds his blood with me/Shall be my brother.*[1] Attributed by the Bard to twenty-seven-year-old English King Henry V on the eve of the Battle of Agincourt in 1415, his call to glory and forging of strong, insufferable bonds between his soldiers would indeed have been appropriate, for the outnumbered English infantry would need courage and willingness to sacrifice themselves for their brothers-in-arms as they faced down French cavalry, and where by the end of the battle the "dead undoubtedly lay thick" on the field in mounds "big and hideous."[2] Journalist Sebastian Junger, studying up close the infantrymen atop a lonely but battle-scarred mountain outpost in Afghanistan, that these "men form friendships that... contain much of the devotion and intensity of a romance... [it is a] world in which human relations are entirely governed by whether you can trust the other person with your life."[3] Psychologist (and Army Ranger) Dave Grossman highlighted these bonds as primary causes for stress, anxiety, and guilt among soldiers—"[t]his bonding is so intense that it is fear of failing these comrades that preoccupies most combatants... [t]he guilt and trauma associated with failing to fully

D. Maurer, *Crisis, Agency, and Law in US Civil-Military Relations*,
DOI 10.1007/978-3-319-53526-5_9

support men who are bonded with friendship and camaraderie on this magnitude is profoundly intense."[4]

On a larger scale, fidelity to one's mission, to one's nation, and to its Constitution is embedded in the oaths of office that new Lieutenants swear upon receiving their commission as officers.[5] It is toward "good faith and allegiance" to the Constitution—and its elevation of civilian authority over military expertise—that uniformed service members ultimately devote their professional activities. It is a loyalty and fidelity MacArthur famously extolled in his "farewell speech" to West Point's Corps of Cadets in 1962:

> The soldier, above all other men, is required to practice the greatest act of religious training - sacrifice. In battle and in the face of danger and death, he discloses those divine attributes which his Maker gave when he created man in his own image. No physical courage and no brute instinct can take the place of the Divine help which alone can sustain him. However horrible the incidents of war may be, the soldier who is called upon to offer and to give his life for his country, is the noblest development of mankind.[6]

The rules of professional responsibility that bind lawyers and guide their conduct relative to their client principals also stress loyalty and fidelity, though far more prosaic and less publically revered as sacred. As courts of law have said:

> One of the cardinal principles confronting every attorney in the representation of a client is the requirement of complete loyalty and service in good faith to the best of his ability. In a criminal case the client is entitled to a fair trial, but not a perfect one. These are fundamental requirements of due process under the Fourteenth Amendment . . . [this] suggest[s] that an attorney should have no conflict of interest and that he must devote his full and faithful efforts toward the defense of his client.[7]

And:

> [A lawyer's] fiduciary duty is of the highest order and he must not represent interests adverse to those of the client . . . he is not permitted to take advantage of his position or superior knowledge to impose upon the client; nor to conceal facts or law, nor in any way deceive him without being held responsible therefor.[8]

Rules, derived from these canons of legal ethics, impart a default presumption that the client—the principal—is correct, at least in terms of the principal's strategic goals or motive. The principal chooses the target and decides to shoot it; the agent helps the principal choose the right weapon, right distance, and the right timing.

> The professional judgment of a lawyer should be exercised, within the bounds of the law, solely for the benefit of his client and free of compromising influences and loyalties. Neither his personal interests, the interests of other clients, nor the desires of third persons should be permitted to dilute his loyalty to his client.[9]

As an example, a lawyer might breach her duty of loyalty to her client when she acquires a large financial interest in the company she represents, and whose financial well-being is at stake in the very litigation she is empowered to manage on behalf of the company. Her zealous, candid, representation of the client company may be jeopardized by her own newly acquired economic interests—she may be disposed toward a lucrative settlement offer or merger that increases her own personal wealth, but poses a major disadvantage to the company's stated policy or strategy. As a result of her conflict, she risks twisting her expert advice, diluting her professional independence to her client in a way that maximizes her own advantages, not for the sole benefit of her client. Similarly, a lawyer who represents two co-defendants in a criminal trial might have his loyalty tested when it becomes clear that the prosecutor could offer a meaningful deal to *one* of his clients provided that defendant turns on the co-conspirator—his *other* client—and testifies against him. Finally, outside forces—for example, public expressions by politically elected leaders favoring swift and harsh justice for detained suspects in a well-known murder investigation—risk swaying the independent calculation and professional judgment of law enforcement or prosecutors in a way that frustrates due process and evidentiary limitations.

Since we are borrowing concepts of legal agency theory's fiduciary duties and applying them to relationships between civilian political leadership and their military agents, another useful source of explanation comes from rules governing *military* lawyers. Military lawyers (unless they are assigned as a defense counsel in a court-martial) represent and advocate for the interests and objectives of the service *as a whole*, through the offices of the chain of commanders whom they advise. A staff judge advocate, usually a colonel, is the senior legal advisor to the division commander, his staff, and the subordinate brigade and battalion and company commanders, on a host of operational law, military justice, and administrative policy questions. He is not, however, their personal legal counsel, much like a corporation's general counsel's office provides legal advice and support for management in its role a collective body of managers, not as personal counsel to the individuals themselves. In this context, each of the armed services has published its own guide for the professional conduct of its uniformed agent lawyers, and they—just like the civilian canons—stress loyalty and fidelity to the "client."

Under the Army's Rules of Professional Conduct for Lawyers, for instance, lawyers are reminded that:

> [w]hen the officers, employees, or members of the Army make decisions for the Army, the decisions ordinarily must be accepted even if their utility or prudence is doubtful. Decisions concerning policy... including ones entailing serious risk, are not as such in the lawyer's province.[10]

Where loyalty to one's principal is clouded by the ambiguous nature of the principal's identity—as an individual or organizational entity—and the agent reasonably believes that the principal's conduct or decision will subject the organization to harm, the Rules permit a range of responses requiring the agent's discretionary judgment. For example, in order to "proceed as is reasonably necessary in the best interest of the Army," the Army's Rules suggest that the lawyer consider the "seriousness of the violation and its consequences, the scope and nature of the representation, the responsibility...and the apparent motivation of the person involved... and any other relevant considerations."[11] Because the client is the *Army itself*, the Rules warn, any preventive or reactive measure the lawyer takes "shall be designed to minimize disruption of the Army and the risk of revealing information relating to the representation to persons outside the Army."[12]

Candor is the other half of this coin. Candor—frank and honest communication—results when both parties feel assured that confidences and necessary secrets are preserved and kept concealed. The client should feel completely free to disclose as much or as little to the agent attorney as he deems necessary to permit the attorney reasonable freedom and independence to carry on legal work for him. When a lawyer promises, and holds true to that promise by remaining loyal to the client's wishes and goals, that the client's personal confidences and secrets will be held "inviolate," the client's interests are advanced by his full disclosure. The lawyer, in an effort to put the client in a position to make the most fully informed decision, will be able to render honest, forthcoming assessments of the legal station that client finds himself in, or might yet if the client pursues his intended goal. Without rules shielding personal confidences about subjects or facts that—if released or shared with others might be embarrassing or hurtful to the client—candor between the two parties is incomplete, narrow, and limited, and the objectives of the principal are at risk of being thwarted or frustrated.

While intimately related, candor and loyalty can work at cross-purposes, and put the agent and principal in jeopardy. An attorney's purposeful disclosure of information about her client or client's legal position without the client's informed consent—say, to a newspaper or other media outlet—with the intent of "shaping" the public's image of the client, or to advance the attorney's attractiveness to other potential future clients is one manifestation of that conflict in ethical canons. It is not surprising, then, that lawyers are also governed by rules in their "transactions with *persons other than* clients"—that is, being truthful in statements to others. One rule states:

In the course of representing a client a lawyer shall not knowingly:

(a) Make a false statement of material fact or law to a third person; or
(b) Fail to disclose a material fact when disclosure is necessary to avoid assisting a criminal or fraudulent act by a client, unless disclosure is [otherwise] prohibited.[13]

In the comments to this model rule, which has been adopted universally by individual state laws and regulations governing licensed attorneys, it is made clear that this kind of agent has an affirmative duty to react to a lie, misrepresentation, or fraud perpetrated by their client. That reaction can come in the form of "withdrawing from representation," or to "disaffirm and opinion, document, or affirmation" that has been published or produced by the client. The comments also advise lawyers that, in "extreme cases," a lawyer may be required to "disclose information relating to the representation [or their client] to avoid being deemed to have assisted the client's crime or fraud."[14]

Another rule governs the "candor toward tribunals," where *tribunal* means any neutral forum that is making a decision that will affect the procedural or substantive rights, property, or interests of the attorney's client—whether it be a court of law, administrative agency, arbitrator, or legislative body.[15] This rule prohibits lawyers from making false statements of fact or law to that tribunal, and prohibits them from *failing to correct* such false statements. It also imposes an affirmative duty to present to that tribunal controlling legal authority that the lawyer knows to be adverse to her client's interests or position (assuming the opposing counsel does not offer it first). Perhaps most importantly, because following the prescription *directly* counters their own client, lawyers who know that their client "intends to engage, is engaging, or has engaged in criminal or fraudulent conduct related to the proceeding shall take reasonable remedial measures, including, if necessary, disclosure to the tribunal."[16]

The intent behind the rule is to protect the integrity of the process—a laudable goal that reinforces predictability of the legal system and the trustworthiness of the players within that system. But friction with other rules, like representing the client with "persuasive force" and maintaining the client's confidences and secrets in order to assure them of the agent's loyalty, can spark turmoil that leads to "extreme deterioration of the client-lawyer relationship."[17]

It is also not surprising, then, given what we know of strategic military and civilian elites—how they relate to one another and what they believe to be their scope of responsibility—that this dual duty of loyalty and candor often makes fateful appearances in fractious civilian-military relations. One famous episode in which the candor and loyalty of military agents toward their civilian principals were publically on display, and seemingly in direct hostility, was the so-called "Revolt of the Admirals."

Revolt of the Admirals

Anticipating massive budget cuts after World War II, and in retaliation for the Defense Department's cancellation of the first "super carrier," eight Navy admirals (including the Chief of Naval Operations) publically testified before Congress in 1949.[18] With extraordinary *candor*, they asserted that the Secretary of Defense, colluding with the Air Force, was systematically dismantling the capabilities of the Navy, diminishing its role relative to the other Services. Moreover, the admirals accused the Secretary of implicitly lying to the public, to Congress, and to the President about the Air Force's priority procurement of a new bomber, inflating its capabilities and shrinking its estimated cost.

Their candor before Congress was not rewarded. When it was time for Chairman of the Joint Chiefs of Staff, General Omar Bradley, to testify that October, he lashed back at his Navy comrades, accusing them of "open rebellion against the civilian control."[19] Nearly all of the admirals involved were forced to resign or retired in the immediate aftermath.[20]

Under Feaver's view of agency, such testimony (an episode of "strategic interaction" in his terms) would be characterized as unproductive "shirking" that could reasonably be "punished" by the civilian leadership.[21] Janowitz, however, might have argued that the admirals were merely behaving as an organized pressure group in the face of external threats to their institution and traditions, and in the absence of any specific legal bar in doing so. Under Huntington's theory, in contrast, the Navy was merely caught between its view of the "functional imperative" (threats to national security) and a "societal imperative" that included a defense establishment in need of post-war downsizing and reorganization in light of new technological capabilities. Under Cohen, it might be reasonable to ask whether the Secretary of Defense had stepped too much into the lane of professional naval expertise, thereby unreasonably stretching the "unequal dialogue" beyond rational limits, and giving the admirals a valid cause of action to bring before Congress. None of these theoretical perspectives on civil-military relations provide any criteria for objectively determining a diagnosis—whether this historic, and very public, confrontation was an unhealthy civil-military conflict, as General Bradley believed.

From the norms gleaned from principal–agent codes of professional responsibility, like the *Model Rules*, this uncertainty becomes far more resolved. First, in order to apply concepts like authority and scope, and to identify the agent and principal, analysis is helped by establishing the fundamental *context* of the episode, rather than assess the action-reaction in a vacuum. Here, the admirals first argued within the Department and sought to change the Navy's policy (and the Secretary's preferences) through internal procedures. When those failed to change course, the senior uniformed leaders of the Navy went to Congress—which has the Constitutional power of funding the Services—to, in effect, complain that the civilian leaders within the Executive Branch were failing in their duties to maintain a well-resourced military capability, thereby degrading the nation's ability to defend itself. This was not a case of unambiguous insubordination or disrespect aimed at a particular official; no order was disobeyed or ignored; no *coup* was planned.

Reviewing this "revolt" now seems to raise the prospect of the so-called Agency Problem which arises when agents are not easily and directly supervised by their principals, and those agents choose to act in a way that dissents from the principals' policy or guidance because they perceive a conflict between their desires or goals and those of their principal.[22] The admirals' candid testimony suggested that the flexing of their *moral* agency, in contravention to the implied or expressed terms of their actual authority, was the fuel animating that strategic civil-military conflict.[23] It was a case of candor against loyalty. In James Burks' terms, they exercised "responsible disobedience."[24] The officers' choice to object to superior civilian authority, and do so publically in front of another party (Congress), violated the civilian *expectation* of loyalty and subordination. But from the perspective of the agents themselves, it was consistent with their oath of office and fulfilled their superior moral obligations to support their *institution* rather than salute and quietly obey the political leadership in the Executive Branch.[25]

From a basic jurisprudential agency framework, the admirals worked for the Department of the Navy, and the Secretary of Defense, and ultimately the President as Commander-in-Chief, by applying their specialized experience and knowledge on behalf of the guiding interests and objectives of the Administration—their principal. On the other hand, the oath they swore was to defend the Constitution, not a particular political party that happened to be elected to govern, or the civilians appointed to upper management by the elected officials. Therefore, the admirals could justify seeking redress from the branch of government that ostensibly represented the public, held the purse, and which served as a check on an Executive they viewed as engaging in conduct that was fraudulent and not in the best interests of the defense establishment as a whole. In this way, they would be acting just a lawyer would when confronted by his client's deliberate fraud or criminality. He would (or could) transfer his fiduciary loyalty to the system—the professional of law and the courts of which he is a member—to protect its integrity over the interests of the client and report it to the appropriate tribunal.

*****

In cases where employees "exercise substantial discretion and are not subject to close supervision" by their employer when performing "managerial, supervisory, professional, or similar highly skilled work responsibilities," the law holds these employees to be in special positions of "trust and confidence."[26] Having the special trust and confidence of their employers, because they have such large discretion and such little oversight, these employees have special fiduciary duties, including that of loyalty. Which is to say that they are—for all intents and purposes—*agents* of their principal.[27] But what happens when the *principal* is unsure of his *agent's* loyalty and candor? In other words, what happens when the principal lacks full trust and confidence in her agent? What measures of "self-help" can the employer-principal engage in, besides summarily firing that employee? To continue with our analogy, strategic military leaders—as agents—are granted extraordinary amounts of discretion and authority to manage the technical aspects of their commands, from personnel assignments and promotions to tactical maneuvers and battlefield decisions, with little direct oversight from the civilian political authority (often far from the field) that granted that discretion and who is ultimately responsible for the course of conduct. Provided that the principal does not presumptively adopt his own agents' scope of responsibility, as Jefferson Davis often did, what self-help measures would such civilian principals rely on when uncertain of their military agent's competence, adherence to their scope of responsibility, candor, or loyalty? Earlier, we saw how Truman dealt with MacArthur and how Obama reacted to McChrystal. But relieving the offending military commander is far from the only self-help remedy that these strategic civilian principals entertain.

Lincoln's Spy

General U.S. Grant was never expected to make much of himself. Unlike George McClellan, Robert E. Lee, and Jefferson Davis, and a host of other Civil War luminaries, Grant lacked the presumed pedigree and personality of a man destined to command large field armies and sway the course of history. Unlike McClellan, he was not a "natural patronizer," and did not consider himself superior to *any*body, let alone *every*body.[28] Grant was probably an alcoholic,[29] introverted, and—outside of the Army—lacked any semblance of professional success. As a young man, he was educated enough (but just barely) to be appointed to a vacancy at the United States Military Academy at West Point, a position his father applied for on his behalf, having been long-time friends with the Congressman from Ohio and from whom the appointment was sought. While a cadet, he admitted that he "did not take hold of my studies with avidity, in fact I rarely ever read over a lesson the second time during my entire cadetship."[30] He did not seem to enjoy his time at the Academy, where five long years seemed to pass for every year on the calendar,[31] and even hoped that a bill, then working its way through Congress, intended to abolish the school, would lead to a soft landing and immediate discharge before he graduated.[32]

As the bill did not pass, of course, Grant began to see himself as perhaps —at most—returning to the Academy to teach mathematics, the one subject he enjoyed. The Mexican War, though, intervened after he graduated, and he served there as an infantry officer, earning a fair reputation for gallantry, and getting to know personally or through reputation many of the officers of the Regular Army, most of whom would later serve in command on both sides during the Civil War. After the war and short assignments in New York and Detroit, and several more years on the frontier—serving in California and the Oregon Territory—he began to fear he could not afford to support his growing family (married, with two children), so he resigned his commission. His resignation, prompted primarily by lousy pay and low chance of promotion, was also—many scholars suggest—hastened by a reputation for drinking to excess, which evidently led to a reprimand from his commanding officer (a point he fails, understandably, to mention in his own Memoirs).[33]

Taking off his uniform, Grant returned to his wife and children outside St. Louis in 1854, seven years before the outbreak of the Rebellion in the South. His agricultural venture was not a success, and he would often find himself resorting to side jobs, as he would with "cord of wood on a wagon and tak[ing] it to the city for sale." He would later come down with "fever and ague" (probably Malaria)—laying him low and underemployed for a year.[34] In 1858, he gave in, selling off his property after four years of toil. He then bought into a partnership in a real estate business with his wife's cousin, but this too proved slow-going and unprosperous.[35] He would move onto one other venture, moving back to Illinois, and serving as a clerk in a brothers' leather store in Galena. It was there, at the beginning of the Civil War, that he found (again) his true calling and returned to the Army, first in charge of mustering new volunteer units into state service on behalf of the governor, and later as a commander of the 21st Illinois Infantry regiment, a rag-tag, undisciplined unit which needed some backbone of experience with the old Regular Army, which Grant of course had in abundance. The unit refused to take the field with the colonel they had elected, but soon found themselves willfully subordinated to the discipline Grant began to impose and expect.[36] This would be the first of his commands, arching their way up to eventually, within four years, to the command of the *all* Union armies as General-in-Chief, and later taking the surrender of the Robert E. Lee in Virginia, and, eventually, the White House for two terms.

A West Pointer with wartime practice south of the border, and therefore credentialed as any at the time to command men in combat, Grant was also known as a "silent and inarticulate man; a man who normally did not confide his thoughts to others, yet a man who seldom if ever hurried towards a conclusion . . . he seems to have been typically non-academic; thinking in facts and not in theories; totally oblivious to his own genius; always willing to listen to others to trust in others when he believed in them, but seldom if ever to be led by them."[37] He still carried himself as a simple and modest soldier, favoring plain unadorned uniforms without the accoutrements attending to his rank and station.[38] Yet, he was remarkably and undeniably competent. And his competence—despite taking and accepting painfully huge numbers of casualties—fueled the esteem with which most troops and commanders held him. It also fueled the confidence of those politicians, President Lincoln first among them, from whom he received a wide leash and which distinguished him from so many other senior, more experienced, Union generals.[39] But it was his competence and growing fame that would lead to political concern, and the famous introduction of an Administration "spy" into General Grant's headquarters.

In early 1863, along the wet Mississippi River valley, Grant's forces were slowly thumping themselves against Confederate strongholds, including the city garrison and railroads of Vicksburg—a lynchpin to the Union's need to open the mighty river, constricting the South's economic lifeline, and tightening a noose around the Confederacy's eastern half.[40] His 45,000 men, however, were weakened by typhoid and dysentery, and the mud flats and numerous bayous along the river impeded the flanking marches he needed to make. He began to make plans that would rely on a joint Navy-Army task force to scurry artillery and other war materiel past the Vicksburg defenses of batteries along the river to points south of the city, then have his army move south along the curvy west bank, rendezvous with the ferrying flotilla, and cross over to the east side, permitting it to march northeast toward Jackson, Mississippi (to the east of Vicksburg), then about-face and head west to the fortified city where he would make a second attempt to capture it by siege.[41]

Fellow generals, and some political leaders and pundits in Washington, were skeptical of his ability to take the city, and in large part resorted to rumor-mongering and gossip to undermine the general's credibility and the Administration's confidence—focusing on Grant's supposed "intemperance" with alcohol and his reported state of universal intoxication during battles. This would not do for a commanding general whose reputation for success, lack of dithering about, and absence of political grandstanding, was catching the eye and ear of President Lincoln. Lincoln liked the homespun, modest, Grant and appreciated his valor and effectiveness. Nevertheless, he wanted assure himself and others that Grant, perhaps despite personal weaknesses, could be the Union's long-sought after Wellington or Washington. Lincoln, through his Secretary of War, Edwin Stanton, dispatched the former managing editor of the New York *Tribune*, Charles A. Dana, now employed as Assistant Secretary of War and the Administration's go-to "troubleshooter."[42] Stanton gave Dana an unusual mission. He would travel to the Western Theater, ostensibly as a Special Commissioner to investigate and inspect the Army's paymaster service, but would, actually, observe Grant's command—of his Army and of himself—and report regularly back to Stanton and Lincoln. His task was to "settle their minds as to Grant, about whom at that time there were many doubts, and against whom there was some complaint."[43]

From a tent near Grant's, surrounded by magnolias, oaks, and shaded by cypress and cottonwood trees around the fertile plantations of Milliken's Bend, Dana was given immediate and total access to the General and his small staff, and an insider's view of the unfolding plan to take Vicksburg that would leave a modern-day embedded journalist stomping mad with jealously. Grant, it is unclear how, knew of Dana's real purpose from the beginning, and wisely kept him close at hand and intimately abreast of the Army's efforts. He need not have worried (if he did), however. Dana's daily dispatches back to Washington revealed a sober commander, in control of himself and his Army, and steadfastly advancing his plans and forces toward his objective of Vicksburg. Dana's independent observations were crucial to convincing the president and secretary of war that Grant was as competent, and as worthy of their confidence, as they had hoped. With such an immediate and detailed accounting of Grant's plan to take Vicksburg, Lincoln was able to remark that the campaign (even before it was successful) was "one of the most brilliant in the world." Months later, after the victory at Vicksburg (and simultaneous Union victory at Gettysburg in Pennsylvania) revealed that the war had begun to look winnable, he would write to his now-favorite general that any past misgivings and concern over Grant's proposals were unwarranted. "You were right, and I was wrong," Lincoln unashamedly conceded.[44]

*****

The Admirals' Revolt and Lincoln's spying on Grant are well-known episodes of civil-military tension that offer us surprising, if less well-known, lessons. They both reveal, when looked at through the prism of jurisprudential agency concepts like loyalty and candor, ways in which to help those parties (and the public watching them) more fairly diagnose that tension as either healthy or unhealthy, functional or pathological. It works just as it would for lawyers, clients, judges, and the public using the same concepts to identify fractious and broken attorney–client relationships.

On the surface, the Admirals' complaint looked like unabashed institutional self-interest and Service parochialism. However, the admirals viewed their effort as a *remedial* measure to correct the Navy civilian leadership's misinformation campaign and its unreasonable breach of the normal civilian scope of authority. In response that "fraud," and breach, the admirals appeared to shift the identity of their *principal* to Congress, which granted them a venue to express their professional views candidly and apolitically. If the parties had been working from commonly accepted fiduciary duties, the risk of the Agency Problem may have been abated. Even if such duties would not have *prevented* the so-called "revolt," all parties and the public would have possessed a common frame and lexicon by which to judge the actions of the admirals and the political leadership. Provided that it was reasonable to recast Congress as the relevant principal under these circumstances, and provided that the admirals' testimony was accurate, material, and within their scope of expertise, the jurisprudential agency view of this civil-military tension looks much less like "open rebellion."

Lincoln's assignment of Charles Dana inside the camp of General Grant is still more evidence that American strategic civil-military relationships can be understood as fiduciary ties between a principal and his agent. It also evidence that remedies available to those principals can shed light on whether certain choices *politicians* make in response to wayward *generals* is symptomatic of a diseased relationship, or a sign of good health instead. Lincoln's choice looks exactly like a concerned principal exercising a clever self-help remedy to gauge whether his investment in a particular employee—in whom much "trust and confidence" has been placed—should be deeper, or whether he should cut his losses and bow to the recommendations of his learned political advisors. It also depicts how candor (or Lincoln's lack of it in attempting to hide Dana's true mission from Grant) interacts with the other fiduciary duty of loyalty. In this case, the former was used to test the latter. Fortunately for both the president and General Grant, loyalty and competence were revealed to be in fully working order. Lincoln was not at risk of being deceived by Grant: He had no compromising influences or split loyalties and was offering his full and faithful effort. But, even if Lincoln had been disappointed in what Dana observed, his secret undercover detective work would still have signaled the cardinal relevance of these fiduciary traits to parties in the strategic civil-military relationship.

Given this strong analogy, and given how important these virtues, traits, and duties seem to be in how strategic elites conform themselves, it seems worth thinking through whether we can use them more deliberately and directly to measure—and to diagnose—these relationships when they seem troubled. The next chapter looks back at the famous Goldwater-Nichols Act, described earlier, to see if it proves a possible statutory host to these duties.

Notes

1. William Shakespeare, *Henry V*, Act IV, scene iii.
2. John Keegan, The Face of Battle 107 (1978).
3. Sebastian Junger, War 155, 234 (2011).
4. Lieutenant Colonel Dave Grossman, On Killing: The Psychological Cost of Learning to Kill in War and Society 90 (1996).
5. This is the same message that Secretary of Defense Ashton Carter imparted to graduates of the U.S. Naval Academy is 2016 ("you not only receive a degree that represents years of studying, striving - you take an oath to a life of service and sacrifice in the finest fighting force the world has ever known. Indeed, you've chosen one of the noblest professions there is - a profession in which you'll be waking up every day to help defend this country and make a better world"), http://www.defense.gov/News/Speeches/Speech-View/Article/783891/remarks-at-us-naval-academy-commencement.
6. Available at http://www.nationalcenter.org/MacArthurFarewell.html.

7. Johns v. Smyth, 176 F. Supp. 949, 952 (E.D. V a. 1959), modified, United States ex rel. Wilkins v. Banmiller, 205 F. Supp. 123, 128 n.5 (E.D. Pa. 1962), aff'd, 325 F.2d 514 (3d Cir. 1963), cert. denied, 379 U.S. 847, 13 L. Ed. 2d 51, 85 S.Ct.87 (1964).
8. Smoot v. Lund, 13 Utah 2d 168, 172, 369 P.2d 933, 936 (1962).
9. American Bar Association (ABA) Model Code of Professional Responsibility (as amended 1980), Canon 5, available at http://www.americanbar.org/content/dam/aba/migrated/cpr/mrpc/mcpr.authcheckdam.pdf.
10. Army Rugulation 27–26 *(Rules of Professional Conduct for Lawyers)*, at R. 1.13 cmt.
11. *Id.* at R. 1.13(*c*).
12. *Id.*
13. SUSAN MARTYN, ET AL., THE LAW GOVERNING LAWYERS 75 (2014) (quoting ABA Model Rules of Professional Conduct, Rule 4.1).
14. *Id.* at 75–76.
15. *Id.* at 11 (quoting Rule 1.0(m)).
16. *Id.* at 64 (quoting Rule 3.3(b)).
17. *Id.* at 67.
18. The author wishes to thank Lieutenant General H.R. McMaster for this reference.
19. Keith D. McFarland, *The 1949 Revolt of the Admirals*, PARAMETERS, June 1981, at 53, 60.
20. *Id.* at 61.
21. Feaver applied his theory to testimony from General Colin Powell and General Norman Schwarzkopf to the Senate Armed Services Committee in 1993. By recommending what amounted to the "Don't Ask, Don't Tell" compromise, they implicitly argued against President Clinton's proposal to end the ban on allowing "open" homosexuals to serve, they engaged in unhealthy "shirking." FEAVER, ARMED SERVANTS, at 202–03; *see* Eric Schmitt, *Compromise on Military Gay Ban Gaining Support Among Senators*, N.Y. TIMES, May 12, 1993, http://www.nytimes.com/1993/05/12/us/compromise-on-military-gay-ban-gaining-support-among-senators.html. The author thanks David E. Johnson for pointing out this example.
22. Eisenhardt, *Agency Theory: An Assessment and Review, supra* note 425, at 58 (describing the "agency problem"). Feaver addresses this as an example of the "moral hazard problem" in principal–agent dynamics, suggesting that the principal should "shape the relationship so as to ensure that his employees [agents] are carrying out his wishes." FEAVER, ARMED SERVANTS, at 55.
23. James Burk, *Responsible Obedience by Military Professionals: the Discretion to do What is Wrong*, at 151–54.
24. *Id.; see also* Owens, *What Military Officers Need to Know About Civil-Military Relations*, at 74 ("officers have an obligation to make their case

as strongly as possible but do not have the right to "insist" that their advice be accepted. However, there must be a 'calculus of dissent'").

25. Milburn, *Breaking Ranks: Dissent and the Military Professional*, at 101. *But see* Paul Yingling, *Breaking Ranks?*, Small Wars J. (Sept. 30, 2010), http://smallwarsjournal.com/jrnl/art/breaking-ranks (arguing that the officer's oath precludes a conscience-based dissent to policy that is post-deliberative). In some cases, strategic military officers may believe that obeying quietly actually advances their long-term goals to protect their institution, thereby justifying what amounts to silence and a lack of candor before Congress. *See, e.g.*, McMaster, Dereliction of Duty, at 327–28, 330–31 (discussing his view that the JCS collectively failed to render proper advice or to "challenge the direction of the administration's military policy" to Congress, leading to short-term benefits for each individual service).
26. Deborah A. DeMott, *Relationships of Trust and Confidence in the Workplace*, 100 Cornell L. Rev. 1255, 1272 (2015).
27. Restatement of Emp'T law § 8.01(a) (2015).
28. T. Harry Williams, Lincoln and his Generals 23 (1952).
29. James M. McPherson, Battle Cry of Freedom 588–89 (1988).
30. Ulysses S. Grant, Personal Memoirs of U.S. Grant 14 (2001).
31. *Id.* at 16.
32. *Id.* at 15.
33. *Id.* at 106, note 1; see also James M. McPherson, Tried By War: Abraham Lincoln as Commander in Chief 72 (2008).
34. Ulysses S. Grant, Personal Memoirs of U.S. Grant, at 106.
35. J.F.C. Fuller, The Generalship of Ulysses S. Grant 72 (1929).
36. Grant, Personal Memoirs, at 123–24; and see Fuller, The Generalship of Ulysses S. Grant, at 72–73.
37. J.F.C. Fuller, The Generalship of Ulysses S. Grant ix (1929).
38. Doris Kearns-Goodwin, Team of Rivals: the Political Genius of Abraham Lincoln 692 (2005); McPherson, Battle Cry of Freedom, 590.
39. One historian called this the "most effective political-military relationship in American history." Matthew Moten, Presidents & Their Generals 153 (2014); see also T. Harry Williams, Lincoln and his Generals 11 (1952) (Lincoln "was willing to discard his judgement of what was good strategy and take the opinion of any general whom he considered able. He was willing to yield power to direct strategic operations to any general who could demonstrate that he was competent to frame and execute strategy").
40. Grant, Personal Memoirs, at 219–20.
41. McPherson, Battle Cry of Freedom, at 588; Grant, Personal Memoirs, at 240.
42. McPherson, Tried By War, at 169.

43. Charles A. Dana, Recollections of the Civil War 20–22 (1898); T. Harry Williams, Lincoln and his Generals, at 222–23; Goodwin, Team of Rivals, at 528–29.
44. Letter to Ulysses S. Grant, July 13, 1863, in Lincoln on War (Harold Holzer ed.) 198 (2011); Goodwin, Team of Rivals, at 528, 534.

CHAPTER 10

Exhibit C: Amending the Goldwater-Nichols Act

Despite Congress's attempt with the Goldwater-Nichols Act to restructure and improve the Department of Defense, the Act is a missed opportunity to provide a "quality assurance/quality control" mechanism for those relationships. While the Act provides *venues* for expressing candid military advice, and expands the influence of some participants, it does not include any standard or norm for how that relationship should or could be expressed in good faith under particular but foreseeable circumstances. It fails in this regard because there is no singular framework on which to create such norms and expectations. It fails because it does not overtly adopt an agency lens.

There are three pieces of evidence pointing toward a conclusion that amending the Act is a reasonable method by which to establish criteria for assessing the health of these relationships in context. First, the Act already portrays, implicitly, these relationships in agency terms, as we saw in Chapter 2. Second, the participants—from Robert Gates to Barrack Obama, and from Stanley McChrystal to Martin Dempsey—already view themselves in this principal–agent dynamic. Third, American military history (McClellan's megalomania, Lincoln's "spying" on Grant, MacArthur's relief by Truman, the "Revolt of the Admirals") is replete with examples of civil-military crises unfolding in terms, and for reasons, that can be described by jurisprudential agency. Adding normative language to the provisions of this Act that already detail roles and organizational responsibilities is a relatively straightforward exercise.

D. Maurer, *Crisis, Agency, and Law in US Civil-Military Relations*,
DOI 10.1007/978-3-319-53526-5_10

Such a diagnostic device sidesteps the disadvantages of other potential sources of criteria. Where military doctrine vaguely but repeatedly reveres constitutional principles of military subordination, and aim "down and in," this code provision aims "up and out" and captures the nuanced dynamic between strategic policy-makers of national security where the line of demarcation between the civilian "ends" and the military "means" is often blurred. Where regulations narrowly prohibit unethical behaviors that place personal ambition and gain above public interests, a code provision targets the continual relationship and the natural tensions that form between these participants when they all believe they are acting ethically, within legal bounds, and in the best interest of the country. Finally, it expresses what many current and former participants in this relationship already intrinsically practice and believe. Even if such criteria fail to *definitively* answer whether a particular episode or "strategic interaction"[1] is unhealthy or flawed, jurisprudential agency norms at least establish criteria that all observers could employ as the common language through which to debate it—a feature currently absent in American civil-military relations literature and public discourse.

Example Draft Text of an Amendment

Policy: In enacting these revisions, it is the intent of Congress, consistent with the congressional declaration of policy in section 3 of the Goldwater-Nichols Defense Reorganization Act of 1986 —

(1) to strengthen civilian control over the Department of Defense;
(2) to improve the military advice provided to the President; the National Security Council; the Secretary of Defense; and the Secretaries of the Armed Services;
(3) to increase the transparency of the information, including the purposes, bases, biases, and limits of the information, expressed between civilian leadership and their military advisors;
(4) to recognize the inherent tensions and ambiguities unique to the relationship that exists and evolves between military and civilian leaders responsible for national security policy-making at the strategic level;
(5) to articulate generic expectations and norms of the civil-military relationship as manifested by the senior civilian and military leaders inside the Department of Defense, including the Office of the

Secretary of Defense, the Joint Chiefs of Staff, the Joint Staff, the Departments of the Army, Navy, and Air Force, and the unified and specified combatant commands;

(6) and to provide a consistent and universal set of criteria by which the American public and participants in the strategic civil-military relationships may infer or adduce the strength and health of those relationships in context.

(7) Violations of these revisions do not create any right or benefit, substantive or procedural, enforceable at law by any person against the United States, its agencies, its officers or employees, or any other person.

[Amended] § 151. Joints Chiefs of Staff: Composition; Functions; Fiduciary Duties

Note: 10 U.S.C. § 151(b) describes the function of the Chairman as the "principal military advisor to the President, The National Security Council, and the Secretary of Defense" and the other members of the Joint Chiefs as "military advisors" to the same. Section 151(c) describes the Chairman's permissive ability to seek the advice of the other members of the Joint Chiefs of Staff and the combatant commanders. Section 151(d) describes the ability of the other members of the Joint Chiefs of Staff to offer advice or a dissenting opinion to the Chairman, the President, the National Security Council, or the Secretary of Defense. Section 151(e) describes the requirement to furnish advice upon request from the President, the Secretary of Defense, or the National Security Council.

(f) in carrying out the functions described in subsections (b), (c), (d), and (e), the Chairman, Vice Chairman, the Chief of Staff of the Army, Chief of Staff of the Air Force, the Chief of Naval Operations, the Commandant of the Marine Corps, and the Chief of the National Guard Bureau shall recognize and abide by the following core principles consistent with their oath of office, and fidelity to the Constitution of the United States:

(1) the relationship between the military officer in the positions listed above and the President of the United States is a fiduciary relationship. In the President's role under Article II of the Constitution as the Commander-in-Chief of the Armed Forces, the President acts as the "principal," relying on the technical expertise, practical experience, and professional judgment of the officers nominated and confirmed as members of the Joint Chiefs of Staff in the execution of the President's constitutional responsibilities and authorities. The individual officer member of the Joint Chiefs of Staff shall act as the agent of the civilian principal, acting in the principal's best interests to the extent that such actions are consistent with the lawful objectives and with the lawful intent of the President.

(2) in fulfilling the expectations of the civilian principal and consistent with the specified advisory functions described in subsection (b), (c), (d), and (e), and in §151(b)(2), § 153 (Chairman: functions), § 154 (Vice Chairman), § 3033(c), (d)(3) and(d) (6) [Chief of Staff of the Army], §5033(c), (d)(3) and (d)(6) [Chief of Naval Operations], § 5043(d), (e)(3) and (e)(6) [Commandant of the Marine Corps], and § 8033(c) and (d)(3) and (d) (6) [Chief of Staff of the Air Force], the military agent:

(A) shall ensure that the agent's scope of responsibility and authority to act on the explicit and implied direction of the President (or other civilian principal relevant under the circumstances) is reasonably clear, unambiguous and transparent to the agent and to third parties;

(B) to the extent that the agent's scope of responsibility and authority to act is ambiguous or apparently inconsistent with earlier direction or guidance from a principal, shall seek clarification from the President (or other civilian principal relevant under the circumstances) before acting in such a manner as to be perceived, or reasonably likely to be perceived by the President (or other civilian principal relevant under the circumstances) as breaching or attempting to breach the agent's authority or expressing a position inconsistent with the policy or proposed policy of the Administration;

(C) shall abide by any lawful restriction imposed by the President (or other civilian principal relevant under the circumstances) on the agent's exercise of independent professional judgment to the extent that it encompasses moral, economic, social, political, or other non-military factors;

(D) shall abide by any lawful restriction imposed by the President (or other civilian principal relevant under the circumstances) on the agent's exercise of independent professional judgment to the extent that the exercise of such judgment communicates the intentions, motivations, constraints, or content of deliberations engaged in by the principal, with or without the agent's knowledge or participation, to third parties;

(E) shall keep the President (or other civilian principal relevant under the circumstances) reasonably informed, promptly comply with reasonable requests for information, and discuss any relevant limitations on the agent's ability to carry out the objectives of the President;

(F) shall explain a matter to the extent reasonably necessary to permit the President (or other civilian principal relevant under the circumstances) to make informed decisions;

(G) if asked by a member of Congress in an official and public forum to offer a professional or personal opinion on a matter the military agent knows or reasonably should know is expected to be withheld in confidence until authorized by the President (or other civilian principal relevant under the circumstances), the agent shall consider whether the public interest, candor toward Congress, and fidelity to Constitution outweigh, under the circumstances, fiduciary duties of confidentiality and loyalty toward the President as Commander in-Chief under the circumstances then known;

(H) if asked by a member of Congress in an official and public forum to offer a professional or personal opinion on matter the officer knows or reasonably should know is contrary to that of his or her political principal and has been tacitly or expressly overridden by a strategy, decision, directive, or order communicated to that officer, the officer shall first presume that his or her opinion is confidential and will not disclose that opinion, or that such an opinion exists, in an official and public forum unless in receipt of express and knowing consent of the principal; if the principal's knowing consent to disclosure is ambiguous or unknown, the agent shall presume no consent has been given;

(I) shall not, consistent with any prohibitions on the disclosure of confidential, secret, or otherwise classified material established under any law, offer to any third party (individual, person, agency, organization, or business entity) a professional or personal opinion on a matter the agent knows or reasonably should know is expected to be withheld in confidence until authorized by the President (or other civilian principal relevant under the circumstances);

(J) may impose the aforementioned duties on any subordinate member of the Armed Forces under circumstances which cast, or are reasonably likely to be interpreted as casting, that military subordinate as an agent in the execution of the President's objectives.

(g) The provisions in (f)(1) and (f)(2) shall apply to all situations in which the military agent knows or reasonably should know under the circumstances that the agent is to perform lawful duties and responsibilities on behalf of a civilian principal appointed by the President.

*****

The aforementioned draft amendment is certainly not intended to be an exhaustive codification of agency-based norms and duties. Nor is it intended to be only applicable to the "choice architects" assigned as members of the Joint Chiefs of Staff. It is easily repeatable, with some modifications, to provisions regulating the specific functions of the Chairman,[2] Vice Chairman,[3] Combatant Commanders,[4] and the senior ranking officers of the Army, Navy, Marine Corps, and Air Force.[5] Likewise, most of it could be adopted by an order or Service regulation to apply to other military "choice architects" positioned to serve as fiduciary agents to civilian principals within the national security establishment. Moreover, to the extent that the draft provision illustrates basic fiduciary duties owed by the military agent, analogous provisions related to the *principal's* role could be added to the Act in sections regulating civilian leadership of the Department of Defense, including the Secretary of Defense[6] and the Service Secretaries.[7] Regardless of how many official job descriptions would be amended to reflect these norms, expectations, and duties, the obvious consequence is the de facto establishment of criteria that may be used by the participants themselves, or the public, to diagnose the health of a strategic civil-military relationship.

*****

Goldwater-Nichols Agency Applied

April-May, 1951
Washington, D.C.

> *I believe that the plan and the policy I have [for countering global communism and China's military effort in support of the North Koreans] offers the greatest hope for not having a third world war.*[8]

As this book opened with short retelling of General MacArthur's ironically triumphant return to the United States after his controversial relief from command, it is now an opportune point to return to that period, just days before his celebration in Chicago, and assess a small slice of his conduct as if a Goldwater-Nichols Act existed (as amended to include fiduciary concepts of Agency described previously).

Though long festering, and itching uncomfortably with untoward remarks to the press about the "web of artificial conditions" that limited his military efforts in a war that was, he said, "without a definite objective," the strategic civil-military crisis finally came to a head.[9] MacArthur's letter to Congressman Joe Martin was the final affront. Yet, without a doubt, he was stunned as much by the *manner* of his relief as by the relief itself. As he described it in his memoirs,

> Since the beginning of time, commanders have been changed, some through whim, some through cause, but never in history was there a more drastic method employed than in my relief—without a hearing, without an opportunity for defense, with no consideration of the past. Up to the moment of my recall, I had been receiving laudatory commendations from the President.[10]

The order recalling him, he would write later, placed him "under duress." He explained, "no office boy, no charwoman, no servant of any sort would have been dismissed with such callous disregard for the ordinary decencies."[11] Strange, given that his grasp of military history should have counseled him that a relief from command in wartime is both rare and critical enough to have no such prescribed set of "ordinary decencies."

With his honor blemished in such a way, did MacArthur breach his duties of fidelity, candor, confidentiality, or scope of responsibility as Truman's agent—after having been so relieved—by accepting Congress' offer to talk to them (and the nation) about his experience? What about his sworn testimony before a combined session of two Senate committees just days later? His "old soldiers never die" speech, considered one of the most famous before Congress of the twentieth century and certainly the most infamous of all by a military officer, certainly touches on his own relief from command and geopolitical decision-making by civilians above his paygrade. As we have seen in earlier chapters, such insouciance with the gospel of civilian control over the military had a history before MacArthur and a history since MacArthur. Former Chairman of the Joint Chiefs of Staff, General Martin Dempsey, offered this bit of counsel in response to recently retired senior generals speaking at the two national party conventions during the 2016 presidential race:

> The military is not a political prize. Politicians should take the advice of senior military leaders but keep them off the stage. The American people should not wonder where their military leaders draw the line between military advice and political preference … as generals, they have an obligation to uphold our apolitical traditions.[12]

One of those generals explained his partisan stance to his audience in a way MacArthur would have understood: “The stakes are enormous. We must not, we could not stand on the sidelines.”[13] Also believing whole-heartedly that the stakes in the Far East were high, and not content with merely fading away into retirement, MacArthur stepped off the sidelines too. Did MacArthur’s candor offer such a prize to anti-Truman Republicans and conservative Democrats, in the form of well-crafted rhetoric and carefully wrought explanations? Did he leave room for others to wonder, or assume, his political preference and thus sharpen the tense disagreement between the nation’s senior military officer and the nation’s commander-in-chief in a time of war?

n the opening moments of his long speech, which “combined pathos with passion, experience with erudition, strategy with philosophy,”[14] MacArthur implied an elevated sense of moral rightness over the administration that had just fired him. He would speak to Congress, he said, from “the highest plane of national interest,” not as an “advocate for any partisan cause,” but only as a humble “fellow American,” who just so happened to be the most informed of participant-observers.[15] “I know war as few other men now living know it,” he said.[16] This is probably true. From his earliest days as an Army Brat living in the desert southwest with his father, Arthur MacArthur (also awarded the Medal of Honor for his courage in the Civil War battle of Missionary Ridge as a teenager), to serving in France in the First World War (where he earned seven Silver Stars for his heroic leadership), to his exploits in the Pacific Theater, to Korea, the man was draped in martial history that he himself helped create if not lead himself. There is a point in his speech where he interrupts his discussion of Asian history and Chinese culture and begins to explain the nuances of tactics and military necessity in that theater. Given the wide arc of Pacific Ocean and land under dominant American control, MacArthur explained that:

> Any predatory attack from Asia must be an amphibious effort. No amphibious force can be successful without control of the sea lanes and the air over those lanes in its avenue of advance. With naval and air supremacy and modest ground elements to defend bases, any major attack from continental Asia toward us or our friends in the Pacific would be doomed to failure. Under such conditions the Pacific no longer represents menacing avenues of approach for a prospective invader—it assumes instead the friendly aspect of a peaceful lake. Our line of defense is a natural one and can be maintained with a minimum of military effort and expense.... The holding of this littoral defense line in the western Pacific is entirely dependent upon holding all segments thereof, for any major breach of that line by an unfriendly power would render vulnerable to determined attack every other major segment. This is a military estimate as to which I have yet to find a military leader who will take exception.[17]

Yet, he did not stop there. Moving beyond mere "military estimates," he not so subtly implied that his former, recent, employment as a field commander beneath the Joint Chiefs of Staff and President Truman, was—to the detriment of his mission in Korea and the United States' authority and reputation more generally—would have been nothing more than advocacy for an unworthy client if it had continued apace without his public objections. Strongly stating that the North Korean invasion of the South was Chinese-led, he argued that Chinese military expansion, manifesting in Korea, made the United Nations' effort on the peninsula into a "new war and an entirely new situation, a situation not contemplated when our forces were [first] committed against the North Korean adversary, a situation which called for new decisions in the diplomatic sphere to permit the realistic adjustment of military strategy." That he had not been allowed to make those "realistic adjustments" by applying naval and air power against Chinese forces directly was evidence he threw in support that no such "new decisions" were being made by those who ought to be making them, tacitly indicting his President for not comprehending that a "new war" had begun. "Such decisions have not been forthcoming," he politely reminded Congress.[18] Civil though it may have sounded, its mere utterance cast aspersions on civil authority.

MacArthur, despite assailing the political administration for ignoring the reality (as he saw it) of the war it asked him to prosecute, considered himself a persecuted professional—attacked by his own side for wanting nothing more than the termination of bloodshed at reasonable (as he calculated it) political cost.

> For entertaining these views, all professionally designed to support our forces committed to Korea and to bring hostilities to an end with the least possible delay and a saving countless American and Allied lives, I have been severely criticized in lay circles . . . despite my understanding that from a military standpoint the above views have been fully shared in the past by practically every military concerned.[19]

Of course, as subsequent testimony before Senate committees and history would later reveal, he had no such universal support among his fellow military strategists.[20]

Though MacArthur disclaimed wisely (though it went without saying given the circumstances) that "everything I say is on my own personal authority, and represents nothing but my own personal views,"[21] it must be asked whether he was in the right to say anything at all at this point. For now, in early May 1951, testifying under oath for three continuous days before a combined session of the Senate Armed Services Committee and the Foreign Relations Committee, he certainly claimed the right to do so. Not only did he answer their probing questions about what advice he had given, in confidence, the White House on the use of military force against China, but he also intimated that not one of them could reasonably second-guess that advice. "I understood the dangers everyday as nobody else, perhaps, understood them,"[22] going on to suggest that the senators should personally visit Korea because only then will they "learn more in forty-eight hours in that atmosphere than you will learn in forty-eight weeks at this distance."[23]

Moreover, he answered a hypothetical question that put himself in the shoes of the President, positing what he would have done if he had the authority: threaten China with an ultimatum, warning her that its concentration of troops at the Yalu river was an act of war, earning an attack from Allied forces from the air to prevent their crossing. "It seems to me," he mused, "that is what common sense would have dictated should have been done."[24] Not stopping with merely condemning the common sense of the superior political authority, which was stalwartly attempting to restrain the spread of violence beyond Korea to avoid entangling with the Soviet Union, MacArthur stated that his unanswered requests were the cause of thousands of predictable and preventable deaths. He exclaimed, "the inertia that exists! There is no policy—there is nothing, I tell you, no plan or anything. . . . This is not war. That is appeasement."[25] It would not be the last time he attacked the Administration with that loaded word in the months to come.

Eventually, the senators came around to asking how he felt he should have responded to political interference with war-waging, or how he believed he ought to present his dissenting views. At that point, he struck a note that would not be shared the majority of senior military officers, even those who tend to comport themselves along the lines described by Cohen as unequal partners. "I believe the theater commander has the responsibility of registering his views as he might see fit, if they are honest views and not in contradiction to any implementing directives that he may have received."[26] Here, his only check on complete candor is honesty—as long as his view reflected the truth, he had carte blanche by virtue of his position. But notice his primary points, for they speak volumes about the General's ultimate Roman stoic self-image.[27] He can and should register his views *as he might see fit*, provided those views are not incongruous with *direct orders.* This short exchange reveals the philosophy animating his conscious choice to sit before Congress. It was within his duty to select both the *forum* and *timing* of his objections, allowing that it could be to the public at large or at a closed hearing in the Capitol or within the West Wing. Moreover, it was for him to do this at any point before, or in the absence of, direct orders that formalized and cemented a policy decision as an action-in-waiting. Therefore, according to his logic, his honest candor could—if he chose—be unrestrained even during sensitive and information-poor deliberative stages of policymaking and strategizing. He held himself accountable to a higher power, beyond that of the Commander-in-Chief he believed to be ignorant, and who was "weakened into a hesitant nervousness indicative of a state of confusion and bewilderment."[28]

> I believe it is in the interest, the public interest, that diverse opinions on any controversial issue shall be fully aired . . . the people are entitled to have the facts, the judgement of the government itself is subject to their opinion and to their control, and in order to exercise that, they are entitled to the truth, the whole truth and nothing but the truth."[29]

This was stirring oratory that would make any proponent of transparent bureaucracies thrilled, but it was clearly assuming that a field commander—vital to military operations and national security but *not* sitting at the apex of legitimate, popularly elected civil government, wielding the entire machinery of government and its grand strategy—is both the archeologist and publicist of that truth, consequences notwithstanding. That view, as articulate as it may have been and consonant with Janowitz's description of the military as public interest group unto itself, was not uncontroverted. General Omar Bradley, then Chairman of the Joint Chiefs of Staff, testified after MacArthur went home to New York City. He resolutely countermanded MacArthur's assertion of duty and his scope of responsibility.

> A field commander very properly estimates his needs from the viewpoint of operations in his own theater or sphere of action... Those responsible for higher direction [like the Joint Chiefs, the Secretaries of State and Defense, and the President] must necessarily base their actions on broader aspects, and on the needs, actual or prospective, of several theaters. The Joint Chiefs of Staff, in view of their global responsibilities and their perspective with respect to the world-wide strategic situation, are in a better position than is any single theater commander to assess the risk of general war.[30]

With that, he condemned MacArthur's substantive views as narrow-headed, parochial, and short-term, even if Mac did have the best interests of *his* troops, mired in the Korean mud, in mind. Because MacArthur knowingly let those views become public, to the consternation of his political principals, General Bradley also implicitly condemned MacArthur's procedural posture—the vocal disagreement, in the media and to Congress, with the ongoing strategizing about the larger war on communism beyond the borders of Korea or even the region of the Far East.

*****

Huntington's objective control theory would have little to add to our ability to judge the appropriateness of MacArthur's testimony. MacArthur, by testifying in his manner, was clearly blending what Huntington called the "functional" and "societal" imperatives. He emphasized to Congress the immediate military threat posed by China's support of North Korea, and so seemed to be demonstrating Huntington's "conservative realism" or the pessimistic planning for the worst case scenario (at least as MacArthur defined it). Also, by stressing that his views were shared by all informed military thinkers, he attempted to establish both the expert nature of, and the "corporateness" of, his opinion, thus enlarging its value and contrasting against the civilian versions of the Korea narrative.

Yet, from General Bradley's perspective, or Truman's, he was not unselfishly performing a service in support of his nation—though, he clearly thought he was. Huntington himself wrote that:

> MacArthur's opposition to the manner in which the government was conducting the Korean War was essentially similar [to the German generals of World War II that politically opposed Hitler's foreign policy]. Both the German officers who joined the resistance to Hitler and General MacArthur forgot that it is not the function of military officers to decide questions of war and peace.[31]

Politics, for MacArthur, was *not* beyond his scope of responsibility or ability, and therefore he swayed into dangerous ground where civilian control of the military was far more relative, ambiguous, or subjective—where the roles, responsibilities, and aptitudes of the senior echelon of political and military leaders fuse.[32] His vocal, public disagreement was a direct renunciation of what Huntington would have called his "executive" function—that is, execute those policy and strategic decisions with the military means allotted to him on behalf of the civilian policy-maker, regardless of personal disagreement. Ultimately, Huntington found MacArthur paradoxical, unable to fit him neatly into any precise bounds of a theory of normal military professionalism that could explain his behavior.

> From the start, MacArthur had been a brilliant soldier but always something more than a soldier: a controversial, ambitious, transcendent figure, too able, too assured, too talented to be confined within the limits of the professional function and responsibility ... [h]is sense of mission and dedication gave rise to a sustained and unbridled optimism which contrasted with the normal professional pessimism. The professional officer exists in a world of grays. MacArthur's universe was one of blacks and whites and loud and clashing colors.[33]

Eliot Cohen's "unequal dialogue" description also seems incapable of judging the health of this relationship or MacArthur's decision to speak to Congress or say what he said. Clearly, since a Third World War was indeed avoided, one can confidently state that Truman's restraint of MacArthur's aggression toward China was the more "prudent" course. Moreover, to the extent that the parties knew or could have suspected that their relative actions were going to be fodder for future debate on the proper degree of civilian authority over military responsibility, Truman's difficult and wildly unpopular decision to fire MacArthur was also a necessary price to pay. On the other hand, given the General's popularity abroad and at home, the vagaries of combat and the ultimate unpredictability of war, one could believe that Truman's choice to assert civilian dominance elevated *that* principle over the potentially more prudent and politically safer choice to yield to MacArthur's war-waging preferences.

Applying jurisprudential agency duties of candor, loyalty, confidence, and scope of responsibility to MacArthur's voluntary contribution to public debate in the halls of Congress, while in uniform and in the immediate wake of his relief, we can argue now in explicit terms—not waiver between less concrete measures. MacArthur's position in Korea is most analogous to that of a modern-day combatant commander, whose duties are described under Goldwater-Nichols Act in 10 U.S.C. section 164. The current statute is quoted as follows, with jurisprudential agency-based amendments italicized.

(b) Responsibilities of Combatant Commanders.—

(1) The commander of a combatant command is responsible to the President and to the Secretary of Defense for the performance of missions assigned to that command by the President or by the Secretary with the approval of the President.

(2) Subject to the direction of the President, the commander of a combatant command—

(A) performs his duties under the authority, direction, and control of the Secretary of Defense; and

(B) is directly responsible to the Secretary for the preparedness of the command to carry out missions assigned to the command.

(c) Command Authority of Combatant Commanders.—

(1) Unless otherwise directed by the President or the Secretary of Defense, the authority, direction, and control of the commander of a combatant command with respect to the commands and forces assigned to that command include the command functions of—

(A) giving authoritative direction to subordinate commands and forces necessary to carry out missions assigned to the command, including authoritative direction over all aspects of military operations, joint training, and logistics;

(B) prescribing the chain of command to the commands and forces within the command;

(C) organizing commands and forces within that command as he considers necessary to carry out missions assigned to the command;

(D) employing forces within that command as he considers necessary to carry out missions assigned to the command;

(E) assigning command functions to subordinate commanders;

(F) coordinating and approving those aspects of administration and support (including control of resources and equipment, internal organization, and training) and discipline necessary to carry out missions assigned to the command; and

(G) exercising the authority with respect to selecting subordinate commanders, selecting combatant command staff, suspending subordinates, and convening courts-martial,

(2)

(A) The Secretary of Defense shall ensure that a commander of a combatant command has sufficient authority, direction, and control over the commands and forces assigned to the command to exercise effective command over those commands and forces. In carrying out this subparagraph, the Secretary shall consult with the Chairman of the Joint Chiefs of Staff.

(B) The Secretary shall periodically review and, after consultation with the Secretaries of the military departments, the Chairman of the Joint Chiefs of Staff, and the commander of the combatant command, assign authority to the commander of the combatant command for those aspects of administration and support that the Secretary considers necessary to carry out missions assigned to the command.

(3) If a commander of a combatant command at any time considers his authority, direction, or control with respect to any of the commands or forces assigned to the command to be insufficient to command effectively, the commander shall promptly inform the Secretary of Defense.

(d) *in carrying out the functions described in subsections (b) and (c), the Combatant Commander shall recognize and abide by the following core principles consistent with their oath of office, and fidelity to the Constitution of the United States:*

(1) the relationship between the military officer in the position listed above and the President of the United States and Secretary of Defense is a fiduciary relationship. In the President's role under Article II of the Constitution as the Commander-in-Chief of the Armed Forces, and through the Secretary of Defense at the President's discretion, the President acts as the "principal," relying on the technical expertise, practical experience, and professional judgment of the officers nominated and confirmed as Combatant Commander in the execution of the President's constitutional responsibilities and authorities. The individual officer shall act as the agent of the civilian principal, acting in the principal's best interests to the extent that such actions are consistent with the lawful objectives and with the lawful intent of the President.

(2) in fulfilling the expectations of the civilian principal and consistent with the specified advisory functions described in subsection (b) and (c), and in §151(b)(2), § 153 (Chairman: functions), § 154 (Vice Chairman), § 3033 (c), (d)(3) and(d) (6) [Chief of Staff of the Army], §5033(c), (d)(3) and (d) (6) [Chief of Naval Operations], § 5043(d), (e)(3) and (e)(6) [Commandant of the Marine Corps], and § 8033(c) and (d)(3) and (d) (6) [Chief of Staff of the Air Force], the military agent:

(A) shall ensure that the agent's scope of responsibility and authority to act on the explicit and implied direction of the President (or other civilian principal relevant under the circumstances, such as the Secretary of Defense), is reasonably clear, unambiguous and transparent to the agent and to third parties;

(B) to the extent that the agent's scope of responsibility and authority to act is ambiguous or apparently inconsistent with earlier direction or guidance from a principal, shall seek clarification from the President (or other civilian principal relevant under the circumstances) before acting in such a manner as to be perceived, or reasonably likely to be perceived by the President (or other civilian principal relevant under the

circumstances) as breaching or attempting to breach the agent's authority or expressing a position inconsistent with the policy or proposed policy of the Administration;

(C) shall abide by any lawful restriction imposed by the President (or other civilian principal relevant under the circumstances) on the agent's exercise of independent professional judgment to the extent that it encompasses moral, economic, social, political, or other non-military factors;

(D) shall abide by any lawful restriction imposed by the President (or other civilian principal relevant under the circumstances) on the agent's exercise of independent professional judgment to the extent that the exercise of such judgment communicates the intentions, motivations, constraints, or content of deliberations engaged in by the principal, with or without the agent's knowledge or participation, to third parties;

(E) shall keep the President (or other civilian principal relevant under the circumstances) reasonably informed, promptly comply with reasonable requests for information, and discuss any relevant limitations on the agent's ability to carry out the objectives of the President;

(F) shall explain a matter to the extent reasonably necessary to permit the President (or other civilian principal relevant under the circumstances) to make informed decisions;

(G) if asked by a member of Congress in an official and public forum to offer a professional or personal opinion on a matter the military agent knows or reasonably should know is expected to be withheld in confidence until authorized by the President (or other civilian principal relevant under the circumstances), the agent shall consider whether the public interest, candor toward Congress, and fidelity to Constitution outweigh, under the circumstances, fiduciary duties of confidentiality and loyalty toward the President as Commander-in-Chief under the circumstances then known;

(H) if asked by a member of Congress in an official and public forum to offer a professional or personal opinion on matter the combatant commander knows or reasonably should know is contrary to that of his or her political principal and has been tacitly or expressly overridden by a strategy, decision, directive, or order communicated to that commander, the commander shall first presume that his or her opinion is confidential and will not disclose that opinion, or that such an opinion exists, in an official and public forum unless in receipt of express and knowing

consent of the principal; if the principal's knowing consent to disclosure is ambiguous or unknown, the agent shall presume no consent has been given;

(J) shall not, consistent with any prohibitions on the disclosure of confidential, secret, or otherwise classified material established under any law, offer to any third party (individual, person, agency, organization, or business entity) a professional or personal opinion on a matter the agent knows or reasonably should know is expected to be withheld in confidence until authorized by the President (or other civilian principal relevant under the circumstances);

(K) may impose the aforementioned duties on any subordinate member of the Armed Forces under circumstances which cast, or are reasonably likely to be interpreted as casting, that military subordinate as an agent in the execution of the President's objectives.

(e) The provisions in (d)(1) and (d)(2) shall apply to all situations in which the military agent knows or reasonably should know under the circumstances that the agent is to perform lawful duties and responsibilities on behalf of a civilian principal appointed by the President.

Given this amended version of the Statute, we can pose some straightforward and very fact-dependent questions about MacArthur and Truman during this period, thereby enlarging and elaborating the context for the former's grandiose rejection of the latter's policy objectives and his decision to stand before Congress to relay it.

First, we can use the amended statute to assess some of the contextual facts that placed MacArthur and Truman in opposition. We can first ask whether MacArthur had the technical expertise, practical experience, and professional judgment to adequately serve as Truman's agent under the circumstances. Under nearly every objective standard of the day, the answer was yes. Yet, as a corollary, we can also ask whether MacArthur's "scope of responsibility"—as Truman's agent—and his authority to act on the explicit and implied direction of the President was "reasonably clear, unambiguous, and transparent" to him. (See section (d)(2)(A).) Third, if his scope of responsibility and authority was even moderately ambiguous or uncertain, did MacArthur seek clarification from his principal, before taking a public position that was mismatched or irreconcilable with Truman's understanding of that scope? (See section (d)(2)(B).) Fourth, did MacArthur's activity and "independent judgment" encompass moral, economic, social, political, and other "non-military" factors—all factors that are reasonably and predictably reserved to the province of the politician? (See section (d)(2)(C).) Fifth, if so, did the General's independent judgment about these non-military factors entertain and acknowledge any known restrictions or limits imposed on him by his principal, the President? (See section (d)(2)(C).) Sixth, did Truman—as principal—impose any lawful restriction on MacArthur's exercise of his judgment to the extent that exercise of judgment communicated the intentions, motives, constraints, or content of ongoing deliberations with his principal? (See section (d)(2)(D).) Consider that Truman told his Cabinet, and the Joint Chiefs of Staff then communicated to MacArthur just four months before his relief and speech in Congress that:

> In light of the present critical international situation, and until further written notice from me, I wish that each one of you would take immediate steps to reduce the number of public speeches pertaining to foreign or military policy made by officials of the departments and agencies of the executive branch. This applies to officials in the field as well as those in Washington. No speech, press release, or other public statement concerning foreign policy should be released until it has received clearance from the Department of State. No speech, press release, or other public statement concerning military policy should be released until it has received clearance from the Department of Defense [and] advance copies of speeches and press releases concerning foreign policy or military policy should be submitted to the White House for information.[34]

Despite this directive, he continued to issue press releases—one of which, at the end of March 1951, boasted of the United Nation's evident tactical success called for the imminent collapse of the enemy military strength. Given that Truman had been negotiating with the other combatant nations over the terms of a possible cease fire, this very pronounced and public statement led instead to the collapse of those political negotiations, much to the chagrin of the Administration.[35]

Seventh, did MacArthur keep Truman reasonably conversant and cognizant? Did he explain his concerns and proposals sufficiently to permit the President to make informed decisions? (See section (d)(2)(E) and (F).) Finally, did MacArthur—knowing that his views on Korea were contrary to that of the Truman administration and had been overridden by policy statements—ever seek the President's express and knowing consent before giving his speech and testifying before Congress? (See section (d)(2)(H)).

Surely, these are not the only questions that could be generated from the application of an amended, Agency-infused, Goldwater-Nichols Act. The answers to each of these questions would certainly birth interesting offspring investigations, and I suspect that many of the answers would appear to paint the protagonists inconsistently. MacArthur, for example, was keenly aware that his views on the war were not mainstream within the Truman administration and were incompatible with known policy. He further recognized the ultimate supremacy of the political, elected, decision-maker, with his advice, ability, and action relegated to that of the influential (and at best persuasive) subject matter expert. It is also evident he attempted to keep his principal reasonably and candidly informed of his actions, constraints, preferences, and recommendations.

All of this points in the direction of an obedient, if disgruntled, agent strenuously working on behalf of his principal yet strained in that work because of conflicting principles. Yet, he did *not* appear to have sought out Truman's permission to reply to Congressman Joe Martin's defiant and anti-Truman letter, nor to speak before Congress on such a wide range of subject matter, touching inevitably on the very areas sparking their disagreement and the controversy of his relief. "The *people*," he said, were entitled to the "truth, the whole truth, and nothing by the truth" regardless of *who* speaks it, or under what pretense of authority or discretion. He also very definitively violated his Commander-in-Chief's explicit order to clear all public statements about political and military policy and strategy with the General's military and civilian principals first. Moreover, the way MacArthur described his service and the context for his military advice and military decisions clearly portray his judgment affected by considerations of moral, economic, social, and political "non-military" factors. Regardless of whether he was right to conclude that such factors ultimately yield *military* events and facts for which he must account, MacArthur should have known that his principal may have had a very different mold in mind for what he expected his senior field commander to consider, let alone share publically.

This, in contrast, does not paint MacArthur as a resolute (if frustrated) agent working on behalf of a higher authority with more responsibility and greater accountability. Rather, it paints him as a petulant, piqued, and morally outraged *co-principal* offended that the less-wizened President not only failed to grasp the geopolitical gravitas of the strategic crossroads the General stood before, but also failed to follow the map he opened for the President. The *other* principal, in Mac's view, failed to defer to his expertise in choosing which fork in the road to take, and then fired him for telling others about this very map his wide, rich experience helped draw.

*****

The critical lesson from this exercise of applying legal Agency concepts to the Goldwater-Nichols Act and reviewing MacArthur's conduct in that light, evidenced by the various ways in which these questions can be addressed and the diverging messages we can interpret from them, is not necessarily the value of any specific *answer* to any of these questions. Instead, the central lesson is the argument that jurisprudential agency theory can provide a lexicon and an objective framework for *asking* those questions in the first place. It is the sum of those questions and answers—taken in the form of reasoned, objective, debate, and analysis of *which* (if any) fiduciary duties were breached or fortified, by *whom*, and *how*—which benefit the public and the actors participating in these recurring "crises" about the nature of power and how each party ought to wield the sword. In the next, final, chapter, I offer one such debate.

Notes

1. Peter D. Feaver, *Crisis as Shirking: An Agency Theory Explanation of the Souring of American Civil-Military Relations*, at 407.
2. 10 U.S.C. § 153.
3. 10 U.S.C. § 154.
4. 10 U.S.C. § 164(b).
5. 10 U.S.C. §§ 3033, 3034, 5033, 5035, 5043, 5044.
6. 10 U.S.C. § 113.
7. 10 U.S.C. §§ 3013 (Secretary of the Army), 5013 (Secretary of the Navy), 8013 (Secretary of the Air Force).
8. H.W. Brands, The General vs. the President 351.
9. William Manchester, American Caesar, 763–64.
10. Douglas MacArthur, Reminiscences 447 (1964).
11. *Id.* at 449.
12. General (retired) Martin E. Dempsey, Letter to the Editor ("Military leaders do not belong at political conventions"), *Washington Post*, July 30, 2016, https://www.washingtonpost.com/opinions/military-leaders-do-not-belong-at-political-conventions/2016/07/30/0e06fc16-568b-11e6-b652-315ae5d4d4dd_story.html?utm_term=.df795671efd5. Dempsey's frustration was directed at retired Marine General John Allen, who spoke

at the Democratic National Convention, and retired Army Lieutenant General Michael Flynn, who spoke at the Republican National Convention.

13. Quoting General (retired) John Allen at the Democratic National Convention. https://www.washingtonpost.com/news/post-politics-live/liveblog/democratic-national-convention-updates/?tid=a_inl#932c496e-bb41-48a2-816f-0299793a6f60.
14. H.W. BRANDS, THE GENERAL VS. THE PRESIDENT 321.
15. MACARTHUR, REMINISCES, 454.
16. BRANDS, 326.
17. MACARTHUR, REMINISCENCES, 456.
18. *Id.* at 458.
19. *Id.*
20. Both General Omar Bradley (then the Chairman of the Joint Chiefs of Staff) and General (retired) George Marshall (then Secretary of Defense) testified and revealed that the differences of opinion over global communism containment strategy were between MacArthur and the leading policy-makers in Washington, not between the military leadership and the civilians in the White House as suggested by MacArthur. See BRANDS, at 353–62.
21. BRANDS, 333.
22. *Id.* at 337.
23. *Id.* at 335.
24. *Id.* at 338–39, 343.
25. *Id.* at 344–45.
26. *Id.* at 348.
27. One biographer calls him a "thundering paradox of a man, noble and ignoble, inspiring and outrageous, arrogant and shy, the best of men and the worst of men, the most protean, most ridiculous, and most sublime. No more baffling, exasperating soldier ever wore a uniform." WILLIAM MANCHESTER, AMERICAN CAESAR, 15.
28. MACARTHUR, REMINISCENCES, 448.
29. BRANDS, 348.
30. *Id.* at 360–61.
31. SAMUEL P. HUNTINGTON, THE SOLDIER AND THE STATE, 77.
32. *Id.* at 353.
33. *Id.* at 369–70.
34. Memorandum from Joint Chiefs of Staff to General MacArthur, December 6, 1950, available at https://www.trumanlibrary.org/exhibit_documents/index.php?pagenumber=5&titleid=186&tldate=1951-04-07&collectionid=firem&PageID=1&groupid=3414.
35. FOREST C. POGUE, GEORGE C. MARSHALL: STATESMAN 1945-1959 (1987), 478–79.

CHAPTER 11

Exhibit D: The Future Fallacy: A Civ-Mil Dialogue

The "future of war" is a persistently present topic of discussion among national security professionals. Last year, the New America Foundation, a think tank, teamed with Arizona State University to create a "Future of War Project."[1] Another Washington think tank—the Center for Strategic and Budgetary Assessments—describes itself as "specializ[ing] in thinking about the future of warfare."[2] Peter W. Singer of Brookings presented a "TED talk" in 2009 on warrior robots that has garnered nearly 1.4 million online views.[3] Both the Navy and the Army have had small, specially selected annual cohorts chartered to be novel, independent, and to "think big thoughts" on the long-term future of their respective Services, "unconstrained" by present policy and doctrine.[4] In early 2015, the Army's Combined Arms Center at Fort Leavenworth sponsored a writing competition on the "future of war." The Army's senior leadership seems to routinely probe the future when faced with a smaller Army and fewer resources than desired, and more threats than are comfortable.[5] It is therefore, a subject ripe for picking as the instigator of civil-military debate, frustration, and tension.

This chapter is a modified version of an earlier essay, *The Future Fallacy: A Conversation About the "Certainty Principle,"* Small Wars Journal (March 12, 2015), http://smallwarsjournal.com/jrnl/art/the-future-fallacy-a-conversation-about-the-%E2%80%9Ccertainty-principle%E2%80%9D.

D. Maurer, *Crisis, Agency, and Law in US Civil-Military Relations*,
DOI 10.1007/978-3-319-53526-5_11

This chapter tries an unconventional approach—a Socratic dialogue[6]—to express a contrarian view of predicting such futures, but one that expresses key themes about the principal–agent dynamic we have seen in earlier chapters. While not dismissing thoughtful, limited attempts to forecast the future as substantively wrong-headed, this dialogue argues that even the attempt to make those forecasts—*especially by those in uniform*—may, under certain conditions, be misguided, distracting, and ultimately undermine the military's credibility in the eyes of the political and civilian side of the relationship. The following dialogue is entirely fictional: What it may lack in realism, it may gain ground in its original take on a persistent problem—figuring out if there really is a "problem."

*****

[Scene: Elihu's Pub & Restaurant, corner of Root Rd. and Mahan Ln., Arlington, Virginia.
Time: Thursday, 20:15]

Special Assistant to the Chairman of the Joint Chiefs of Staff [SA-CJCS]: Hey there, stranger! I know it's late today, but thanks for sitting down with me.
Want a beer, Tom?

Professional Staff Member, Senate Armed Services Committee [PSM-SASC]: [taking his seat at the bar] Sure, Jane. Thanks. Not a problem—you know we always have
time to chat. With the hearing coming up next week, I assumed you'd call.
The Committee is obviously working hard to make sure the "event" [making air quotes with his fingers] goes better than last time. You remember.

SA-CJCS: [sigh] Well, I was a back-bencher, as they say. I can't—and won't—take credit for that... *event.* I know the General certainly doesn't want to be put in a position like that again—he was caught between his role as a confident and advisor to the President and the Senator's request for a personal opinion about a subject that was still being batted around inside the Administration.[7]

...Your guys really put him in a tight spot, you knew it, and you kept *squeezing*.

PSM-SASC: I got it. But understand: Goldwater-Nichols[8] requires him to respond to Congress with his *candid* opinion when asked...the Committee has a right to know what you all are thinking in the Building. Besides, your guy has been in a unique position—not really on the Joint Chiefs, not really in the NSC...he's just like Maxwell Taylor was in the early 60's, before Kennedy made him Chairman.[9]

And you all get it wrong as often as you get it right, so Congress has a legitimate interest in...let's say, *helping the process along* by injecting a little transparency.[10]

SA-CJCS: Tom, first, you all inject a lot of things, none of which I'd say aid in "transparency."

Second, Goldwater-Nichols does *not* make the Chairman, or even any of the other Service Chiefs, or really any senior strategic leader an open back door into the President's head on national security. Especially if they're still deliberative. That's exactly what happened last time. The esteemed Senator harangued our guy for five minutes on how he was evading the questions and trying to skirt around fully disclosing the expert military opinion...And it was so obvious what the Senator wanted to do: spot some friction between the military and the NSC,[11] portray it as a divide, and pry it open for the *Post* and the *Times*.

PSM-SASC: [chuckling] Well that's a bit unfair! I know what's in the law, and I know how the Committee views its role under that law. Despite what you may think, they all have good intentions—just sometimes, I admit, it's hard to see the long-range good they're envisioning, and it tastes and smells a lot like farce and "I need my sound bite this week"...Sometimes.

	. . . Sometimes, frankly, you guys deserve it.
SA-CJCS:	Look, I don't want argue. But we both know my guy's going to be confirmed at the end of the day unless he seriously steps on it. He's had good press, the troops downrange love him, he gets along with everybody in the Building,[12] and the President trusts him (if you believe the Secretary's memoirs). I'm just here tonight to smooth the way a bit. Is there anything he needs to be wary of? I don't need specifics, just don't blindside us with some obscure reference to an Inspector General complaint filed by a civilian GS-6 at Redstone Arsenal two years ago.
PSM-SASC:	No, no. [Pausing, staring into his now half-empty bottle] . . . I'll tell you what, though: that article he wrote a few months ago . . . you know the one about a terrorist's dirty bomb and the follow-on human stampede during the Kumbh Mela festival in India?[13]
SA-CJCS:	Yeah, yeah . . . in *Foreign Affairs*. I thought it was pretty good. I mean, it wasn't science fiction, Tom: it was not out of the range of plausible, and it addressed issues of interoperability, regional engagement, the Pacific Pivot, counter-terrorism. Thought it was pretty comprehensive.
PSM-SASC:	. . . Comments about *content* aside, *why* did he write it?
SA-CJCS:	[turning in her bar stool to face her friend] . . . You know why he wrote it. His Service got seriously screwed during the last round of budget talks, and half the civies in the Pentagon were *happy* about it; the intelligentsia of retired lieutenant colonels and lieutenant generals at think tanks in town are penning monographs about how future war doesn't need his particular competitive advantages anymore; and, *by the way*, he spent the better part of the last five years in one sandbox or another with little to no consistent and unambiguous political end state for him to use. He's been beaten, battered, and rejected. I guess he felt the time was right to express

himself... he vetted it, of course. The SecDef told the VP about it before my guy was finished with the draft, and he sent over a copy to the White House the week before it came out online. No one was surprised. This wasn't a *Rolling Stone* incident.[14]

PSM-SASC: I'll tell you what was surprising. And I say "surprising" because your guy has a lot of credibility, even *deference* on the Hill—but his essay turned a few heads, to be straight with you.

SA-CJCS: [with a droll sarcastic grin] You mean they actually took time read someth–

PSM-SASC: –something besides poll numbers? Funny, but yes, they did. Or at least asked me about it.

SA-CJCS: So what's the issue? He sees the writing on the wall and how it isn't exactly painted with dollar signs for Defense. He's concerned. He wants the job, and wanted to be sure he could articulate the basis for the arguments he thinks he'll have to make on the Hill and in the Oval Office after he's confirmed.

PSM-SASC: [nodding] He's probably going to have to do that a lot sooner than you think. The Committee is likely to bring up the essay.

SA-CJCS: Alright, I'll bite. So what? They disagree?

PSM-SASC: He shouldn't have tried to predict the future.

SA-CJCS: Uggh... He wasn't dressed up as Nostradamus, Tom —he was making educated guesses and some pretty commonsense recommendations.

PSM-SASC: That's just it, Jane. Guesses. We get it—he's the four-star subject matter expert with a chest full of medals and combat scars. But you guys take that expert label and stretch it over everything that touches national security like it was pair of yoga pants.

SA-CJCS: [with mock indignation] I own a couple of those!

PSM-SASC: Seriously—he went, in the minds of some of the members anyway, a bit too far. Remember Colin Powell's op-eds back in '92 when he was still the Chairman? He basically applauded his boss, Bush I, and implicitly bashed the proposed foreign policy of Clinton, like a *month* before the election.[15]

SA-CJCS: Well, it didn't work, did it? Clinton got elected; we ended up with boots in the Balkans.

PSM-SASC: Whether he influenced the electorate or not is not my point. My point is that we again have this very well-regarded four-star general, nominated to be the senior ranking military officer in this country, arguably the most influential military officer in the world, and he's writing about what he thinks the future of war will be ten . . . twenty . . . thirty years down the road? . . . Are you kidding me? There's a problem with weather forecasting, and you know it.

Future capabilities—ours or the other guy's—are not the same as future intentions.

There are certain members of the Committee who are starting to raise the "BS" flag—or at least thinking about how that might look if they do confront him on it. Which should give you guys some serious tactical pause next time you want your general or admiral to look like Clausewitz in a three thousand word "thought piece."

SA-CJCS: What is the concern? Why "BS?"

PSM-SASC: Alright, look. Here's what he did. He proposed a set of hypothetical facts, right, set in some dismal dystopian future, constructed on what he asserts are reasonable, foreseeable trends, data points, and conditions that he currently observes. From somebody else's vantage, though, the question of motivation is important. You only make those kind of predictions, when you're positioned like the General is, in order to do one of two things. [holding up one finger] First, to justify departing from some status quo or even a proposal you don't like. Oh, you don't like the idea of dropping below a 500,000 Active Duty Army?[16] Then suggest the future is sure to return to tank-on-tank maneuver and attrition warfare between nation states fighting over dwindling natural resources or access in the global commons. Say it's the smallest standing army since before Pearl Harbor. Don't like the idea of falling behind our near-peer competitors in advanced weapon technology while we spend our money and time fighting dirty little savage wars in the "human domain?" Then focus on trends that suggest those peers are shrinking the US overmatch gap: "Watch out, here they come! Bring me some drones!"[17]

SA-CJCS: Come on, Tom. Aren't you being a bit over the top? The General does not have an agenda he's trying to work, other than setting up the Services and Combatant Commands to be in the best possible position to be ready should something warrant their direct or indirect involvement, across a range of entirely plausible "bad days." Being conservative and aiming to prepare for the worst is kind of what we do.[18]

PSM-SASC: Jane, sometimes being "realistic" [again with the air quotes] doesn't mean you have to be conservative. Sometimes it just means being a "realist" about what you know, what you don't know, and why you don't know it. Not once, just to give you an example from his essay that comes to mind, did he ever caveat that his claims were nothing much more than assumptions. Merely writing something in a declarative sentence does not, usually, turn an assumption into a fact that everybody agrees on.[19]

SA-CJCS: Ha! That was "declarative!"...So now you're quibbling with his writing style?

PSM-SASC: No. It's not a stylistic complaint; it's a substance complaint. Stating that the future will feature a combination of violent non-state actors dominating in ungoverned spaces wielding hybrid strategies and capabilities[20] is an example that's in his essay. Like him, we all see Boko Haram[21] ...we see AQIM,[22] and the Committee certainly sees ISIS.[23] We understand the challenge that the military has if facing off against these guys. We also understand that it is a different fight than COIN,[24] and a different fight than a coalition of the willing to oust a dictator, and definitely different than responding to a humanitarian or environmental crisis. But saying that these threats "represent" the future operational and strategic environment, and therefore our military strength should be directed at figuring out how to fight them convincingly and with some finality is hyperbole. How does he know? How can he even suppose what other countries might do—think "self-help"—if we don't step in? His argument is premised on buttery assumptions like (and I'm paraphrasing) that the more we know and understand, on the ground, the better we can get ahead of an escalating conflict in Phase 0 or Phase 1.[25]

The Army's Regionally Aligned Forces idea is built on that "engagement"[26] narrative, and it hasn't been entirely evidenced by the record, you might say.[27] We've been in Europe for how long? Did we see Russia's moves in Ukraine coming? How long we're we in Iraq? Did we get ahead of ISIS? Or did we create the conditions for it?

I don't know the answer, but your General has to appreciate that his vision of the future, in all its bloody and uncertain glory, is pretty darn speculative. And oh by the way, it also seems to ignore that whole "war is a continuation of politics with the addition of other means" gospel that every colonel I know quotes at me, like I'm not familiar with Clausewitz.[28] It's like they think politics will trigger the military tool-of-choice, but then all politics stops whilst the armies engage.

What they don't understand is that politics is also like the crock pot that conflict slowly simmers in . . . Politics and policy shape how we look at the world and view our place in the community of nations. When was the last time the President's National Security Strategy was actually read and dissected by the uniformed guys? To them, it's merely a reference cited in other sources, like the NMS,[29] and doctrine.[30] Everything written and published coming out of the services is going to be "nested" within the overall NSS, but that usually just means getting the same terms on the page, in roughly the same order, and written for a slightly different audience. But doctrine is like *bedrock*—it hardly ever moves, and when it does move, it does so at the margins—the pebbles at the surface. National policy—I mean at the Oval Office and a couple of places on Hill—is supposed to be flexible and wayward and unstable and inconsistent. It's more like that loose soil and gravel on top of sediment. It is supposed to respond to the winds of public opinion, even if it is uninformed, and it is has a lot of external audiences out there to influence. If the NSS *can* change every so often—even within a single Administration—why are you military guys always so shocked and upset that politics is unpredictable?

SA-CJCS: The unpredictability is upsetting because—and you're right—doctrine is hard to move around. We live and breathe doctrine[31] because it not only helps us create useful heuristics and makes planning for uncertainty easier to swallow, but it helps us stop what seems like utter entropy... the spreading disorder and chaos... it's about establishing *coherence*[32]—don't laugh at me!... Besides, did you ever stop to consider how much of what we say in the press is theater, aimed at each other?

PSM-SASC: Fair enough. You've been up there, you've seen the members in action. Everything is theater. But that doesn't make it senseless. The other reason why someone like the General would want to write that sort of essay is because he doesn't actually want change—"the status quo norm is just fine, thank you very much, and my best military advice to you is to not try to fix what isn't broken."

Take women in combat jobs, or even as Rangers, or ending Don't Ask, Don't Tell. One easy way to avoid uncomfortable or new directions is to argue that the nothing currently justifies the change; another is to say that making the change would dismantle unit cohesion and esprit de corps, and all that slippery slope jazz. None of which, by the way, has the military ever claimed with convincing evidence to back it up. Those arguments are premised on *me*, the audience, believing that *you* are the expert in such matters and that I'm better off following your advice, lest we put national security at risk.[33] Scare tactics, dressed up as conservative realism.

Part of the job of Congress is to act as backseat driver. Not all of your norms and SOPs are grounded in reality, and sometimes *we* need to point it out.

SA-CJCS: Wait a sec, are you saying that the Service Chiefs or Commanders are not in the best possible position to know what would happen to the institution or their units if certain fundamental changes are imposed from the outside? They may not have visibility down to a platoon's barracks, but there *is* a reason why we don't promote and select our leaders from the outside. They have to be grown from lieutenant on up, and with that comes experiential learning and a feel for how a unit behaves, its networks, its motivations, and its constraints—just like your Committee Chairs…you don't get that without seniority and experience and respect, all three of which are related.

PSM-SASC: True. I *agree* with you: your generals and admirals have the experience to give them their bona fides, credentials. And certainly I can understand how a commander would have a tough time making a go of it with a division if he'd never been a brigade or battalion commander. So the credentialing is important internally within the Services. But that isn't necessarily the same thing as credibility. And without credibility, there is no trust. And without trust, well-…you get my drift. They certainly are "better positioned" (to use your words) to "know" how the ship sails, the tanks fires, the plane flies, and the troops think. But they're also conditioned—you can't argue here—by the institution they grew up in and sacrificed for.

Maybe they're not short-sighted, ill-intentioned, or "institutionalized," but they sure are biased—or at least it looks like that when you hear multiple voices from the same organization or Service saying or doing the same things as if were a cultural personality trait.[34] I'm not saying anything new here, Jane. I mean, consider the 1920s: Coolidge was pressured by the War and Navy departments into court-martialing Colonel Billy Mitchell for stating the obvious truth: that our leaders were blind and unwilling to consider air power as the next major influence on war.[35] The Navy had its traditional view and the Army had its view and neither one wanted an independent air force that owned that new "domain." Mitchell was ultimately vindicated, but was trashed by his own team.

SA-CJCS: Mitchell never really had a team. Tom, I've read that bit of history too. As I recall, he wasn't court-martialed for being a prophet—he was court-martialed for being arrogant, undisciplined, and throwing his senior leaders under the bus in a very public way in the newspapers. Besides, you're arguing against yourself now. You're proving my point that it takes someone in uniform to point out the current trends that signal big changes are coming and to warn the rest of us that we had better rethink our doctrine or we'll get steamrolled and it will seem like it came out of nowhere. Mitchell may have been wrong in his "means," but his "ways" were justified by the "ends" he had in mind, don't you think?

PSM-SASC: So what were the General's "ends," then?

SA-CJCS: Like I said, he's concerned about the "fiscally constrained environment" disabling our ability to respond effectively to future ambiguity, instability, and uncertain degrees of conflict. We don't have a good understanding of why these threats grow, sustain themselves, and are able to fluster us with limited technical capacity, limited numbers, and a *raging* desire to hate anything that doesn't reflect their vision of paradise on earth.

He's concerned, like every senior officer before him, that the *politics* will get in the way of a clear-sighted strategy, and that we'll get caught unprepared. This RAF-thing the army wants to do—it may have some kinks to work out, but ultimately it is about eliminating Clausewitz's friction and chance[36] to the maximum extent possible . . . not through technology alone, but serious and substantial investment in time and presence. If our partnering abroad leads to collaboration, it increases our influence, and demonstrates our resolve and commitment, and we can exercise some better degree of control.[37]

PSM-SASC: There's your assumption again. You're trying to support an argument with a statement whose truth is taken as accepted without further evidence. You said partnering increases our influence and demonstrates our resolve, and therefore gives us a stronger, steadier hand on the reigns. You're assuming that those positives (like demonstrated commitment) will translate into a positive outcome we want (that is, control: a reduction in friction and chance). It also assumes we know where we're going—just because we have a map doesn't mean we have a destination. We collaborated with the Saudis in 1990 and look what it did to bin Laden.[38] And who exactly is "partnering abroad," Jane? The S-3[39] of a battalion for three weeks in West Africa, before the battalion minus shows up for three months of "mil-to-mil engagement?" For ninety-five percent of those soldiers, it will be the one and only time they deploy there. That's not making a strategic mark or institutionalizing the knowledge they learn or the relationships they make.

SA-CJCS: Okay, I'm familiar with the current drawbacks with implementation, but the Army is still trying to figure what the best practice looks like. Regardless of organizational design and the TTPs,[40] I think, ultimately, RAF[41] is about something much larger: discriminating judgment (what to think and why), discriminating action (what to do or not to do), and discriminating lethality (what to destroy and what to build) at any and every scale of military force, across the Range of

Military Operations.[42] I grant you it's not exactly the Special Forces model yet, but it looks a lot better than where we were in February 2003.

PSM-SASC: So it's ambiguity and uncertainty that are bugging him the most, then?

SA-CJCS: Exactly. He was doing what every leader ought to do: first, understand the conditions you're walking into. "Recon the future." Know where you want to go, spot the ambush on the way, map your route through the terrain, and figure out what you need to bring with you to get there safely.

PSM-SASC: [smiling] A fine metaphor, my friend. Let me buy you another beer.

SA-CJCS: Thanks.

PSM-SASC: Ambiguity and uncertainty. But I can't help but thinking: maybe all this is much more straightforward. I mean, who was the Greek who sai—

SA-CJCS: Thuycidides. "Fear, honor, interest."[43] Why nations go to war.

PSM-SASC: Right, and you've got one of your own three-stars writing op-eds and articles talking, quite persuasively, about how the nature of war has never really changed and won't change: it's uncertain, it's political, and it's human.[44]

That for all the talk of "revolutions in military affairs" in the 1990s,[45] especially after Gulf War 1, it wasn't a stealth bomber with precision-guided munitions that could ever hope to stabilize post-war Iraq in the 2000s. The Air Force or SOF[46] may have been able to screw with the Taliban, initially, but what about ten years after that?

Turns out you all were right about "network-centric operations"—just not that kind of network. We all know drones controlled out of Nevada, and squadrons out of Bragg, aren't going to affect much in the human domain except a whole lot of broken things that somebody has to rebuild. That "somebody" is usually us.

And those are *political* choices with *political* implications. Beyond that, making forecasts about we think will happen in some hot spot over the long term, based on what see right now, is just wrong-headed and easily disproven . . . And we keep doing it.[47]

SA-CJCS: So, you said solving this was simple?

PSM-SASC: Not simple, no. The solutions are never simple. The simple thing is what your guy could have said, but didn't. He *could* have written that, from his perspective, after x number of years wearing the uniform, deploying to such and such, and having been educated by so and so at this school and that, his job regarding the "future character of war" is expectation-management.

Instead of donning his prophet's hat, he should have said that every actor, with any bit of influence and power, has some animating ambition in life. Sometimes it is simply to increase his influence and power. Sometimes it is moral outrage that we simply cannot appreciate, let alone persuade them to "keep calm and carry on"; sometimes its sheer survival instinct, or retribution. Sometimes his animating ambitions put him at cross-purposes with our own. Sometimes, there is no negotiation, no reasoning to be done. That actor's value system drives his motivation, his intent.[48] If he has the right resources, and the opportunity to use them presents itself, then you have the trifecta: means, motive, and opportunity.

There will always be enemies of the state, lurking and building and planning, waiting for those three elements to align. It's not always going to be an army crossing a border with tanks, or shelling a city . . . But, sometimes, it will be. It's not always going to be a mosque that gets blown up, or a kidnapped civilian teenager that incites the masses to hysterical war fervor. (There's your Clausewitz again.)[49] But sometimes it will be. What I'm saying is, I think, is that you can look at the pace of communication and the ease by which we can talk to each other across the globe, and say, "Wow! It's been accelerating, and it's going to keep going that way—faster and faster." And you can plan accordingly to develop sophisticated cyber tools to get ahead of message or to shape it to our will, to take down centers of gravity with finesse and a key stroke without ever putting boots on the ground. Or if you do put them on the ground, they're of the commando/Delta/SEAL/Ranger variety because of the speed by which you can get them on station and "mission complete."

Or, you could say something like: "the velocity of information is an interesting and impactful cultural phenomenon." Does it mean that the Internet is the harbinger of those evil means, motives, and opportunities? Does it mean that SOF units should be the dominant tool-of-choice for future combat operations? Does it mean a revolution in military affairs, as Andy Krepinevich defines it, is afoot?[50] I don't know, *and neither do you.*

You could assume that having regionally-aligned forces with persistent presence in some corner of the world will give you better insight into the area, more warning if things sour, more opportunity to influence or exert pressure, faster response times, and greater ability to prevent war or to win one.[51]

Or, as the general *could* have written, it might just mean we anger a whole lot more people with these "extended reconnaissance operations"[52] and end up *hampering*, not extending, our political, social, and diplomatic reach. We win in the short term, lose in the long term. There is simply too much complexity out there to allow for blanket assertions of strategy that are nothing but best-case assumptions based on present-sense impressions . . . what is happening right now need not describe even the *near* future, let alone the far future. Why couldn't he have accepted that as a premise with as much validity as any other he asserted?

SA-CJCS: Where are you taking me with this, Tom? It seems to me that what you're saying is that the military can't ever make an educated guess about how conflict, how war-fighting, is going to look. That seems awfully cynical, and not really all that true. There isn't really a war-fighting "uncertainty principle." Didn't Clausewitz say that we *can* "forecast" tomorrow's animating will of the enemy based on what it is today?[53] Isn't that even more true today than it was in the 1820s? Shinseki was right when told the Senate that occupying Iraq would likely take hundreds of thousands of troops.[54] The politicos just vilified him, lampooned him.[55] Even Patton wrote on article on tank warfare right after World War I, in which he sarcastically admitted to being heretical for having the gall, as a serving officer, to discuss the potential future of a war-fighting capability that was against the party line.[56] Patton turned out be right too.

We often get the specifics wrong, but the big trends are not hard to see.[57] If we don't say "wait a minute, you need to really think hard about not funding this program because of reasons A, B, and C," then we're not doing our job as advisors and experts. Did you read General Bolger's mea culpa?[58] He admitted that he and his fellow flag officers deserved a lot of blame for Iraq and Afghanistan for failing to question their own assumptions (and those of the civilian leadership) and believe that "more time" was all that was needed to get those countries to a place we could comfortably leave.[59]

PSM-SASC: So if they had spoken up, or done so more forcefully, do you think the politicians would have bowed their heads and said, "You're right, we're not prepared for this just yet. Let's go back and study modern Middle Eastern history for a few years so that we can understand our enemies?"

What if the politicians had ignored them? To whom would the generals have complained? Would they have all retired and then written scathing op-eds?[60] Would they have testified before Congress?[61] Or would they have executed *anyway*, knowing the mission was doomed and their soldiers would die for it? Jane, I get it. Your next boss is thinking about a lot more right now than a paper he wrote. I'm sure he expects the Committee to hit him hard with questions on health of the force, sex assault victims, and that new tank slash transport slash scout vehicle Scylla I saw being touted as the next big thing at the AUSA conference.[62] But he needs to be cautious about his predictions, even if he thinks of himself as the smartest dude in the room on the subject of future war. It's all too easy to debate him, to retort that he's projecting his present anxieties onto the future.[63]

SA-CJCS: Of course he's "projecting!" How else can he drive the military, or even just his Service, to think long-term about what they're doing? [sighing] I'm sorry I raised my voice, Tom... Let's say he goes quiet, doesn't speak up and doesn't try to articulate that we'll likely get bogged down, with uncertain or inconsistent coalition support, in some underdeveloped megacity fighting alongside undertrained and undisciplined paramilitaries against ideologically-committed insurgents for long stretches... that the way in which we ended ops in Iraq and Afghanistan—that's going to be the *norm*, not a definitive peace conference plus parade. That the average Joe on the ground will have to be culturally-sensitive, language-adept, and proficient with a UAV.[64] But if the General doesn't say these things, repeatedly, in all kinds of forums and to all kinds of audiences, how can he push, prod, or ram the military into preparing for the inevitable?

PSM-SASC: I'm not suggesting that he's even wrong in his prediction, Jane. I'm also not suggesting that he shouldn't talk about it. But what I am suggesting is that he must, must, must caveat his predictions.

You all seem to act like there is some "certainty principle"—that, if you can just know a little bit more, you'll be able to act first, fastest, and with proper amounts of force. You'll somehow be able to accurately measure and quantify as many variables as you want without impacting any of them in the process. That notion is as naïve in the so-called human domain as it is in physics.

First, in my humble opinion, the general should probably steer clear of definitive declarations, like saying certain undesirable conditions are "inevitable." Just because cities are getting larger and we've found ourselves fighting inside them recently doesn't make urban operations in a megacity a foregone conclusion, or even a remote possibility.[65]

Second, and related, he should readily and repeatedly acknowledge where he's making assumptions and predictions based on what he defines as patterns that will extend into the future.

Third, he should be clear about how he has come to believe such-and-such actually is a "pattern" and why—based on his experience—he thinks it is worth worrying about.

Fourth—am I at number four now?—he needs to understand his audience, and tailor what he's saying to that audience. He shouldn't have a problem with that. He doesn't address a graduating class of cadets the same why he addresses a veteran's group or the one or two-stars that seek out his counsel, or Congress.

And even in Congress, not all are created equal; they need differentiated details in order judge something or fund something they know little about. Every audience will have its own distinct depth of knowledge, its own preconceptions, its own biases, and its own experts, and its own degree of deference to your expert. I think it's important, and a good thing too, that your guy vetted the essay first with OSD[66] and the White House…it shows that he's not detached from his "principal"—that as an "agent"[67] he can be trusted to be candid and forthcoming, but within bounds established by his civilian superiors.

SA-CJCS: I thought you were upset about the article…now you're saying it was the right thing to do? Have I had too much of this fine local micro-brew you're paying for?

PSM-SASC: Funny girl. No. I personally welcomed the outside-the-box pre-mortem[68] he wrote. I liked the creativity and that he found the time to write it himself... He did write it himself, yes?

SA-CJCS: [shaking her head while grinning] You've heard him brief before; you've seen him lecture at CNAS[69]; what in the world makes you think he'd let anyone else's words be attributed to him?

PSM-SASC: ...Thought so. [motions for bartender; orders two shots of bourbon] I guess what I was saying was that he needs to carefully identify what "principal" he's advising under the circumstances when he writes something like that. Was it the administration? Was it his Service? Was it the Joint Staff or other Chiefs? Was it Congress? Was it the media?

SA-CJCS: Not to speak for the General, but I'd guess he was aiming it all of the above.

PSM-SASC: Okay. Okay, I think I know what I would do—if I were in his shoes.

SA-CJCS: Oh, by all means, share!

PSM-SASC: Look, you said yourself that he's most concerned with ambiguity and uncertainty; that he feels some compulsion or duty to shape the future readiness of the military; and that he's "firing for effect" on a large and diverse audience. Right?

SA-CJCS: Sure.

PSM-SASC: Thanks for playing along [smirking]. So, if those three things are true, then—as Herr Clausewitz wrote—everything in war is simple.[70] Instead of making predictions and forecasts about what the future of war will look like, such a wide variety of audiences and a broad purpose suggests he would have been better off breaking the idea down into its most basic and fundamental elements—those basics that will never change.

SA-CJCS: And those would be?

PSM-SASC: Well, try to imagine a war... strike that: any scale of armed conflict, at any time, between any set of belligerents . . . doesn't matter if they were states, terrorists, or gangs of marauders!

Hmm, even better: imagine you were designing a war game completely from scratch—you had no directions, no guidance, no examples. You want to create a dynamic in which multiple agents use various tools they have available to achieve some objective, which may or may not seem aggressive or threatening to another agent and its interests.

It strikes me as fairly obvious that any war, at any scale, over any period of time includes some population of belligerents—even in a cyber war, somebody is writing the codes for the software and somebody's ability to do something downstream is going to be affected. That's what scares you so much: the reality that war, from the large to the small, can we waged by those who are never exposed to physical danger or proximity to harm, and would never look like a conventional, traditional combatant.

Then there's the sub-population of civilians and non-combatants—the bystanders, the refugees, the innocent or ambivalent on-lookers. That leads me to think of audiences again. Somebody, somewhere, is watching what you do and how you do it—whether it's an ally in support, or an undecided party waiting to see who is worth supporting. They're the spectators. Some have an interest in what you do, some think they do not. The media too, obviously, which could enable or disable your local tactics or long-term security by how they report, what they report, and the impression they leave on others.

You'll laugh at me, but I liken it to the Tonight Show: you have the host and the guests bantering back and forth, you have a live audience, and at home watching on television; you have the mainstream media reporting on any lively or unexpected incident during the show; you have the not-so-mainstream media posting, tweeting, and sharing clips of the show; you have the crew manning the teleprompters, cue cards, stage props, wardrobe and make-up, and cameras; you have the network executives and corporations watching the ratings. Every single person in those various types of audiences have a role and potential impact on the show—either directly and immediately (say, a wrong cue card, a bad joke, no laughing) or indirectly (pulling an advertisement, hiring a new host, inviting new guests, airing at a different time).

And there's got to be some form of an adversary . . . of course, antagonists come in many flavors and degrees, so I can't say that it will always be a clean-cut "us versus them" situation. Clearly, the conflict happens *some*where . . . a geographic place is going to be impacted, even if it the fight isn't over territory per se. It might be contiguous and local, or widespread. Even some of your generals weigh in and say geography is affected by climate change, so even that has some elemental role too.[71] . . . Some form of weapon will be used. You're rolling your eyes at me! Again, I'm generalizing here to illustrate my point about generic conflict at any scale.

I suppose I mean broad categorizations of weapons: conventional or unconventional. The means may be highly technological, sophisticated, or simply a cell phone taped to an artillery round on the side of an unpaved dirt road running alongside a canal. Nothing says that each party has parity, or that each party sticks to one kind or another over the course of the conflict. Then, there's going to be some standard or typical practice in how those means are employed—the tactics used—which of course might vary over time and location and might very well be as asymmetrical or unconventional as the means used.

Finally, I think an important piece that is always there is information . . . I don't mean just propaganda or psy-ops, but really any and all data about the conflict and its players, what they know about each other, what they think they know about each other, what they want to know, and what they might not ever know. So, I'd sum it all up as a *stew* of people, locations, adversaries, means, tactics, audiences, and information, stirred by big spoon of uncertainty.

...But [chuckling] I don't really know! I *do* know that the general could help untangle some of this thorny problem by giving each of those basic elements some kind of weight...some normative value that is relative, based on context. Any rational decision, I would think, would factor in one or more of those elements in order to do anything resembling the use of force—or even its threat...Even the art of command is a function of information and applying systems (be they weapons, sensors, or people) to manage information, shape it, or produce it for some effect. *That's* where his expert knowledge and experience comes in. He could then describe, given a desired strategic goal *set by the politicians*, how he would adapt his military to that element and describe how that adaptation would work (or cost) if that strategy or policy or expectation changed...as they're wont to do given enough time. [staring down at his empty glass]...I have had entirely too much to drink.

SA-CJCS: You probably have! But as you were talking just then, you mentioned adaptation, and I think that has to mean something much bigger than a platoon on the ground adapting to new tactics.

PSM-SASC: I agree...

SA-CJCS: You mentioned "means, motive, and opportunity" earlier. Maybe that's how you can judge the relative value or weight of each of those basic, self-evident, elements in context. It doesn't really allow you to predict what they'll do next, but I suppose it widens the menu of what they might do, and why. What you're saying is that all that the military can do is adapt, and do so in a way doesn't affect the apparent or actual legitimacy of the politics that wields the sword[72] in the first place.

You know all this talk about how the nature of war never changes but the character of war probably does change?[73] If we don't understand those changes—who fights, who is victimized by the fighting, the tools used to fight... let's say, for example, how ISIS swept through north-western Iraq so easily—then we're stuck playing catch-up, which leaves us at the defensive disadvantage.

Or, let's say, we get ahead of those changes... say, the use of precision-guided munitions during the first Gulf War, or stealth technology, or armed drones... then we're at the cutting edge and trying to prevent everybody else from catching on to the new rules of the game we just wrote.

But that division between "nature" and "character" is artificial and misleading. It takes one surprising event to convince everybody learned on the subject that yet another "revolution in military affairs" is taking place. But all that has really happened is that some other actor had a different motive, opportunity, and means. Given their motive, and given the opportunity, they used whatever means they had available and the net effect under the circumstances was some snowflake-like aggregation of information, tactics, people, weaponry, adversaries, and locations—all your "self-evident" components of conflict. That, my friend, is the so-called changing character of a conflict, nothing more...

.... Saying that there is something akin to a generic character of war that is nearly universal at a particular time period but also subject to change, and that this change is both subject to diagnosis is like saying the same silly thing about a disease! Can you imagine the Centers for Disease Control saying something like, "Folks, no need to be alarmed: we know that this particular strain of flu has begun to mutate and is resistant to all currently available vaccines... but there's hope: the nature of flu never changes, and we're hard at work identifying the traits of the particular character of this strain, so we'll be fine in the end!"

The doctors may be able to create a new vaccine, thereby ending a pandemic. But from the perspective of each unique patient, or prospective victim, with their own unique combination of general health, immune system strength, exposure to the virus, access to care, and preventative steps they might take, those blanket descriptions do very little in terms of fair warning, medical advice, or diagnosis. I think you're saying the same is true of combat at a small scale or war at a larger scale.

PSM-SASC: Yes, I suppose that is what I'm saying. I'm glad I'm not as incoherent tonight as I feel. I think I might be aping off what I read of John Warden—his "five rings"—infrastructure, populations, military, command and control, organics[74]... I can't take credit for originality.

SA-CJCS: Well, Warden's rings were really just classes of potential targets of offensive operations—some more vulnerable than others and each had certain merit or priority as a target.

But what you're saying is another level of abstraction up, I guess you could say. It isn't just about knowing your enemy's vulnerability. It's about understanding how each of the universal basic elements are networked together—how they relate to one another and how they influence one another over time, based in part on what we do to that system, which in turn should be a function of what we know or want to know about that system.[75] Reminds me of Sun Tzu: stimulate your enemy to discover its patterns of behavior.[76]

PSM-SASC: Oh, going Eastern Zen on me now?

SA-CJCS: Adaptation—if it means something more strategic than updating battle drills on the fly—comes in two directions. First, it can be *internally-oriented* adaptation. You identify your own mistakes (including misinterpreting policy constraints or the policy latitude you *think* you have). You correct those mistakes in order to either (a) regain the status quo ante or (b) to gain an advantage. You also identify your own successes. You act in a way that attempts to keep that knowledge or behavior that was successful in order to either (a) sustain the advantage or (b) increase your relative advantage. But I suppose there is also *externally-oriented* adaption too. You ID the mistakes of your adversary. You try to exploit that mistake, in order to either (a) regain the status quo ante, or (b) capture an advantage you didn't already have. You also have to ID your adversary's successes. You then adapt by neutralizing the effect of that success, or acting to prevent its repetition.

You know when you first mentioned "adapting," I thought you were saying we should be reactionary. But the more I think about it, adaptation is really both reactive *and* activist. I guess you could say its giant feedback loop, or really two feedback loops.[77] How you set yourself up to create stable loops, those in which you can readily see and interpret the signals accurately enough to base your adaptations on, is the key.

PSM-SASC: Right. And I think all your General had to do was to explain that it is his job—the job of the senior leaders in the military—to create those crystal-clear feedback loops that give maximum time and maximum space for the policy-makers to think, decide, react, or be proactive.

...And it *isn't* the military's job is to decide when enough time or enough space is there—they don't get to define "maximum." I picture it in my head like a giant box, and the four outer walls of the box are the bounds of legitimacy. The four walls might be dashed lines in reality, and they might shrink or expand the area inside the box over time, or unexpectedly, but they mark the known limits on the use of force: the how, where, when, the "with what," and the all-important "why." Of course that box is going to dilate over time. But if the military steps outside the walls, it violates the sacrosanct rule of civilian policy control: it has become its own political force, not just a pressure group or interest group.[78]

But as long as the military stays inside the four walls of that legitimizing frame, if you will, then it is responsive and leashed appropriately to the political decision-makers.

From *our* perspective on the Hill, the military's job to create and then preserve the political freedom of maneuver and freedom of choice. I know that's anathema to the Services, who teach their youngsters about being *a*political, staying out of the debates, being objective, so they don't appear critical or subversive of civilian authority. But I guarantee the senior generals and admirals get it. Knowing how and why the military ways and means mesh with the existing, future, or even possible, "ends" of politicians is not heretical at all—it's smart leading. Anything that you do, whether it's a "strategic corporal" on the ground or the Chairman on Sunday morning talk show, that restricts those freedoms is going to look like you're boxing in your bosses.[79]

SA-CJCS: I don't disagree with you . . . not sure I agree with you either. I suppose I could argue that sometimes, sometimes, the politicians *need* to be boxed in by those most aware of the danger they are placing the nation in. If the military doesn't cry foul, who will? . . . But maybe I've had too much to drink. Trust me: I'm not speaking for the Chairman right now, or the General who expects that job soon.

PSM-SASC: No worries. And you know I'm not speaking for the Committee. I don't know exactly what direction they'll take the General in next week, but I just wanted you to know—my dear friend—that the usual praise mixed with posturing will probably touch on the future of war as the General sees it. Nobody really wants to see someone like him get lectured by a senator on his core competence. Just don't let your guy back right into it—his assumptions will make that a lot easier.

SA-CJCS: Well... as always, thank you, Tom. You certainly took advantage of this "opportunity" tonight, and your "motive" was pure... [smiling] Your "means" on the other hand...

PSM-SASC: I know. I talk too much and start get all metaphorical. Blame the bourbon!

SA-CJCS: [standing up] I know you too well to blame the drinks! Besides, that's why you've worked for the Committee for so long.

PSM-SASC: [shaking Jane's hand, standing up, and laying out a few crumpled dollar bills on the bar]... Did you watch the game last night? How about that interception?... Couldn't believe it when I saw the replay... and they replayed it from every angle over and over and over...

SA-CJCS: [nodding and walking Tom out of the bar] It was a great catch. But you were wrong, by the way, earlier... Clausewitz did say "everything in war is very simple." But he also said "the simplest thing is difficult."[80]... And we don't get the luxury of a replay video in slo-mo.

Notes

1. http://www.newamerica.org/future-of-war/.
2. http://csbaonline.org/research/future-warfare-and-concepts/.
3. Peter W. Singer, "Military robots the future of war," (Feb 2009), TED.com, http://www.ted.com/talks/pw_singer_on_robots_of_war?language=en.
4. The Chief of Naval Operations' Strategic Studies Group, worked out of the Naval War College in Newport, Rhode Island, and the Chief of Staff of the Army's Strategic Studies Group, works out of Arlington, Virginia. Both organizations are staffed by small, platoon-sized interdisciplinary teams of junior and senior officers and civilians, reporting directly to their Service Chiefs. The author served as a Fellow on the Army's Strategic Studies Group from 2013–14.
5. See, e.g., 32nd Chief of Staff of the Army, General Gordon Sullivan, "Moving Into the twenty-first Century," *Military Review*, July 1993, 3–11; General Gordon Sullivan, "A Vision for the Future," *Military Review*, May-June 1995,

3–14; see also 38th Chief of Staff of the Army, General Ray Odierno, "The Force of Tomorrow," *Foreign Policy*, Feb. 4, 2013, available at http://foreignpolicy.com/2013/02/04/the-force-of-tomorrow/.

6. See, e.g., REBECCA GOLDSTEIN, PLATO AT THE GOOGLEPLEX (2013), at 4–5, 40–41 (suggesting that Plato's literary use of the dialogue to expose presumptions and false certitudes served artistic and rational philosophical purposes: to "render violence to our sense of ourselves and our world, our sense of ourselves in the world... [to be] disorienting").
7. See, e.g., Nominations of Gen Martin E. Dempsey, USA, for Reappointment to the Grade of General and Reappointment as Chairman of the Joint Chiefs of Staff; and ADM James A. Winnfeld, Jr., USN, for Reappointment to the Grade of Admiral and Reappointment as Vice Chairman of the Joint Chiefs of Staff, Before the Senate Comm. on the Armed Forces, 113th Cong. 782–85 (2013) (statement of General Martin E. Dempsey), http://www.armed-services.senate.gov/hearings/2013/07/18/nominations.
8. Goldwater-Nichols Defense Reorganization Act of 1986, Pub. L. No. 99-433, 100 Stat. 992 (1986) (codified as amended in scattered sections of 10 U.S.C., especially 10 U.S.C. §§ 151–155 (relating to the Chairman and Vice Chairman of the Joint Chiefs of Staff and the Joint Staff) and 161–166 (relating to the Unified Combatant Commands)).
9. RICHARD REEVES, PRESIDENT KENNEDY: PROFILE OF POWER (1993), at 183; compare H.R. MCMASTER, DERELICTION OF DUTY (1997), at 10–17 (describing the former Army Chief of Staff Maxwell Taylor's role as the "Military Representative to the President").
10. See, e.g., Legislative Reorganization Act of 1946, Pub. L. No. 79–601, 60 Stat. 812 (1946); the Senate Armed Services Committee website, at http://www.armed-services.senate.gov/about/history.
11. The National Security Council. See, e.g., http://www.whitehouse.gov/administration/eop/nsc/.
12. Euphemism for the Pentagon.
13. The Kumbh Mela is the world's largest religious festival. The festival lasts two months and occurs only once every third year, rotating among four Indian cities. It is notable not just for its infrequency, but also for its population. On the outskirts of Allahabad in northern India, where the Maha Kumbh Mela festival occurs only every twelfth year, a megacity of forty-five million faithful Hindu pilgrims temporarily blossoms in a ten square mile patch of earth at the confluence of two heavily polluted rivers. This urbanization springs out of nothing, on ground that just months earlier had been submerged beneath the Monsoon-engorged Ganga and Yamuna rivers. In late autumn, the rivers recede and the floodplains become ground zero for the rapid building of an impermanent civilization. See Laura Spinney, "Karma of the Crowd,"

National Geographic (Feb 2014); Romit Guha, "Why We Shouldn't Be Surprised by the Kumbh Mela Stampede," The Wall Street Journal (11 Feb 2013), available at http://blogs.wsj.com/indiarealtime/2013/02/11/why-we-shouldnt-be-surprised-by-the-kumbh-mela-stampede/; see also Tarun Khanna, "Studying India's Maha Kumbh Mela Festival," Harvard Business Review Blog Network (25 Jan 2013), available at http://blogs.hbr.org/2013/01/a-closer-look-at-one-of-indias/; as well as the event's official website: http://kumbhmelaallahabad.gov.in/english/index.html. The reference to a "dirty bomb" is entirely fictional, and refers to the character's use of the Kumbh Mela festival as the hypothetical ground zero for an international armed conflict.

14. Michael Hastings, "The Runaway General," *Rolling Stone*, June 22, 2010, http://www.rollingstone.com/politics/news/the-runaway-general-20100622; Marybeth P. Ulrich, "The General Stanley McChrystal Affair: A Case Study in Civil-Military Relations," *Parameters* (Spring 2011), 86–100.
15. General Colin L. Powell, "Why Generals Get Nervous," New York Times, October 8, 1992, http://www.nytimes.com/1992/10/08/opinion/why-generals-get-nervous.html.
16. Carl H. Builder, The Masks of War: American Military Styles in Strategy and Analysis 22 (1989), (suggesting that a key element of the Army service "personality" is its choice to "measure" itself (i.e., its readiness to fight) in terms of personnel "end strength" of its Active Duty force, rather than number of deployable divisions or tanks).
17. For a modern example of the Services getting nervous about the future of war and the nation's ability to prepare for it, see General Raymond T. Odierno, General James F. Amos, and Admiral William H. McRaven, Strategic Landpower White Paper: Winning the Clash of Wills (United States Army Training and Doctrine Command, 2013), available at http://www.tradoc.army.mil/FrontPageContent/Docs/Strategic%20Landpower%20White%20Paper.pdf.
18. Samuel P. Huntington, The Soldier and the State: The Theory and Politics of Civil-Military Relations 61–66 (1957).
19. Andrew J. Bacevich, Breach of Trust 91–93 (2013) (discussing the Army leadership's propensity, in the early 1990s, to declare that the Persian Gulf War was both a validation of its post-Vietnam War preparation to fight conventional armies [i.e., the Soviets] and a harbinger of things to come in the twenty-first Century).
20. Frank G. Hoffman, "Hybrid Warfare and Challenges," *Joint Forces Quarterly* (First Quarter, 2009), 34–39.
21. International Crisis Group, Curbing Violence in Nigeria (II): The Boko Haram Insurgency (April 3, 2014), available at http://old.crisisgroup.

org/_/media/Files/africa/west-africa/nigeria/216-curbing-violence-in-nigeria-ii-the-boko-haram-insurgency.pdf.
22. Organization of al-Qa'ida in the Land of the Islamic Maghreb. See Council on Foreign Relations, Background paper (Jan. 8, 2014), available at http://www.cfr.org/terrorist-organizations-and-networks/al-qaeda-islamic-maghreb-aqim/p12717.
23. Islamic State of Iraq and the Levant. See, e.g., Ben Hubbard and Eric Schmitt, "Military Skill and Terrorist Technique Fuel Success of ISIS," New York Times (Aug. 27, 2014), http://www.nytimes.com/2014/08/28/world/middleeast/army-know-how-seen-as-factor-in-isis-successes.html?_r=0.
24. Acronym typically used as shorthand for American counterinsurgency doctrine and practice. See, e.g., Joint Publication 3–24, Counterinsurgency (Government Printing Office: Washington, D.C., 2013).
25. Joint Publication 3–0, Joint Operations V-6, Figure V-3 (Aug. 11, 2011), http://www.dtic.mil/doctrine/new_pubs/jp3_0.pdf.
26. Training and Doctrine Command (TRADOC) Pamphlet 525-8-5, U.S. Army Functional Concept for Engagement (Feb. 24, 2014).
27. Rosa Brooks, "Portrait of the Army as a Work in Progress," *Foreign Policy* (May 2014), http://foreignpolicy.com/2014/05/08/portrait-of-the-army-as-a-work-in-progress/.
28. Carl von Clausewitz, On War (Michael Howard, Peter Paret eds., trans., Princeton University Press 1984) (1832), at 605.
29. National Military Strategy.
30. Dep't of Defense, Joint Publication 1, Doctrine for the Armed Forces of the United States, at II-3 (Government Printing Office: Washington, D.C., 2013).
31. Dep't of Defense, Joint Pub. 1-02, Dep't of Defense Dictionary of Military and Associated Terms, 73 (8 Nov. 2010). The individual Services' definitions are identical. Compare, Naval Doctrine Pub. 1, Naval Warfare, 48 (March 2010), and Army Doctrine Pub. 1-02, Operational Terms and Military Symbols, Glossary-1, (31 Aug. 2012).
32. Barry Posen, The Sources of Military Doctrine 14 (1984); Morris Janowitz, The Professional Soldier: A Social and Political Portrait 257 (1960).
33. Eric Schmitt, "Compromise on Military Gay Ban Gaining Support Among Senators," New York Times, May 12, 1993, http://www.nytimes.com/1993/05/12/us/compromise-on-military-gay-ban-gaining-support-among-senators.html; General Colin L. Powell, "U.S. Forces: Challenges Ahead," *Foreign Affairs* (Winter 1992/93), http://www.cfr/org/world/us-forces-challenges-ahead/p7508.

34. Carl H. Builder, The Masks of War: American Military Styles in Strategy and Analysis (1989), at 4, 7–8, 12 ("[t]he institutional self-interests are most evident in peacetime and among the senior officers of the services. It is the 'fathers' of the institution who must look after their institution's well-being, for they have been entrusted with its care").
35. David E. Johnson, Fast Tanks and Heavy Bombers 87–90 (2003).
36. Carl von Clausewitz, On War 120-21 (Michael Howard, Peter Paret eds., trans., Princeton University Press 1984) (1832).
37. General Robert Cone, "Building Strategic Landpower," *Army* (October 2013), available at http://www1.ausa.org/publications/armymagazine/archive/2013/10/Documents/Cone_GreenBook2013.pdf.
38. U.S. National Commission on Terrorist Attacks Upon the United States, The 9/11 Commission Report (Washington, D.C.: U.S. Government Printing Office, 2002), 57–59.
39. The senior staff officer at a battalion, brigade, or regiment who is responsible for plans, training, and operations.
40. Tactics, Techniques, and Procedures.
41. Regional Alignment of Forces.
42. Joint Publication 3-0, Joint Operations V-6 (Aug. 11, 2011), http://www.dtic.mil/doctrine/new_pubs/jp3_0.pdf.
43. Karl Walling, "Thucydides on Policy, Strategy, and War Termination," *Naval War College Review* (Autumn 2013), 47–85, at 58.
44. H.R. McMaster, "The Pipe Dream of Easy War," The New York Times, July 20, 2013, available at http://www.nytimes.com/2013/07/21/opinion/sunday/the-pipe-dream-of-easy-war.html; H.R. McMaster, "Discussing the Continuities of War and the Future of Warfare: The Defense Entrepreneurs Forum," *Small Wars Journal*, Oct 13, 2014, http://smallwarsjournal.com/jrnl/art/discussing-the-continuities-of-war-and-the-future-of-war fare-the-defense-entrepreneurs-foru.
45. Steven Metz & James Kievit, "Strategy and the Revolution in Military Affairs: From Theory to Policy," Strategic Studies Institute (June 27, 1995), available at http://www.au.af.mil/au/awc/awcgate/ssi/stratrma.pdf; Donald H. Rumsfeld, "Transforming the Military," *Foreign Affairs* (May/June 2002), https://www.foreignaffairs.com/articles/2002-05-01/transforming-military.
46. Special Operations Forces.
47. Robert A. Johnson, "Predicting Future War," *Parameters* 44(1) (Spring 2014), 65, 66.
48. M.L.R. Smith, "Explaining Strategic Theory," *Infinity Journal*, issue 4 (2011), 27.
49. Clausewitz, On War, 89.

50. Andrew F. Krepinevich, "Cavalry to Computer: The Pattern of Military Revolutions," *The National Interest*, No. 37, Fall 1994 (defining them as "the application of new technologies into a significant number of military systems combines with innovative operational concepts and organizational adaptation in a way that fundamentally alters the character and conduct of conflict... [m]ilitary revolutions comprise four elements: technological change, systems development, operational innovation, and organizational adaptation. Each of these elements is in itself a necessary, but not a sufficient, condition for realizing the large gains in military effectiveness that characterize military revolutions").
51. Department of the Army, Training and Doctrine Command (TRADOC) Pamphlet, 525-3-1, The U.S. Army Operating Concept: Win in a Complex World 2020–2040 (October 31, 2014), at 17.
52. Andrew J. Bacevich, Breach of Trust 169 (2013) (referring to engagement as "persistent meddling").
53. Clausewitz, On War, 78.
54. "Army chief: Force to occupy Iraq massive," USATODAY.com (Feb. 25, 2003), http://usatoday30.usatoday.com/news/world/iraq/2003-02-25-iraq-us_x.htm.
55. Eric Schmitt, "Threats and Responses: Military Spending; Pentagon Contradicts General On Iraq Occupation Force's Size," N.Y. Times, Feb. 28, 2003, http://www.nytimes.com/2003/02/28/us/threats-responses-military-spending-pentagon-contradicts-general-iraq-occupation.html.
56. Major George S. Patton, "Tanks in Future Wars," *Cavalry Journal* (May 1920), in Military Essays and Articles of George S. Patton (Charles M. Province ed.), at 342, available at http://www.pattonhq.com/pdffiles/vintagetext.pdf.
57. Robert A. Johnson, "Predicting Future War," *Parameters* 44(1) (Spring 2014), 65, 68.
58. Lieutenant General (retired) Daniel Bolger, Why We Lost: A General's Inside Account of the Iraq and Afghanistan Wars (2014).
59. Ibid, at xv–xvi.
60. See, e.g., Lieutenant General Greg Newbold, "Why Iraq Was a Mistake," *Time* (April 9, 2006), http://content.time.com/time/magazine/article/0,9171,1181629,00.html; Don M. Snider, *Dissent and Strategic Leadership of the Military Professions* (2008), available at http://www.strategicstudiesinstitute.army.mil/pdffiles/PUB849.pdf (discussing the ethics of dissent by "strategic" leaders in uniform, based on a study of the 2006 public "revolt of the [retired] generals" in opposition to the Iraq war).
61. Keith D. McFarland, "The 1949 Revolt of the Admirals," *Parameters* (June 1981), at 53–63.

62. The Association of the United States Army (AUSA) holds an annual meeting and exhibition in Washington, D.C. See http://ausameetings.org/2015annualmeeting/.
63. Robert A. Johnson, "Predicting Future War," *Parameters* 44(1) (Spring 2014), 65, 70–71.
64. Unmanned Aerial Vehicles; also known as Remotely-Piloted Vehicles; also known as "Drones."
65. Michael Bailey, et al., "A Proposed Framework for Appreciating Megacities: A U.S. Army Perspective," *Small Wars Journal* (April 21, 2014), http://smallwarsjournal.com/jrnl/art/a-proposed-framework-for-appreciating-megacities-a-us-army-perspective-0; see generally David Kilcullen, Out of the Mountains: The Coming Age of the Urban Guerrilla (2013).
66. Office of the Secretary of Defense.
67. Peter D. Feaver, Armed Servants: Agency, Oversight, and Civil-Military Relations 3, 9 (2003); and see Peter D. Feaver, "Crisis as Shirking: An Agency Theory Explanation of the Souring of American Civil-Military Relations," *Armed Forces & Society* (Spring 1998), at 407.
68. Gary Klein, "Performing a Project Premortem," *Harvard Business Review* (September 2007), https://hbr.org/2007/09/performing-a-project-premortem.
69. Center for a New American Security, a Washington, D.C.-based national security-focused think tank. See http://www.cnas.org/.
70. Clausewitz, On War, 119.
71. Sherri Goodman and Gordon Sullivan, "Climate Change is 'Threat Multiplier'," Politico.com (Feb. 7, 2013), available at http://www.politico.com/story/2013/02/climate-change-is-threat-multiplier-087338.
72. Mackubin Thomas Owens, "What Military Officers Need to Know About Civil-Military Relations," *Naval War College Review* (Spring 2012), at 67, 67.
73. See, e.g., General Ray Odierno, "The Force of Tomorrow," Foreign Policy.com (Feb. 4, 2013), http://foreignpolicy.com/2013/02/04/the-force-of-tomorrow/ (highlighting the speed of information access and dissemination, the advent of groups linked by ideology working in "ungoverned spaces" or "failed states," and the local influence of regional powers displacing that of global powers); see also Hew Strachan, "The Changing Character of War," Europaeum Lecture, November 9, 2006, at 10–11, available at http://www.europaeum.org/files/publications/pamphlets/HewStrachan.pdf (proposing five enduring elements, or nature, of "war:" the use or threat of use of force; "contention" between two or more actors; some intensity and duration to the conflict; a public, not private, legitimacy or sanction for the use of force; some aim or goal).

74. John A. Warden III, "The Enemy as a System," *Airpower Journal*, Vol. 9, No. 1, (Spring 1995), at 40–55.
75. Michael Handel, Masters of War, at xxiii ("war will remain a dynamic and reciprocal activity in which both sides adapt to successive challenges").
76. Sun Tzu, Art of War, 192–93.
77. Donella H. Meadows, Thinking in Systems 25–34 (2008).
78. Morris Janowitz, The Professional Soldier: A Social and Political Portrait 138–39 (1960).
79. Robert M. Gates, Duty: Memoirs of a Secretary at War 368–70 (2014).
80. Clausewitz, On War, 119.

CHAPTER 12

Closing Argument

This book opened by posing an argument: American strategic civil-military relationships are haunted by an inability to diagnose whether they are pathological or healthy. Neither the parties themselves nor the public can accurately and objectively unravel whether certain actions or inactions are symptoms of a diseased interaction, or whether they are sure signs of a proper and well-ordered immune system, a proper—if nuanced and unequal—collaboration. The phrase "crisis" is too often tossed around, despite a dearth of evidence pointing toward the much-feared *coup*, and no unambiguous "winner" or "loser" in the resultant clash. That is, unless we have an objective and neutral framework for understanding what those relationships actually are in form and function.

By looking at case studies and "fingerprints" of those actually serving in these strategic leadership roles—Secretaries of Defense (e.g., Rumsfeld, Gates, and McNamara), Presidents (Lincoln, Jefferson Davis of the CSA, Bush, Clinton, and Obama), Chairmen of the JCS (Powell, Taylor), combat commanders (MacArthur, McChrystal, McClellan, Grant) and others—and by closely reviewing all that the law has done to structure these relationships, we have seen how closely aligned they really are to common and well-known principal–agent relationships. Just as lawyers and clients have published norms and codes of conduct that guide these principal–agent interactions and establish expectations that are used by both parties, and the public, to gauge their health, so too can we imagine existing legal structures like the Goldwater-Nichols Act as means by which

D. Maurer, *Crisis, Agency, and Law in US Civil-Military Relations*,
DOI 10.1007/978-3-319-53526-5_12

to reinvigorate civil-military relationships with norms and expectations. Duties of candor, confidence, loyalty, confidentiality, and clear but necessarily tailored "scopes of responsibility," permit us to not only enter into these relationships with mutual assurances, but allow the public a means by which to judge and hold accountable these parties when their conduct violates those principal–agent standards, customs, and norms.

With publically pronounced fiduciary duties like these, it is possible to relook old examples of supposed civil-military crises through a new grading scale. Assessing President Kennedy's choice to distance himself from his senior military advisors after the Bay of Pigs, and later inserting General Maxwell Taylor as his a quasi-civilian chief military counselor rather than his Joint Chiefs, illustrates how one principal chose to erect unconventional barriers between himself and his military agents, but did so based on principles of trust and confidence. These, in turn, entailed scaling back one agent organization's scope of responsibility in the favor of ballooning another agent's authority. Reviewing Lincoln's patient reaction to General McClellan's obstinacy and General Grant's supposed intoxication, or Truman's reaction to General MacArthur's arrogant attempt to shift wartime policy, illustrates various ways by which civilian principals reign in their wayward agents, either curtailing their grasp for too much authority at the expense of the principal's larger aims, or helping to ensure their loyalty and fidelity to the mission for which that agent was chosen to execute.

*****

The argument that opened this book was based on three premises. First, that the civilians and military leaders occupying the grand strategy-making posts in American national security are of separate castes—that is, like long-separated twins, they share common traits despite unequal environmental conditioning. Because both of these parties despite their particular upbringings and specified roles share the common, overarching goal of national security, and because both of them are naturally impacted, and can themselves affect or manipulate the authentic conditions that shape a conflict, and because—ultimately—both are inside the same system, or ecology, together constrained by their sum total of means, motives and opportunities, they are more symbiotic and aligned than what we tend to consider as antithetical or bifurcated parties. Therefore, the very nature of conflict tends to reinforce or highlight the *difference by degree principle.*

Rather than occupying separate poles, these parties find themselves more or less distanced from each other only by steps along a spectrum.

The exact distance they are from each other is never firmly established or codified and will often shift or spasm as the principal grants more or less responsibility and independence to his agent—like Lincoln did with Grant—or the agent grapples for more independence as Colin Powell did during the waning days of the Bush Administration as he contemplated what changes Bill Clinton foreshadowed for the military. Nevertheless, one constant remains clear: the *principle of amateur authority over professional specialization*. Regardless of how emphatically frustrated the military agent may be, she may never enact laws herself nor deliberately undermine the credibility and confidence of her civilian principal without—*at least*—the *prospect* of recrimination. The military agent is always, intentionally, bounded by the fence line built by the civilian principal. MacArthur and McChrystal were relieved of their commands; the "revolting" Navy admirals were publically censured by a revered General and forced to retire by civilian political appointees. The principal, without the technical and professional training and real-world experience, is an *amateur* in the field of war as compared to the military leader. But, as seen through the various cases and controversies described earlier, this inferiority in expertise is practically irrelevant. It is no different than a client, ignorant of the rules of criminal procedure, is the final authority on the direction in which she wishes her agent attorney to steer the representation in court, even if it seems contrary to what the agent would do themselves. It is those definitive objectives and aims for which the lawyer, like the military leader, must remain faithful, diligent, competent, candid, and at the end of the day subservient and deferential.

That faithful and competent diligence the military agent must perform, in deference to the preferences of the principal, demonstrates the *advice-action-ability principle*, our third premise, in practice. Because the civilian political authority is an amateur relative to the specialized professionalism of the military agent, and because the civilian has legitimate, accepted, power to direct the conduct of his agent who is employed on his behalf, it is obvious that the civilian relies on the military leader for three functions that are beyond the time or competence of the civilian. The civilian relies on the *advice* of his military agent, advice coming from a detached perspective or point of view but tailored to the known aims of the client, and supported by that agent's military knowledge, experience, and judgement. This advice, if accepted by the principal, triggers *action*: the agent executes, manages, and plans to employ skills or resources under his direct control in order to achieve aims of the civilian, which in turn frees the civilian principal to more freely act (or choose not to act), supervise, and evaluate the ongoing execution of his goals. But in order to warrant the principal's reliance on either the agent's advice or action, the principal must be convinced of the agent's *ability*. That is, a suite of specialized skills or knowledge that—as a professional—the agent has accumulated and developed for the express purpose of providing that advice and action to others, performing functions on their behalf. This explains Lincoln's use of Charles Dana to spy on Grant as he prepared to take Vicksburg, working to assure himself that the trust he had given to Grant was not misplaced and undermined by either incompetent generalship, naked and competitive political ambition, or human fallibility. It also explains Kennedy and McNamara's purposeful emasculation of the uniformed Joint Chiefs when they failed to provide useful and constructive advice that, if followed, would enable the Administration to avoid war with the Soviet Union, and it clarifies why Kennedy relied so heavily on General Maxwell Taylor, to the point of creating an entirely new high-level advisory position out of whole-cloth, potentially in conflict with the ambitions and ideas of other, conventional, strategic military leaders.

*****

It is foolhardy to predict how future wars will unfold, where they will be found, what characteristics will define the enemy, weapons of choice, specific targets, their animating ambitions or how these will define how wars will be fought. It is equally foolhardy to predict just how future exchanges, collaborations, or feuds between civilian and military leaders will reveal themselves—what "crises" they will expose, what choices these actors make, and how those differences are resolved or contained.

But it is *not* foolhardy—indeed it is entirely reasonable and responsible—to try to describe the underlying nature of the relationship between the strategic civilian and military protagonists that must lead us through those wars, or at least work to avoid them. When we do so, we see that the form and function of those parties is one strikingly marked by the traits of the typical principal–agent relationship. As a result, the obligations we ascribe to principals and their agents, fiduciary concepts like duties of care, competence, candor, loyalty, confidentiality, and scope of responsibility, provide intelligible, defined, and convenient diagnostic devices. They not only help us understand those parties and their choices in the *context* (preparing for, deterring, avoiding, or fighting a war) for which those two actors are mutually engaged and mutually dependent. These duties also form what Lincoln would have called a “fit and necessary measure.” This *necessary measure*—in the end—establishes a proper, nonpartisan, and impartial framework for the public to hold these strategic leaders accountable for their choices and for those leaders to understand how expectations are derived from the nature of their professional relationship.

Index

A
Abizaid, John, 22
Actor's value system, 190
Advice action-ability principle, 12, 213
Agency, 82–89
  application of, 132
  applying to civil-military relations generally, 27
  fingerprints of, 95–98
  incorporation into Goldwater-Nichols Act, 155–160, 168–170
  jurisprudential version of; Agency Problem, 104; agent, definition of, 103; authority, definitions of, 105, 111; candor between agent and principal, 140–141; de facto fiduciary relationship, 27; defined, 102–105; distinct from economic model of, 102–103; fiduciary, definition of, 104; inherent duties of, 104; loyalty and fidelity to principal, 137–142; meeting of the minds, 103; principal, definition of, 104
  law of, 27
  legal concept of, 103
  microeconomic model of, (*see* Feaver, Peter)
Agency-based norms, 160
Agency Problem, 104, 144
Agent, 193
  definition of, 103
Amar, Akhil Reed, 37–38
American "civil-military crisis", 4
American civil-military relations, 12
American counterinsurgency campaigns, 76
American foreign policy, 20
American national security, strategy-making posts in, 212
Anxiety, 137
Armed conflict, 195–196
Army's Regionally Aligned Forces, 183

D. Maurer, *Crisis, Agency, and Law in US Civil-Military Relations*,
DOI 10.1007/978-3-319-53526-5

Army's Rules of Professional Conduct for Lawyers, 140
Association of the United States Army (AUSA) conference, 193, 209n62
Authority, definition of, 105, 111
Autonomy, 131

B

Bales, Robert, 59
Bay of Pigs, 13, 101, 105n1, 120, 212
Betts, Richard, 24
Black, Hugo, 134
Boko Haram, 183
Bradley, Omar, 143, 176n20
Bragg, Braxton, 110
  discord in headquarters of, 115
  mediation by Jefferson Davis, 1863, 114
  relationship to Jefferson Davis, 111
Brands, H. W., 7
Brodie, Bernard, 40
Bureaucratic foot-dragging, 83
Burks, James, 144
Bush, George W., 20, 22, 42, 133, 181, 211, 213

C

Candor toward tribunals, 141–142
Case law
  failure to address strategic behavior among military elites relative to civilian leaders, 46
  inability to over prescriptive diagnostic tool or norms of behavior, 48–53; court-martial prosecution of Howe, Henry, 49; court-martial prosecution of Mitchell, William (Billy), 49–50; political question doctrine, 49, 67n88
  Youngstown Sheet & Tube Co. v. Sawyer (The Steel Seizure Case), 60n2, 61n8, 132–136
Casey, George
  "out of balance" statement, 21
Castro, Fidel, 101
Central Intelligence Agency, 101
Certainty principle, 193
Chairman of Joint Chiefs of Staff, 105n6
  Under Goldwater-Nichols Act, 43–44
Changing character of war, 10
Chinese army
  "military assessment" of, 3
  pronouncements and military forecasts of, 6
  use of military force against, 164
Chinese culture, 162
Choice architecture, 41
Churchill, Winston
  on role in Middle East Campaign, 32n42
Citizenship, obligations of, 54
Civil–military conflict, 41, 144
Civil–military crisis, 4, 7, 18
  contrarian view of, 25, 31n36
  indicators of, 24–25
  as "lymphoma", 22
Civil–military debate, 177
Civil–military fusion, 78–79
Civil–military relations/relationship, 57, 82, 102, 109, 125, 156, 211
  administrative regulations focus on, 53–55
  "agency theory" of, 89
  case law remains silent on, 48–53
  constitution structures, 37–41
  diagnosing health of, 8–9, 17, 177

difficulty in publicizing disputes in, 82
Feaver's view of, 12
generic expectations and norms of, 156–157
inability to diagnose, 24–27
"key condition" of, 58
lack of "neutral principles" for evaluating, 25, 34n56
legislation organizes, 41–48
military doctrine, 55–60
perceived influences on, 26
permissible conduct in, 49
problem of, 77
quality of, 8
role differentiation, 27n3
scholarship, from Huntington to Owens, 88
signal symptoms of, 17
strategic problem of, 20–24
tacit elements of, 105
theory, 80
three axes of, 24
Civil–military tension, 11
jurisprudential agency view of, 149
Civil War, 109, 116, 146
Civ–mil dialogue, 177–203
Clausewitz, Carl von, 7
friction and chance, 189
on role of political factors and influence in management of war, 19, 33n48
on "stout defense" applied to MacArthur's post-relief actions, 7
Cleburne, Patrick, 115
Clinton, Bill, 182, 213
Cohen, Eliot, 79–82
criticism of "normal" theory of civil-military relations, 80
opinion of McChrystal, 70n115
skepticism of lawyer analogy, 79
"unequal dialogue" between civilian and military elites, 81
"unequal dialogue" description, 167–168
"unequal dialogue" perspective, 11, 81, 111
Coherence, 185
Cold War, 13, 88, 109
Cold War-era theory, 75
Combatant Commander, 13, 85, 98, 160, 168
campaigns in Middle East, 21
command authority of, 168–170
geographic, 84
under Goldwater-Nichols Act, 44
potent combination of, 46
requirements from, 44
responsibilities of, 168
Service chiefs and, 45
Combatant Commands (COCOMs), 45
Combat operations, 191
Confiscation, 4
Conflict
armed, 195–196
Korean, 133
"self-evident" components of, 199
Congress
addresses organizational efficiency and generic responsibility for ethical conduct, 48
as amended 1949, 42
Defense Reorganization Act of 1958, 43
extent of legislative role in civil-military relationships, 41
Goldwater-Nichols Act of 1986, 43–44, 155–159
Iraq Liberation Act 1998, 41

Congress (*cont.*)
Joint Committee on the Conduct of the War, 1861; Purpose of , 39; Report of 1863, 61n19
National Security Act of 1947, 42
Conservative realism, 77, 166–167
Constitution, United States
Article I, purpose of, 38
Article II, purpose of, 38
Frankfurter, Felix on Separation of Powers, 38
"gloss" on Executive and Legislative Authority created by precedence, 40
on making military strategy, silence of, 39
relevance as cause for civil-military relationship confusion, 37–41
on sharing of power between executive and legislative branches, 40
Control, forms of, 75–77
Coup d'état, 5
definition of, 28n4
effect of lack of American experience with, 25
Cuban Missile Crisis, 13, 22, 101, 123
Cyber war, 196

D

Dana, Charles
spying on Grant, 149
as troubleshooter for Lincoln and Stanton, 148
Daniel, John Moncure, 112
Davis, Jefferson, 124, 131
case of, 110–117
decision to not relieve Bragg, 115
disagreement with Cleburne, 115–116
disagreement with Lee, 116–117
on generalship, 114
"greedy for military fame", 112
"infallible egotism" of, 112
letter to Braxton Bragg, 110
military experience of, 112
modes of success, 110
nomination of, 113
public expectations of battle, 113
role in history, 110–111
self-image as "General-in-Chief", 112
strategic civil-military relations under, 112
veto of act creating position of General-in-Chief and General Staff, 115
view of own presidential authority, 111
De facto fiduciary relationship, 27
Defense Reorganization Act of 1958, 43
Defense Reorganization Plan 1953, 43
Dempsey, Martin E., 13, 97–98, 155, 161–162, 175n12, 204n7
on generals speaking at political rallies, 161
on importance of candor with civilian leaders, 97–98
Desch, Michael, 26, 81–82
Difference by Degree Principle, 11
Discretionary authority, 135–136
Doctrine (military)
definition of, 55–56
as missed opportunity to prescribe norms and standards of military behavior, 55–60
Dubik, James, 14
on agency (as employer-employee dynamic), 86, 94n90
attack on Agency Theory, 86

Feaver's theory, 86
microeconomic principal-agent theory, criticism of, 83

E
Eisenhower, Dwight D.
on civilian responsibility for defense establishment, 43
on Defense Reorganization Plan 1953, 43
national security policies, 118–119
Emancipation Proclamation, 117
Exercise considerable initiative, 79
Externally-oriented adaption, 201

F
Fallon, William
resignation of, 21, 30n24
Feaver, Peter, 82–89
application of Agency Theory, 85
civilian leader; privileged position of, 82–83; right to be wrong, 82
civil-military relations as game of "strategic interaction", 83
microeconomic principal-agent theory; as alternative to "normal" (Huntington) theory, 80–81; criticisms of, 85; Dubik, James, on, 85–87
military leaders; working, shirking by, 83
principal–agent framework, 84, 85
rational actor model, 103
theory of civil-military relations, 102–103
view of agency, 143
view of civil-military relations, 12
Fidelity, 137–142
Fiduciary, definition of, 104
Fiduciary loyalty, 144
First World War, 49
Fiscally constrained environment, 187
Foreign policy, 2
Franks, Tommy, 42
as CENTCOM Commander, 41–42, 46
feelings toward JCS, 46
Frémont, John, 7
conflict with Lincoln over emancipation in Western Theater, 4–5
Frémont-Lincoln crisis, 5
Future of war, 177–203

G
Game-theoretic approach, 82
Gates, Robert, 20, 95, 155
on candor and authority, 96
on loyalty of senior officer to president, 96
on officers speaking on politically sensitive issues, 96
relationship with senior officers, 96
as Secretary of Defense as broker, 95
Global War on Terror, 46
Goldwater-Nichols Act, 58, 88, 155–156, 179, 211–212
agency applied, 160–175
composition, 157–160
congressional declaration of policy, 156–157
draft text of an amendment, 156–157
fiduciary duties, 157–160
functions, 157–160
Joints Chiefs of Staff, 157–160

Goldwater-Nichols Act of 1986, 43–44
  application of tenets during Persian Gulf War, 45
Goldwater-Nichols Defense Reorganization Act, 156, 204n8
Grant, Ulysses
  background of, 145–146
  being "spied" on by Charles Dana, 149
  siege of Vicksburg, 147–148
Gray, Colin, 23
Grossman, Dave, 137
Group cohesion, 84
Guilt among soldiers, 137
Gulf War, 45

H

Hagel, Chuck, 21
  resignation of, 21, 30n25
Hastings, Michael, 205n14
Hoover, Herbert, 7
Hunter, David
  relief of, 15n8
Huntington, Samuel, 75–77, 143
  alternative theory, 82
  analogy of military officers to doctors, lawyers, 79
  corporateness, 75
  criticism by Emile Simpson, 18, 90
  "executive" function, 167
  "functional" and "societal" imperatives, 166–167
  imperatives; functional, societal, 75
  MacArthur, discussion of, 166–167
  "management of violence", 76
  objective control theory, 77, 102, 166–167
  officers, "responsibilities" of, 77
  outdated assumptions, 85
  on politics being beyond scope of military competence, 77
  soldier and the state, seminal status of, 75
Hussein, Saddam, 41

I

Institutional authority, 8
Insubordination, 2
Internally-oriented adaptation, 200
International Crisis Group, 205n21
Iraq, 192
  American invasion of, 41
  "surge strategy" in, 22
Iraq Liberation Act of 1998, 41, 42

J

Jackson, Robert, 132, 134
  on equilbrium, 136
  framework, 135–136
  on president's executive power, 135
Janowitz, Morris, 78–79
  analogy of military officers to doctors, lawyers, 79
  blurring of distinct spheres of responsibility ("fusion"), 78
  military as pressure group, 78–79
Joint Chiefs of Staff (JCS), 13, 44
  Kennedy's expectations of after Bay of Pigs (, *see* Kennedy, John F.)
  use of during Cuban Missile Crisis, 101
Joint Ethics Regulation (JER), 54, 55
Junger, Sebastian, 137
Jurisprudential agency framework, 144, 155
Jurisprudential version of agency
  Agency Problem, 104
  agent, definition of, 103

authority, definitions of, 105, 111
candor between agent and principal, 140–141
de facto fiduciary relationship, 27
defined, 102–105
distinct from economic model of, 102–103
fiduciary, definition of, 104
inherent duties of, 104
loyalty and fidelity to the principal, 137–142
meeting of the minds, 103
principal, definition of, 104

K

Keegan, John, 11
on how politics does not test "worth" but battle does, 11
Kennedy, John F., 120, 212
expectations of JCS after Bay of Pigs, 101
feelings toward "experts", 122–123
use of JCS during Cuban Missile Crisis, 101–102
Kissinger, Henry, 40
Korea, 164
Korean conflict, 2–3, 133
Korean War, 43
Krepinevich, Andy, 191
Kumbh Mela festival, 180, 204n13

L

Law of agency, 27
Lee, Robert E., 116, 147
Legal agency theory, 139
Legalized insubordination, 121
Legislative Reorganization Act of 1946, 204n10
Limited war, 121
Lincoln, Abraham
conflict with Frémont over emancipation in Western Theater, 4–5
deference/good generals, 151n39
fit and necessary measure, 215
public order, 5
spy, 145–150
use of Charles Dana to spy on Grant, 140
Loyalty, 140

M

MacArthur, Douglas, 50, 97
activity and "independent judgment", 172–173
as "center of controversy", 5
Chicago homecoming parade, 1–3, 15n1
conduct, 175
as "co-principal", 174
exercise of judgment, 173
fact-dependent questions about, 172
farewell speech, 138
interviews with foreign newspapers, 5
letter to Congressman Martin, 5, 161
on obedience to orders, 97
objective control theory applied to, 166–167
"Old Soldiers Never Die" Speech, 162–163
Omar Bradley, criticism by, 166
reaction to relief from command, 161
relationship to Mitchell, 68n97
relative popularity of, 33n53
relief, 7

MacArthur, Douglas (*cont.*)
restrictions on public pronouncements of military and foreign policy, 173
role in court-martial of "Billy" Mitchell, 49
on role of theater commander, 165, 166
scope of responsibility, 172
sense of moral rightness, 162
service and context for military advice, 174
substantive views, 166
testimony to combined session of Senate Armed Services Committee and Foreign Relations Committee, 164
visit to Chicago, 3–4
war-waging preferences, 168
Macgregor, Douglas, 56
Management of violence, 76
Marshall, George, 176n20
Martin, Joe, 161
McCain, John, 13
McChrystal, Stanley, 155
Eliot Cohen's opinion of, 70n115
Inspector General report on, 70n116
resignation in 2010, 30n23, 96
Rolling Stone Article, 70n115
Tom Ricks on chilling effect of relief, 70n115
McClellan, George, 7, 20, 22, 117–119, 131
letter to Lincoln, 118
letter to wife, Mary, after First Battle of Bull Run, 20
Note to Lincoln 1861, 118
Note to Lincoln 1862, 115
McKiernan, David
resignation of, 30n22
McNamara, Robert, 22, 102
management of Vietnam War, 22
McPherson, James, 112
Mexican-American War, 113
Mexican War, 146
Microeconomic model of Agency, *see* Feaver, Peter
Microeconomic principal–agent theory, 83
"Military assessment" of Chinese army, 3
Military conclusion, 3
Military doctrine, regulations and, 8
Military lawyers, 139
Military officer, relationship between, 157–158
Military professionalism, 119, 167
Military receivership, 2
Mitchell, Billy, 187
Mitchell, William (Billy)
Bolger, Daniel, 192
court-martial prosecution of, 49–50, 187
as "military bureaucratic insurgent", 50
relationship to MacArthur, 68n97
Montesquieu's theory on separation of powers, 38
Mullen, Michael, 98
on limiting "decision-space" of civilians, 98
on obedience to civilian decisions, despite disagreement, 98

N

National policy, 184
National Security Act of 1947, 42, 88
National security agenda, 119
National Security Council, 79, 123
National security, policy-makers of, 156
National Security Strategy, 183

New America Foundation, 177
Newbold, Greg, 208n60
Nixon, Richard, 133

O

Oath of Office (for military officers), 30n77, 46
Obama, Barack, 13, 155
  congressional authorization, 39
  decision to deploy forces in Libya, 39
  decision to not deploy forces in Syria, 39
  election in 2008, 21
  public opinion about, following acceptance of McChrystal resignation, 52
  on trust relationship to senior military, 9
Objective Control, *see* Huntington, Samuel
Objective control theory, 77, 166–167
Operation Iraqi Freedom, 42
Organizational culture, 10
Owens, Mackubin Thomas, 87
  for civil-military relationships, 88
  on "criteria" for judging civil-military relationships, 87

P

Police force security, 2
Policy-making paralysis, 21–22
Political interference with military, 5
Political process as source of legitimacy, 24
Post-Vietnam War preparation, 205n19
Powell, Colin, 7, 181
  Foreign Affairs article 1992, 23, 32n40, 180
  New York Times op-ed 1992, 35n70
Principal-agent framework, 82
Principal-agent relationship, 118, 211
Principal, definition of, 104
Principle of Amateur Authority Over Professional Specialization, 11
  See also Unequal dialogue
"Proconsular arrogance", 5
Professionalism, 75–77
Professional responsibility, 138
  principal–agent codes of, 143

R

Rank insubordination, 5
Rational actors, 82–89
Regulations, 53–55
  Executive Order 12674 (Principles of Ethical Conduct for Government Officers and Employees, 53–54
  on failure to prescribe norms or standards of behavior for civilian or military elite, 53
  focus on personal financial responsibilities and avoiding conflicts of interest, 53
  Joint Ethics Regulation, 54
Responsible citizenship, 55
Responsible disobedience, 144
Revolt of the Admirals
  background, 142–145
  as remedial measure of agents, 149
Revolutions in military affairs, 189
Ricks, Tom
  on President-Elect Donald Trump, 21, 26n26
Ridgeway, Matthew, 7, 13, 118, 119, 131–132
  discouragement with Eisenhower's New Look strategy, 118–119
  relationship with Secretary of Defense Wilson, 119

Ridgeway, Matthew (*cont.*)
on retirement after one tour as Chief of Staff, 128n57
Rodman, Peter, 23
Roosevelt, Eleanor, 9
Roosevelt, Theodore
on directing Army officers, 19
on use of presidential authority, 62n24
Rumsfeld, Donald, 13, 42, 46
on military as "rival political faction", 30n18
on transforming military, 20, 30n18

S

Scope of Responsibility and Authority, 109
case of Jefferson Davis, 110–117
Maxwell Taylor, 119–125
Mcclellan's megalomania and Ridgeway's recalcitrance, 117–119
Scope of responsibility and representation, 111, 131, 172, 212
Agency Theory's, 133
Alexander's, 109
defined, 111
expanding and shrinking, 117
framework, 125
lawyer's, 111–112
using case law to determine relative "boundaries" of, 131
Self-dealing, 104
Self-help as tool for principal, 145, 150
Service parochialism, 149
Services and Combatant Commands, 183
Shinseki, Eric, 13
statement to Senate Armed Service Committee 2003, 20, 30n17
Significant field of human endeavor, 75
Sinclair, Jeffrey, 59
Snider, Don
on "jurisdictional" fights, 73n173
Socially-approved purposes, 76
Social networks, 84
Strategic civil-military relationship, 20–24, 44
guidance to participants in, 47
nature of, 48
participants in, 54, 95
unequal dialogue, 81
Strategic interaction, 156
Strategic Studies Group (SSG), 14
Stress, 137, 140
Sullivan, Gordon, 203n5
"The Surge", 22

T

Taft-Hartley Act, 134
Taylor, Maxwell, 25, 101, 119–125, 131–132, 212
as Chairman of the Joint Chiefs of Staff, 122
criticism of Eisenhower New Look strategy, 118–119
Cuba Study Group, participation in, 121
on duty of senior military officers to consider "far more than purely military matters", 123
experience in Pentagon, 120
expression of support, 123
"legalized insubordination" of, 121
as military representative to the president, 121, 178
unique advocacy, 123
views while serving as Kennedy's Chairman, 124

"TED talk" in 2009, 177
Temporary political administration, 2
Thaler, Richard, 12
Training and Doctrine Command (TRADOC), 206n26, 208n51
Truman, Harry S., 134, 163, 173
  civilian dominance, 168
  contextual facts, 172
  fact-dependent questions about, 172
  relative popularity of, 33n53
Trump, Donald, 21
Tuchman, Barbara
  American Army as "neutral instrument of state policy", 29n11

U
Unequal dialogue
  as support for *Principle of Amateur Authority*, 11
  See also Cohen, Eliot
Unequal partnerships, 79–82
Uniform Code of Military Justice (UCMJ), 50–51
  application to Howe and Mitchell, 53
  possible criminal sanctions under, 50
United Nations Security Council Resolution, 39
Use of term; "agents", 45–46
  proposed amendment of, 157–158, 168

V
Vietnam War, 25, 85, 102

W
Wage Stabilization Board, 133
Wartime relationships, 11
Weapons, categorizations of, 197
White, Thomas
  view on civilian "defense intellectuals", 34n58
Wilson, Charles, 119
Woodward, Bob, 96
World War III, 102

Y
Yingling, Paul
  "failure in generalship" article in armed forces 2007, 31n29
Youngstown case (1952), 132–133, 136

Z
Zinni, Anthony, 41

The manufacturer's authorised representative in the EU is Springer Nature Customer Service Centre GmbH, Europaplatz 3, 69115 Heidelberg, Germany. If you have any concerns regarding our products, please contact ProductSafety@springernature.com

Printed and bound by CPI Group (UK) Ltd, Croydon, CR0 4YY
22/09/2026
02221067-0004